Tentative Transgressions

Tentative Transgressions

Homosexuality, AIDS, and the Theater in Brazil

Severino J. Albuquerque

THE UNIVERSITY OF WISCONSIN PRESS

The University of Wisconsin Press
1930 Monroe Street
Madison, Wisconsin 53711

www.wisc.edu/wisconsinpress/

3 Henrietta Street
London WC2E 8LU, England

5 4 3 2 1

Printed in the United States of America

Library of Congress Cataloging-in-Publication Data

Albuquerque, Severino João Medeiros.
Tentative transgressions: homosexuality, AIDS, and the theater in Brazil / Severino J. Albuquerque.
p. cm.
Includes bibliographical references and index.
ISBN 0-299-18924-4 (pbk.: alk. paper)
1. Brazilian drama—20th century—History and criticism. 2. Homosexuality in literature. 3. AIDS (Disease) in literature. 4. Literature and society—Brazil. I. Title.
PQ9595.H65 A43 2003
869.2´4209353—dc21

2003005649

para Afonso e Meta

Contents

Preface

The research for this book began as a project on representations of AIDS in Brazil—artistic and otherwise. As the work progressed I soon became aware of the forbidding scope of the project and decided to limit myself to artistic depictions, only to be again confronted with the enormity of the enterprise. I was then drawn to focus on stage representations, not only because of my previous interest in and familiarity with Brazilian theater but also because representations of AIDS in Brazilian theater stand out—both in quality and quantity.

This book is a descriptive and historical analysis of homosexuality in (or hidden in) Brazilian theater. While it is not a history of homoeroticism or same-sex-centered Brazilian theater since the early colonial period, as I was writing the introductory chapter I became convinced that in order to better understand theatrical representations of homosexuality after 1970 and, especially, of AIDS in Brazil, it was necessary first to track representations of homosexuality in Brazilian theater throughout the twentieth century, starting with modernism's evasiveness in that regard. It was also evident that considerable attention had to be given to distinctive aspects of the theater in Brazil, especially its traditional reluctance to portray transgression. Continually inflected by such factors as gender, race, age, and sexual orientation, theater is a prime locus for a study of the representation of transgression; yet in Brazil such depictions have been for the most part hesitant, tentative, even apologetic. In twentieth-century Brazil, theater faced new challenges—and offered new rewards—as it interacted with elements intrinsic to a culture characterized by male rule, social disparities, and economic dependence. In such a milieu, with the boundaries of gender, class, and race constantly shifting in response to power struggles that often—and all too easily—lead to violence, difference assumes fresh overtones, and transgression new meanings.

I was fortunate to have at my disposal key studies of Brazilian sexual culture conducted by scholars trained in North America (notably, Richard Parker and James Green) and in Brazil (João Silvério Trevisan, Luiz Mott, and Jurandir Freire Costa). The sources and theory I have used in this project, from social criticism to queer theory—Brazilian, North American, and European in origin—bespeak a flexible critical orientation. Because I believe a pioneering work such as this one must give priority to historicizing and contextualizing the subject, however, I did not set out to undertake extensive theorizing here. Chapter 1 is animated by the ideas of Parker, Green, Trevisan, Mott, and Costa, as well as those of Amy Kaminsky, Henning Bech, Rommel Mendès-Leite, and others. It lays the groundwork for the subsequent chapters through a consideration of the intersections of transgression, homosexuality, and the stage in Brazil.

In chapter 2, I examine Brazilian modernism's evasiveness in dealing with the theater in general (the first genuinely modernist play was not produced until 1942) and, especially, in representing homosexuality. Drawing on the work of Judith Butler and Eve Kosofsky Sedgwick, I consider how intersecting anxieties at the heart of Brazilian modernist intellectual production led otherwise great playwrights Oswald de Andrade and Nelson Rodrigues to seriously misrepresent male and female homosexuality in their theater; with reference to the work of Andrew Hewitt, George Mosse, and others, I look at the convergence of masculinity, fascism, and homosexuality in the first half of the twentieth century and how it may have affected some of the plays of this period. In addition, because the focus of chapter 2 is the work of Oswald, Nelson, and neorealist Plínio Marcos, this part of the book problematizes the representation of homosexuality by heterosexual dramatists. Since this project attempts to trace the representation of homosexuality as transgression in Brazilian theater, the tentativeness of such representation is analyzed against the backdrop of a mostly hostile environment. And because homosexual-accented (not to mention homosexual-authored) plays from the period covered in chapter 2 have proved nearly impossible to locate, I have focused on canonical authors such as Oswald and Nelson, who nevertheless wrote a large corpus of iconoclastic drama.

Chapter 3 tracks one of the most fascinating periods of the homosexual-themed drama in Brazil, when two decades of military dictatorship (1964–1985) ironically gave rise to some of the most creative stage representations of homosexuality in the history of the Brazilian theater. This was particularly true in the years that followed the 1979 revocation of the repressive Ato Institucional Número 5, or Institutional Act Number 5, which had conferred on the president dictatorial powers. The somewhat freer atmosphere that prevailed in the 1980s made possible the formation of a number of gay rights organizations and the appearance of several openly gay playwrights. In examining their contributions I turn to several of the historians, theorists, and critics mentioned in chapter 1, especially Trevisan and Mendès-Leite, as well as to Bataille and his critic Joseph Libertson; In chapter 3, I also draw on the exciting work of younger scholars such as José Esteban Muñóz, Rebecca Schneider, and Don Kulick.

With the onset of AIDS in Brazil in the mid-1980s the game changed entirely; for the rest of the decade and through most of the 1990s the crisis at the center of gay life also became the main focus of gay-accented theater in Brazil. The theater of Caio Fernando Abreu and others has helped to cast light on how a peripheral society dominated by inequity and violence represents its confrontations with difference. The several paradigms around which the chapter is constructed illustrate the diverse approaches Brazilian playwrights have taken as they react to the emergency. As a reading of chapter 4 will show, my understanding of AIDS and its ramifications has been shaped by the work of several theorists and critics, including Richard Parker, Alberto Sandoval, David Román, and Fernando Arenas.

Some of the research for this book was conducted during trips to Brazil over a period of five years, starting with a longer stay in Rio de Janeiro and São Paulo in 1996, and followed by shorter visits in 1997, 1998, 1999, and 2000. I am indebted to a number of individuals in Brazil and the United States for their invaluable assistance and support. In Brazil, I want to express my gratitude to Afonso Rosa, Márcio Dowsley, and Meta Loei, without whose love, friendship, and hospitality the field research for this book could not have been completed. I also would like to thank the following artists, scholars, and theater people: in Rio de Janeiro, Gilberto Gawronski, Marcos Breda, Luiz Arthur Nunes, Vagner de Almeida, Richard Parker, Marcelo Secron Bessa, Italo Moriconi, Silviano Santiago, Ana Maria Bulhões, Mari Mancuso, and Victor Hugo Pereira (who has an amazing talent for locating hard-to-find playscripts and books); in São Paulo, João Roberto Faria, Alberto Guzik, Naum Alves de Souza, Luis Alberto de Abreu, the late Zeno Wilde, and Silvana Garcia and her staff at the Arquivo Multimeios of the Centro Cultural São Paulo; Homero Cavalcanti Nunes, Gilda Villela Brandão, Reinaldo Lessa, Celso Brandão, Luciano Carvalho, Alex Teixeira, Lula Nogueira, and Lúcia Guiomar in Maceió; and Pedrinho Nicácio and Jomard Muniz de Brito in Recife.

The staff of the Interlibrary Loan Office at the University of Wisconsin's Memorial Library was tireless in locating little-known books and articles. Several colleagues, fellow fighters for the cause of disseminating Brazilian theater in the United States, were always available for information and support, especially Fred Clark (North Carolina), Leslie Damasceno (Duke), David George (Lake Forest College), and Margo Milleret (New Mexico). In addition, Jurandir Oliveira (Cornell) remained a constant source of encouragement throughout the project, as did Alberto Sandoval (Mount Holyoke College), who was particularly selfless in his careful reading of chapter 4. Leslie Damasceno, Fernando Arenas (Minnesota), and James N. Green (California State at Long Beach) wrote thorough, perceptive reports on different drafts of the manuscript; I am forever indebted to them for their time, generosity, and extremely useful corrections and suggestions. I also wish to express my gratitude to colleagues at the University of Wisconsin, especially Mark Streeter for the careful editing of the early version of the manuscript, Ron Kuka for opening the way to publication, and Ellen Sapega, my colleague in the Portuguese program in Madison, for all the clippings and newspapers she kept passing on to me. Francisco Scarano, as director of Latin American, Caribbean and Iberian Studies, kindly released me from teaching and other duties during a summer that was crucial for the writing of the manuscript. At the University of Wisconsin Press, acquisitions editor Raphael Kadushin was unfailingly encouraging throughout the writing and rewriting of the manuscript.

Portions of this book grew out of earlier versions of papers given at professional meetings and also a keynote speech at the Carolina Foreign Language and Literature Conference in 1997. A section of chapter 2 has appeared in *Confuencia* 17 (2002, pp.12-25), and sections of chapter 4 have appeared in *Romance Language Annual* 8 (1996, pp. 358–62), *Romance Studies* 29 (1997, pp. 65–73), and *Brasil/Brazil* 20 (1998, pp. 81–98). I am grateful to the editors and publishers of these journals (including Maney

Publishing of Leeds, UK, for *Romance Studies*) for their permission to include these materials in the present work. The photographs are reproduced by permission of the Divisão de Pesquisas (Arquivo Multimeios) of the Centro Cultural São Paulo, São Paulo, Brazil; individual photographers are credited with each photograph reproduced in this book.

Following Brazilian convention, I use first names to refer to authors and playwrights (Oswald, Nelson, and Caio, for example, instead of Oswald de Andrade, Nelson Rodrigues, and Caio Fernando Abreu), except when tradition dictates use of last names (Machado de Assis) and pseudonyms (João do Rio) or in cases where there is no clear preference for one name over the other (as in Zeno Wilde and Mauro Rasi).

Unless otherwise noted, translations are my own. Translations of play titles are also mine, except when a published translation exists; in such cases, titles are in italics (books) or in quotes (text in anthology).

Tentative Transgressions

chapter 1

Transgression, Homosexuality, and the Theater in Brazil

Featured prominently in the long profile that Brazil's leading newsweekly occasionally dedicates to the nation's notables, soccer star Renato Gaúcho (the professional name of Renato Portaluppi, b. 1962) declared in 1993 that "real men don't die of AIDS" and in the same breath that he has no use for condoms, since "only gay men contract the disease" (Alves 1993: 102). Speaking to *Veja* magazine more than a decade after the condition was first detected in Brazil, the popular athlete had no qualms airing his opinion because he knew his sentiment to be shared by many others who believe that male homosexuality is a threat to masculinity. AIDS, moreover, according to this line of thought, is at once transgression and punishment. Predicated on a notion of de facto compulsory heterosexuality (Rich 1980) and failing to comprehend the concept of deed and consequence even at a basic level this position continues to be embraced by a sizable segment of the population, even after two decades of familiarity with the syndrome.

Key figures in Brazilian society, soccer stars (most of whom are not as outspoken or controversial as Renato Gaúcho)[1] enjoy an authority and prestige that even other celebrities lack. A select few are revered as national treasures and symbols, and national consciousness reserves a veritable pantheon for the most distinguished soccer heroes from the past. Their idealization never seriously challenged by a society largely uninterested in the transgressive elements attending the sport,[2] these oracles of popular wisdom are looked up to by the young as trendsetters and role models. No other sport, except perhaps auto racing, has soccer's visibility or aura of machismo.[3] To this day, even as the national women's soccer team makes outstanding achievements,[4] women are discouraged from playing soccer or even attending soccer games. The few women who insist on playing the sport do so at the risk of ridicule and marginalization, and lesbian players are all too often subjected to disturbing violations of their right to privacy.[5] These are but a few instances of how, in Brazil and elsewhere, "gender norms are policed . . . in the service of shoring up heterosexual hegemony" (Butler 1999: xii).

In an environment still steeped in the positivist thought that characterized the founding of the republic in 1889, the *pátria,* or fatherland—ironically, a feminine noun connoting male heroism—encompasses the pursuit of privileges to which women are for the most part not entitled. It should come as no surprise, then, that such a culture sees its international men's soccer matches as a battle against an enemy nation[6] yet does not seem to believe the national honor is at stake in women's matches. Women's soccer games are seen as quaint exercises, curiosities, signs of modernity and of female advancement in society rather than matters of national urgency. As essential as any other cultural category to an understanding of Brazil, the country's gendered performances of soccer are constructed on the denial of an individual's freedom to choose a role.[7] Individuals come to discover the implications, concrete or implied, subjective or objective, that attempts to challenge imposed roles have for their material lives (de Lauretis 1987: 3).

Throughout this book I use "transgression" in the general sense of an act, process, or instance of infringement or violation of an existing law, command, or duty; or, as the well-known Foucauldian definition puts it, "the crossing of a boundary—a going further." I favor this interpretation over an exclusively literary or artistic understanding of the term, the sort suggested in Robert R. Wilson's frequently quoted 1989 article, "Play, Transgression, and Carnival." While I share Wilson's enthusiasm for transgression's positive, liberating energy, I worry that the notion of transgression has fallen prey to Wilson's and other late-twentieth-century attempts to conceptualize postmodernism in purely aesthetic terms. Angelia R. Wilson (1997) has written perceptively on the dangers of an exclusively aesthetic focus on transgression. Her point of departure is British sociologist Elizabeth Wilson's article "Is Transgression Transgressive?" which criticizes the substitution of an aesthetic interest in transgression for politics. At the same time she concurs, Angelia Wilson expresses her own worries about the risk that transgression may be understood other than in terms of political transformation. To avoid such a danger, she calls for a stronger stand:

> Transgression for its own sake may be personally enjoyable, but as a political tactic its message is too important to leave to interpretation by the "heterosexual other." If we are to establish as political the very terms through which identity is articulated, then surely we must be clear about that message. And in so doing we must be sensitive to the collage of identities—racial, economic, religious—that individuals struggle to balance in understanding themselves. (Wilson 1997: 105)[8]

In Brazil, most rules pertaining to social behavior and ethical conduct are part of the moral code of the patriarchal family prevalent since the early days of the colonial period and still very influential today. In addition, official policies in effect throughout most of Brazil's history (and until as recently as the military dictatorship that ruled the nation from 1964 to 1985) have emphasized population increase as a way to occupy the immense territory and thwart foreign invasion and occupation. This situation has been compounded by the Catholic Church's opposition to sex outside of marriage and to virtually all forms of birth control, a position unlikely to change with an increasingly conservative hierarchy in the Vatican and in the Brazilian Church itself. Those who do not conform to expectations are identified as sexual Others, and Other, according to Jonathan Dollimore (1991: 34), is an amalgam of variously perceived forms of difference, including a perception of the Other as an "object of displacement for fears within/of the same." The possibilities for the occurrence and identification of transgression are for Dollimore, "profoundly affected by the cultural construction of subjectivity"; different forms of subjectivity contrast but also interconnect. In Brazil, the prevalent assumptions about sexual identity so cogently expressed by soccer star Renato Gaúcho have not allowed for the questioning of the conflicts or the exploration of interconnections, and as a result those who do not conform to societal expectations of sex and gender are relegated to the margins as objects of displacement.

In Brazil as elsewhere, names and naming are vital tools in the not always subtle contest for cultural control[9] (for instance, the incorporation of the term *gaúcho* in Renato Portaluppi's professional name not only identifies the player's origin—from the state of Rio Grande do Sul—but, more importantly, suggests the macho qualities associated with the mythical rancher of the South American pampas). The line of thinking espoused in his remarks on the subject of AIDS also echoes the feelings and acts of those who in the early eighties collectively decided on a name for the disease in Brazil. Instead of using the more logical "SIDA" (for *Síndrome de Imunodeficiência Adquirida*), standard in Portugal and other countries where Romance languages are spoken, Brazil adopted the English acronym AIDS. The explanations normally advanced to account for the unexpected usage are disparate. Some claim the imported term is consistent with the widespread use of English words in a country so fond of North American ways and wares. Others, less plausibly, insist that "AIDS" caught on because when the disease was first detected in Brazil the acronym was used by English-proficient doctors and intellectuals in highly visible and frequent media interviews and statements. But the explanation that seems to hold most sway among cultural critics is that heavily Catholic Brazil rejected a term that is pronounced exactly as "Cida," the short form or nickname for women named Maria Aparecida, after the patron saint of Brazil, Nossa Senhora Aparecida (literally, Our Lady [who] Appeared).[10]

I start with HIV infection and disease because in Brazil the spectacle of AIDS (to use Simon Watney's phrase) has too often been staged at the basest levels and has included a good deal of exaggeration and pathos. Since AIDS is conceptualized primarily as a sexual disease (regardless of how it was contracted), it is, through a process of associative thinking, suggestive of diseases like syphilis and gonorrhea and also of transgression, sin, and death. To the minds of many, then, AIDS has come to represent the ultimate transgression because it evokes images of sexual aberration and male homosexual sex, especially anal penetration. Performing an association between the disease and receptive anal sex, AIDS, according to this line of thinking, is punishment for abdication of the male prerogative of penetration and subjugation. Whereas in the pre-AIDS era the loss of a man's *honra* (honor, a key concept in patriarchal society) as a consequence of being penetrated was serious debasement, an AIDS diagnosis and death from the disease became the utmost disgrace. For that reason, a female carrier of the virus, while still ostracized, would be subjected to significantly less severe reprehension.

AIDS in Brazil, then, has exacerbated homophobia, a fear rooted in the denial of sexual difference. In Brazil, as in most of the world, homosexuals are hated because they provoke erotic anxieties, above all the bigot's fear of his own homosexual desires. As Leo Bersani (1995) has shown in *Homos*, homophobia is a defense against the idea that anal intercourse allows gay men to experience the intimidating gratifications of female sexuality, that it threatens to abolish the difference between the sexes.

This considerable repression notwithstanding, anal eroticism plays a key role in Brazilian erotic ideology. As Richard Parker (1992: 235) explains,

> precisely because the restrictions and taboos associated with the anus and its functions are perhaps more extreme than in the case of any other part of the body, nowhere is the transgressive logic of the erotic more powerful than in the eroticization of anal intercourse. It is fully in keeping with this logic that anal intercourse should be given special importance within this system of meanings and that the *bunda* (literally, the "behind" or "ass") of both men and women should be treated as almost a national fetish reproduced in a whole range of images and media.[11]

Men and women who transgress their culturally prescribed sexual roles (*atividade* or the dominating/penetrator/inserter role for men, and *passividade* or the submissive/penetrated/insertee role for women) are subjected to considerably more severe stigmatization than those who engage in homosexual sex but do not upset the culturally condoned roles of domination (for men) and submission (for women).[12] Whereas anal intercourse is taboo in many cultural contexts, in Brazil it is the issue of power that often overrides the pursuit of pleasure.

Phallocentrism is likewise not limited to Brazil. There, as in other parts of the world, the key factor is less the common biological gender of the partners than the social roles each performs, and one's same-sex object preference is less important than one's gender role (Parker 1995: 244, 246). Gender role and an awareness of difference are intrinsically tied to the establishment of identity, and a desire for the sexual Other produces an image of the self. In still staunchly patriarchal Brazil, however, men whose gender role and identity lead them to abdicate their penetrating prerogatives and choose to be anally receptive are the object of considerable scorn from a majority who repress their desire for the Other and will hence relegate those men to the lowest of stations.[13]

Treated by the Inquisition in colonial Brazil as a form of supreme transgression, sodomy (meaning, almost always, anal intercourse) and especially, same-sex sodomy, acquired a stigma combining sin and crime that remains indelibly imprinted on the Brazilian collective unconscious. Often called *pecado nefando* (abominable sin) and other circumlocutions by the inquisitors and theologians of the time, anal coitus was second only to Judaism and crimes against the Catholic faith among the preoccupations of the inquisitors.[14] Historians and cultural critics have registered their surprise at the inquisitors' copious documentation of sexual transgressions, reflecting perhaps not so much the frequency of those practices as the interest that the defenders of the faith had in the subject. Ironically, the several visits of the Holy Office to Brazil from the late sixteenth to the early eighteenth century ended up providing detailed and even appealing descriptions (Mott 1988; Trevisan 1986: 39–59) of the very transgressions the inquests set out to eradicate.

The important outcome of the visitations of the Holy Office to colonial outposts was not so much the documentation (abundant as it is) of sodomy as "the extent to which they forged a link between sexual behavior and language. . . . The Inquisition not only described the aberrations of sexual conduct in colonial life, but invested them with meaning." (Parker 1991: 72). Sexual sin virtually subsumes the overall concept of sin and acquires a new sense of moral crime; therefore, "the subjective meaning of sexual practices is reconstructed at a very different level . . . and sex itself becomes a source of danger, of pollution, and even of evil that plays across the body but takes root within the soul" (Parker 1991: 74).

The medical and scientific models of sexual life that gradually prevailed in late-nineteenth-century Brazil put a premium on procreation, assuring heterosexuals uncontested privileges. Sexual difference was equated with abnormality, deviance, perversion, and disease and deemed in need of prevention or a cure. While sodomites were denounced by chroniclers, inquisitors, and assorted moralists and punished by the legal institutions of the colony and empire, no public health measures were taken in an attempt to prevent transgression. It was not until *higienismo* came to prevail in late-nineteenth-century Brazilian medicine that preventative measures began to be promoted (Costa 1979: 247).[15] Modern medicine would approach perceived sexual deviation no differently than it would sexually transmissible disease—as sicknesses—and called for vigorous prevention and treatment. Disease, as Parker (1991: 84) points out, came "to function not simply as a way of labeling the unacceptable, but as a way of regulating and controlling it."

In the twentieth century, industrialization and rapid urbanization with their attendant social liberalization encroached on traditional perspectives. While the ruling elites continued to struggle to find ways of reining in putatively unusual and dangerous sexual practices, modest social advances encouraged some to advocate a different conceptualization of the problem: rather than attacking deviance per se, it was a matter of enlightening an ill-informed, unaccepting populace. While the notion of homosexuality as deviance remained strong until the 1970s, a gradual change did occur during the first two thirds of the twentieth century. The slowly evolving picture was influenced by a moderate dissemination of feminist thinking and an incipient gay liberation movement in the late 1970s and early 1980s. This process was aided, ironically, by a military regime that was inconsistent in matters sexual, an apt example being the spread of *pornochanchadas*, or soft-core porn movies, in the 1960s and 1970s. Likewise, the coterminous growth of the television industry (especially the Globo network, the first to reach the entire country) offered this shift a modicum of additional (if lukewarm and often ambiguous) support as it homogenized the nation—its tastes, language, and opinions—through sitcoms, variety shows, and soap operas. Although, to the best of my knowledge, there are no published studies of how the growth of television in Brazil has influenced societal attitudes regarding homosexuality, one can safely say that at the very least, television has made gays and lesbians more visible. Male and female couples and gay and lesbian individuals have appeared mostly in *telenovelas*, soap operas with plots dealing with topics as diverse as adoption, divorce, body building, AIDS, immigration, alternative religions, land invasions, and presidential impeachment. Most homosexual characters in Brazilian television have appeared on the shows of the Globo network and during the 8:00 P.M. primetime slot, sometimes in prominent roles and sometimes presented in a positive light; on the other hand, lamentably, these characters tend to be cast as the proverbial effeminate gay man and masculine lesbian.[16] The latter form of representation is especially prevalent in sensationalist programs such as the one hosted by the popular Ratinho, or "Little Rat" (often called Brazil's Jerry Springer), and in speeches by and interviews with fundamentalist Protestant ministers (*pastores evangélicos*) and Catholic priests. Notorious for these statements is a young, telegenic Catholic priest, Father Marcelo Rossi. A particularly vicious diatribe by Father Rossi in the widely watched Sunday evening program *Fantástico,* on 22 November 1998, led the militant Grupo Identidade (based in Campinas, in the state of São Paulo) to file a libel suit against the priest. The suit was later withdrawn, following the priest's awkward recantation on national television a few days later.

The onset of AIDS in Brazil represented a major setback to the process of relative liberalism with regard to homosexuality, as scientific investigation and medical pursuits often became enmeshed with moral condemnation and religious discourse. Earlier notions of aberration regained the prominence they had been losing for decades and returned with renewed fervor. Fearful for their civil rights and personal safety, traditionally ostracized segments (now called "high-risk groups") retreated further into obscurity and anonymity; their moving beyond the reach of prevention and education efforts only accelerated the rate of infection. In the political arena, conservative forces pinned responsibility for the rapidly spreading disease on the liberalizing trends of the recent past (especially the decade and a half following the 1979 repeal of Ato Institucional Número 5, or Institutional Act Number Five), and their proponents were charged with direct responsibility for the quickly spreading disease. In Brazil, as in much of the world, AIDS is the most fitting metaphor of our time, linking sex, race, class, politics, and perceptions of the Other. No longer ignored or circumscribed, the gay male was quickly identified as the aberrant Other in the AIDS scene.[17] Denounced as promiscuous and pernicious, gay males took the brunt of the rhetorical blow. In the absence of an organized community and seriously lacking in political awareness as participants in a culture unwilling to acknowledge the personal as political, they were for the most part unable to counter the attacks.[18] As infection rates for other groups began to increase and the links between disease, race, and class became more apparent, new alliances were formed and AIDS organizations created. At the same time, a few politicized gay individuals worked strenuously to decrease the antihomosexual tone in print and broadcast media. Their intervention was very important for the positive developments that began to occur in the mid to late 1980s. New pedagogies of AIDS began to appear, and preventative campaigns and measures were more visible. Seriously hit by the epidemic, theater became an invaluable partner in the effort to associate art with education, entertainment with civics, drama with activism. A remarkable example is Vagner de Almeida's Oficina de Teatro Expressionista in Rio de Janeiro, or Expressionist Theater Workshop, (examined, along with other efforts, in chapter 4), which employs performance as a tool in community building and strives to take the theater to those who are least likely to get involved in or be reached by any form of consciousness raising.

The ideology of the erotic in Brazil is so dependent on transgression that cultural critics concerned with AIDS prevention dismiss as ludicrous any attempt to disentangle risk, danger, and taboo practices from desire, excitement, and sexual pleasure. Psychoanalyst and cultural critic Jurandir Freire Costa (1992) feels that the term "homosexuality" should be dropped altogether in Brazil, arguing in *A inocência e o vício* (Innocence and vice) that a belief in the existence of a "homosexual sexuality" predisposes those at risk against adopting preventative measures. Other critics concur and propose that interventions aimed at reducing risk and promoting safer sex in Brazil should avoid seeing this transgressive ideology of the erotic as an obstacle; instead, a certain "Brazilian constitutive bisexuality" should be taken for granted. As Parker (1992: 238) states, "a more effective strategy might be to seek to draw on it by focusing on the eroticization of practices that actually result in effective risk reduction." In João Silvério Trevisan's 1998 study of "*a crise do masculino*" (the crisis of the male), which is the subtitle of his *Seis balas num buraco só* (Shooting six bullets into the same hole), the issue is placed within the context of violence. Trevisan sees repressed homosocial desire as a key factor in the very high levels of male violence in contemporary Brazil and illustrates his argument with a close look at the notorious 1997 incident in a small town in the state of Rio Grande do Norte where a twenty-six-year-old former army soldier called Genildo (no last name is given) murdered fifteen people (including his wife and in-laws) before being gunned down by the police. Genildo had planned to kill numerous others, all named in a detailed list he kept. Although he cultivated intensely homoerotic friendships, the former soldier had decided to exact vengeance, he explained in a bitter letter-cum-testament, on everyone he believed was circulating rumors that he liked men (Trevisan 1998: 197–211).

Digesting Brazilian Inversions

Several key categories in Brazilian culture are inextricably related to transgression.[19] Foremost among these categories are cannibalism (or anthropophagy) and carnivalization. Building on one of the Tupi[20] rituals that colonizers most loathed, a Brazilian modernist group adopted cannibalism as a cultural metaphor. Led by Oswald de Andrade (1890–1954), Tarsila do Amaral (1886–1973) and Raul Bopp (1898–1984), the *Grupo Antropófago* published *Revista de Antropofagia* in 1928–1929, the first issue of which included Oswald's celebrated *Manifesto antropófago* (The anthropophagous manifesto). Later in life, Oswald elaborated on the initial metaphor, proposing the notion of "cultural anthropophagy," which sees Brazil as a peripheral consumer and adapter of foreign influences. Accepting as inevitable the importation of hegemonic cultural artifacts, cultural anthropophagy posits that Brazil, at the receiving end in this process, developed a strategy of creative resistance whereby imported ideas and trends are ingested and then digested, that is, transformed through contact with the autochthonous element or mindset and, finally, absorbed or incorporated into the texture of Brazilian life; whatever is not compatible with Brazilian culture is then rejected, or excreted.

In Brazilian culture, the imagery borrowed from the digestive function becomes more complex as it intersects with signation derived from sexual usage. Thus, for example, *fome* (hunger) and *apetite* (appetite) can imply sexual desire; *gostoso* or *gostosa* (tasty) can refer to a physically attractive person; and *comer* (to eat) can mean to fuck (penetrate). Richard Parker (1991: 115) provides abundant examples of the Brazilian eroticization of parts of the body and functions related to eating, cuisine, and the digestive process: "A language of tastes and smells, of food and eating, dominates erotic metaphor ... [and] structure[s] the hierarchy of gender." Transgressiveness is compounded, Parker (1991: 116) points out, as we consider that "nowhere is this alternative understanding of the body and its pleasures more pronounced than in the remarkable emphasis that is placed on the *bunda* (ass, buttocks)" in Brazil, for "just as the emphasis on the *bunda* seems to exceed the emphasis given to even the *boca* (mouth) in the erotic esthetics of the body, the importance of anal intercourse in the structures of erotic practice is more powerfully evident than any other single aspect of erotic ideology" (127). Later, reflecting on the intersections of cannibalism and carnival, he writes:

> Given all of the sexual and sensual connotations of the act of eating in Brazilian culture, the symbolism of anthropophagy is especially well suited to the semantic structure of the *carnaval.* The transgression of a food taboo can easily be linked to the transgression of sexual taboos in a symbolic construct focused on devouring the flesh of another human body in order to incorporate it within one's own. As a symbol of incorporation, then, anthropophagy can be invested with layers of meaning ranging from cannibalism itself, to the act of sexual intercourse, to the mixture of races and cultures that is taken as definitive of Brazilian reality. (149)

Parker's notions can be complemented with other insights about food, eating, and homosexuality in Brazil. Although not per se an indicator of homosexuality,[21] cannibalism among most of the Tupi tribes was a matter of "androphagia," that is, the eating of men by men. Because of their perceived bravery and corresponding privileges, only men were considered worthy of being eaten after death, their qualities preserved and their flesh absorbed by each *abaporu* ("one who eats"). Because they were not allowed to go to war, women were not considered brave and so their flesh was not cannibalized. Cannibalism was, however, blind to race: *tapuia,* or foreign males (i.e., Europeans and natives of other indigenous nations) deemed courageous were fair game for ritual consumption.

Other insights come to mind as we consider these issues in the context of AIDS and homosexuality. Here, in the most likely route of infection, it is the unprotected "eater" (anal penetrator) who transmits the virus. He can thus be seen as an agent of agony and death as the virus wreaks havoc on the immune system. An additional parallel with HIV infection needs to be examined in this regard. Because in the West AIDS was seen originally as a plague (and is still viewed as such in some parts of the world), this imagery needs to be taken into account. The parallels start with the belief that a plague is something that comes from the outside—from another body, another land—and that, as mentioned above, HIV/AIDS was in all likelihood brought into Brazil from the outside. It was, therefore, "imported" and as such—"*Só me interessa o que não é meu*" (I am only interested in what is not mine), goes one of the axioms of Oswald's *Manifesto antropófago* (Andrade 1928: 3)—in need of being anthropophagized. How does a culture approach such a destructive import? How does one deal with devastation coming from the outside (of the body, the country)? What recourse does anthropophagy have when incorporation is no longer a choice? What lessons can be derived from older models? Does anthropophagy still relate to the image of the conqueror as predator—environmental or otherwise—in the age of AIDS? As suggested in chapter 4, the theater, in confronting the AIDS crisis in Brazil, has contributed a variety of responses to such issues.

The other key category that needs to be considered at this point is carnival. The annual celebration was introduced in Brazil by the Portuguese during the colonial period, functioning, as in other parts of the world, as an occasion for "the cheerful vulgarity of the powerless [to be] used as a weapon against the pretense and hypocrisy of the powerful" (Stam 1982:47). Carnival evolved from merely a pre-Lenten street festival with pagan origins into a complex category. In Bakhtinian terms, the carnivalesque is a dismissal of the prescribed ways of doing things, with the obliteration of barriers, limits, and norms, a violent disruption of hierarchic positions. A prime site for the inversion of gender roles, carnival offers the possibility for transgressive performance. Although performative representations of sexual identity are not unique to Brazil or to Latin America, transvestism occupies center stage as the ritualized spectacle of enormous proportions that is Brazilian Carnival.[22] Furthermore, in its intrinsic ambiguity, transvestism comprises simultaneously a critique of and paean to such notions as frivolity and exoticism (a situation on which Gilberto Gawronski grounds much of his performance of *Dama da noite* [Queen of the night], examined in chapter 4). And carrying, as it does, no small amount of woman bashing, this practice accords well with a male-dominated society. Brazil's brand of phallocentrism thus deems homosexuality more palatable, or less threatening, if it is restricted to male-to-female-transvestism. When Luiz Mott (1995: 222) claims that "if a Brazilian is discreetly gay or lesbian or is aggressively transvestite, s/he won't suffer too much discrimination," he must have in mind male-to-female transvestism; the picture is somewhat different when it comes to female-to-male transvestism, where social sanctions seem more likely to obtain.

Often recognized as a defining trait of Brazilian national identity, the carnivalesque is, as Peter Stallybrass and Allon White (1986: 18) point out in *The Politics and Poetics of Transgression*, undeniably useful as a model that is at once utopian and counterhegemonic; as such it will function, in Roberto da Matta's terms, as a privileged locus of inversion. Carnival, nevertheless, raises serious political problems, chief among them its nostalgia, licensed complicity (i.e., its failure to topple the dominant culture), and uncritical populism. The latter is of particular consequence to issues of marginality and inversion, including transvestism, in Brazil. For, as Stallybrass and White state, "carnival often violently abuses and demonizes *weaker*, not stronger, social groups—women, ethnic and religious minorities, those who 'don't belong'—in a process of *displaced abjection*" (19).

In order to understand the Brazilian concept of inversion, one must take into account the prominent role ambiguity plays in Brazilian sexuality.[23] Valued and cultivated since the earliest colonial period by a culture whose very center encourages the expansion of its contours in areas ranging from religion to criminal law, ambiguity has become a key factor in the daily negotiations that define the process of social survival in Brazil. A central notion here is the double standard of sexual morality prevalent in the country. Bolstered by the nation's patriarchal tradition, the double standard oscillates between private life and public conduct (*casa* and *rua*, respectively, in Roberto da Matta's terms (1991) and is a major factor in the game of appearances that Rommel Mendès-Leite (1993) has called "ambigusexuality." The Brazilian culture of sexuality, Mendès-Leite argues, is a system in which three identifiable levels can link the social actor (or sexual individual) with his or her character. The first of these levels is the *role*, or "the number of expectations to which the actor 'would have' to correspond" (274); the second is the "interpretation" the individual gives his or her role, an interpretation that often fails to match what society expects of him or her; the third, which Mendès-Leite calls "performance," is "a level at which the actor tries to give his audience the impression that his interpretation is very close to the original role (more than it perhaps originally was meant to be)." It follows that the more fluid the social roles in a given society, the larger the number of possible interpretations and performances will be. In Brazil, as in other Latin American countries, sexual orientation is for the most part construed from an individual's performance, with the game of appearances (sometimes called "social make-up") being an integral component in the formation of such an image. In homosocial relations, this kind of duplicity or polymorphism exacerbates a real, or perceived, and often craved element of risk. In fact, one can argue that together Mendès-Leite's three levels function as major players in a situation Parker (1992: 238) describes as "an ideology of the erotic which is heavily focused on a certain kind of danger or risk [and is] central to the constitution of desire, excitement, and ultimately, sexual pleasure." In the final analysis, these notions seem to suggest erotic pleasure itself is defined "not merely as just a physical sensation but as a cultural construct" (230).

Ambigusexuality and the notion of inversion prevalent in Brazilian culture helped the elaboration of a particular construct where homosexuality is the simultaneous focus of both abjection and fascination. "The classificatory body of a culture," Stallybrass and White (1986: 20) write, "is always double, always structured in relation to its negation, its inverse." With two forms of subjectivity giving rise to contrary registers of being, a seemingly fundamental rule of the logic of identity formation—"what is excluded at the overt level of identity formation is productive of new objects of desire" (25)—came to obtain in Brazil.

This identity formation process works notably at the symbolic level. As Barbara Babcock (1978: 14) writes in her introduction to *The Reversible World*, symbolic inversion encompasses "any act of expressive behaviour which inverts, contradicts, abrogates, or in some fashion presents an alternative to commonly held cultural codes, values and norms be they linguistic, literary or artistic, religious, social and political." Theater is then a privileged locus for an examination of a situation where "what is socially peripheral is often symbolically central" (32). And if, as Marcel Détienne (1979: ix) has stated, "to discover the complete horizon of a society's symbolic values, it is also necessary to map out its transgressions, interrogate its deviants, discern phenomena of rejection and refusal," this book attempts to claim for the theater an important role in such elucidation.

Beyond Inversion

The vital role of the theater extends beyond the clarification of a society's symbolic values or the untangling of its notions of deviance. Since theater is in a unique position to give voice to those who cannot speak or who can speak but are not heard or properly understood, the notion of the subaltern—with all its attending ambiguities and contradictions inevitably enters the discussion. As the subject in such an elucidation, the subaltern is seen in this book as a gendered subject. In the seminal if controversial essay "Can the Subaltern Speak?" Gayatri Chakravorty Spivak (1988) problematizes the production and reception of subaltern speech in light of its dependence on dominant discourses. While discussing the subaltern as female, Spivak postulates the impossibility of a retrieval of the subaltern's voice, as demonstrated by any attempt to plot the circumstances from which the subaltern speaks, but "cannot be heard or read" (308). Writing about the suitability of the application of Western methodologies to "third world" texts, Spivak (1987: 246) insists on such gendered status for the subaltern—in opposition to the European and North American position that "homogenizes the Third World and sees it only in the context of nationalism and ethnicity." These points are key to an understanding of the concepts of inversion and of the sexual gendered subject as well as to resistance to such notions as they appear in a number of the plays examined in the following chapters. Because of the additional layers of perceived transgression and marginality prompted by the arrival of HIV and AIDS, in chapter 4 I return to a consideration of the subaltern spaces created by the epidemic in Brazil and the role the theater has played in making the subaltern heard.

In a society such as Brazil—subaltern and dependent on the one hand, and carnivalizing and cannibalistic on the other—the notion of inversion plays a vital role. Keeping in mind the widely discussed views of Bakhtin and da Matta on carnivalization in general and those of João Silvério Trevisan and Richard Parker on homosexuality in Brazil in particular,[24]

I proceed to use the pertinent ideas put forth by Eve Kosofsky Sedgwick (1990) in *Epistemology of the Closet* and Judith Butler (1991) in "Imitation and Gender Insubordination."

Sedgwick (1990: 87) rejects the traditional homophobic "inversion trope," that is, the concept of "inversion" as *anima muliebris in corpore virili inclusa* (a woman's soul caught in a man's body) or vice versa, since it is grounded on the perpetuation of the idea of an essential heterosexual desire, the attraction between male and female, regardless of the sex of the bodies housing such elements. Related to this notion but in part contradictory to it is the trope of "gender separatism," which, according to Sedgwick, "tends to reassimilate to one another identification and desire, where inversion models, by contrast, depend on their distinctness" (88). The complex relationship between the two models in the last one hundred years or so (since the foundation in 1897, by Magnus Hirschfeld and others, of the German movement for homosexual rights) is crucial for an understanding of gender asymmetry, oppression, and resistance, Sedgwick argues. Of foremost interest here is the fact that, if one accepts the "gender inversion" topos, with its notion of a male homosexual's tendency to identify with the heterosexual woman, or of the female homosexual's with the heterosexual man, a new homosexual identity based on egalitarian roles could not have appeared, and the post-Stonewall models of gay self-imaging could have only led to a relational impasse, something we know now did not occur.

In her analysis of the homosexual individual's alleged inversion and imitation of the opposite heterosexual gender, Judith Butler appends a long discussion to the axiom "gender is a kind of imitation for which there is no original" (which she prefers to reword as "a kind of imitation that produces the very notion of the original as an *effect* and consequence of the imitation itself"); she concludes that mere inversions are impossible, for "the entire framework of copy and origin proves radically unstable as each position inverts into the other and confounds the possibility of any stable way to locate the temporal or logical priority of either term" (1991: 22). Elaborating on the idea put forth by Derrida (1981) in "The Double Session" that inversion is to be understood through a careful study of mimetic displacement, Butler asserts that "if the structure of gender imitation is such that the imitat*ed* is to some degree produced—or, rather, *re*produced—by imitation, . . . then to claim that gay and lesbian identities are implicated in heterosexual norms or in hegemonic culture generally is not to *derive* gayness from straightness. On the contrary, *imitation* does not copy that which is prior, but produces and *inverts* the very terms of priority and derivativeness" (21). It is my contention here that most of the plays depicting the experience of gays and lesbians in Brazilian theater until about 1970 reflect the impact of a situation Butler describes as "the parodic or imitative effect of gay identities works neither to copy nor to emulate heterosexuality but rather, to expose heterosexuality as an incessant and *panicked* imitation of its own naturalized idealization" (22–23). These works shed light on the intersection of anxieties (if not panics)—sexual, social, political—at the center of intellectual production in mid-twentieth-century Brazil. As chapter 2 attempts to make clear, it was precisely these anxieties that led otherwise great playwrights Oswald de Andrade and Nelson Rodrigues (1912–1980) to so misrepresent male and female homosexuality in their theater; and perhaps more seriously, these anxieties kept Lúcio Cardoso (1912–1968) from expressing his true gay sensibility and blossoming into the outstanding playwright he was perhaps destined to be.

The often disappointing attempts of these writers at gay and lesbian representation reflects perhaps a failure to comprehend the full extent of gender and power in Brazil as such forces intersect with homosexuality. The issue is further complicated by the nature of bisexuality in the country and the attending race and class considerations that are less likely to exist in the West, where a more general brand of bisexuality obtains, one that posits a man (or woman) who is simultaneously a same that is not and a same that is like its partner. In this regard Sedgwick's discussion (1990: 160) of *The Portrait of Dorian Gray* is elucidating, especially her remarks about the "linguistically unappealable classification of anyone who shares one's gender as being 'the same' as oneself, and anyone who does not share one's gender as being the Other." While Oswald and Nelson were for the most part unable to avoid such pitfalls, their works do on occasion present glimpses of understanding, most notably in Nelson's *Beijo no asfalto* (publ. and perf. 1961; A kiss on the asphalt).

Staging Transgression

In a self-reflecting process, the theater has been a privileged stage for the playing out of vastly different approaches to difference and transgression in Brazil. It is my intention in this book to attend directly to transgressive, counteractive elements in Brazilian theater, elements that come to the fore as the theater has an impact on and is, in turn, influenced by a society organized according to diverse perspectives on negation and inversion. Through its provocative, if often hesitant, representations of transgression, the Brazilian theater enriches culture with ideas indispensable to self-reflection and fundamental for cultural survival. However, an examination of transgressive theater demands a rethinking of agency, of who speaks for the oppressed and what is said on their behalf. Such a rethinking plays a political role when it results in or provides contestations to power and authority, issues normally silenced by mainstream canonical theater.

In considering the role of a transgressive theater in the defining of a collective identity around a common experience of oppression and marginalization, one should take into account a central trait of Brazilian culture, namely, an inclination to reject conflict, in favor of what Sérgio Buarque de Hollanda refers to as *"cordialidade,"* or cordiality, a defining attribute of the national character. Inevitably, this mythical harmonious socialization entails a disturbing need to accommodate opposites and evade marginality. It also leads to the widespread belief inculcated among numerous oppressed groups that one must not push the envelope or incite the wrath of those in power. To adjust to such a state of affairs, then, contestation should be cautious, protest temperate, and, as the title of this book suggests, stage transgression should be tentative.

Ultimately, such a study needs to consider to what extent, and with what degree of success, marginalized groups such as Brazilian homosexuals have questioned their representation by mainstream authors, challenged stereotypes presented on stage, offered alternative images of who they are, rejected subdued, tentative contestation, and opted, finally, for meaningful transgression.

Largely owing to its transgressive role, theater has been the site for political battles in different periods of Brazilian history when censorship served as a potent tool for ever-alert power holders in their crusades against dissent.[25] For the military regime in the 1960s and 1970s, the theater was closely associated with what they termed "subversion" and hence in need of being restrained by measures ranging from censorship and arson to arrests, torture, and the disappearance of individuals. The dictatorship's peculiar notion of subversion made no distinction between guerilla warfare and political dissent on an intellectual level and often treated sexual transgression as merely another type of social and political unrest.

From early on, the role of theater as sociopolitical metastage where issues of national importance are played out has been punctuated by ambivalence. In fact, a key conflict has shaped the existence of the theater in Brazil from its inception to the present—an attraction to and rejection of the experience of the different and the disenfranchised. The many gestures toward inclusion and solidarity and the equally forceful movement away from it have taken diverse forms and guises throughout the history of the dramatic arts in Brazil.

This phenomenon is best understood in light of the workings and assumptions of an authoritarian culture and strictly hierarchical society in which the author has the sanction and the weight of authority behind him (and it's usually a him—a white, educated, middle- or upper-class, heterosexual, European-oriented male who has the support of the political, cultural, literary, theatrical establishment) as he builds his career and clinches his place in the canon. In its diverse guises, that authority could be the Catholic Church (as in the case of sixteenth-century missionary playwright José de Anchieta [1534–1597] who represented in his *autos* [brief, one-act plays] the indigenous peoples he sought to convert), the moneyed establishment of the Luso-Brazilian empire (as with Gonçalves de Magalhães [1811–1882] and José de Alencar [1829–1877] who portrayed Jews, slaves, and prostitutes), or a university-trained intellectual elite (as was the case of Gianfrancesco Guarnieri [b. 1934] whose plays offered representations of striking factory workers in mid-twentieth-century São Paulo).

"Repugnance and fascination," write Stallybrass and White (1986: 4–5), "are the twin poles of the process in which a *political* imperative to reject and eliminate the debasing 'low' conflicts powerfully and unpredictably with a desire for this Other." As a prime locus for the moral and political indoctrination of the native population, theater affords us an opportunity to understand how the holders of authority dealt with difference (social, racial, sexual) in the first century of colonization. From the beginning of the Portuguese domination of Brazil, there emerged what Stallybrass and White have referred to as "the low-Other [, a social category that] is despised and denied at the level of political organization and social being whilst it is instrumentally constitutive of the shared imaginary repertoires of the dominant culture" (5–6). Theater was an instrument of catechism that borrowed the low-Other's cultural artifacts (indigenous dances, music and songs, body painting, musical instruments, weaponry, legends, and so on) while urging the same low-Other to renounce their inherent identity in favor of the imposed culture. In sixteenth-century Portugal theater was not regarded as a reputable activity, and in the colony it was viewed with considerable suspicion, acceptable only as a tool of indoctrination.

With the death of Anchieta and a series of shifts in colonial policy that placed less emphasis on indoctrination, theater became virtually invisible for over a century. Notwithstanding a minor infusion of Spanish plays (presented in the original or in Portuguese translation or adaptation for the enjoyment of government officials and members of a tiny business elite), the situation hardly changed between 1581 and 1640, the period when the Spanish crown ruled Portugal and its colonies, and Brazil was essentially a colony of a colony. The discovery of vast reserves of gold and diamonds in Minas Gerais during the eighteenth century created a more welcoming atmosphere for the arts, which included the opening of theaters in Vila Rica, Sabará, and other mining towns. A distinct shift in geo-economics was taking place at the time, with the center of power moving away from the formerly privileged sugar-producing Northeast and its two poles, Recife and Salvador, toward the metal-rich Southeast; this shift was confirmed in 1763 when Salvador lost its condition of colonial capital to Rio de Janeiro. The slow but steady growth of a few colonial cities in southern Brazil enabled the opening of a few "opera houses" in Rio de Janeiro, Cuiabá, São Paulo, and elsewhere. But acting and actors were still held in contempt and the traditional ban on women on the stage (mostly as a consequence of Jesuit praxis), prevalent since the beginning of theatrical activity in Brazil, was actually reinforced with a 1780 royal decree that extended the prohibition to other parts of the building, including theater wings, dressing rooms, and boxes.

It was not until the arrival of the Portuguese court in Rio de Janeiro in 1808 and the declaration of independence from Portugal some years later (1822) that truly favorable winds began to blow the theater's way.[26] But even then, the craft was generally taken up only by "disreputable individuals"—persons of mixed race and impoverished adolescent boys who made a living as performers in mostly decrepit houses. However, as the elites began to frequent the theater, foreign companies (mostly Italian, French, Spanish, and Portuguese) were invited for what often became extended sojourns in the young nation. As a result, white actors began to predominate on stage and nonwhite performers were given secondary or subservient roles.

The decree forbidding women from performing was revoked in 1800, although it had not been uncommon even while the ban was in effect for some companies to include women. But even after female actors were able to legally join their male counterparts on stage, their reputations remained subject to suspicion throughout the nineteenth century; in fact, "up to the beginning of the twentieth century public health authorities demanded medical certificates from actresses to prove that they were not carrying any diseases" (Trevisan 1986: 91). It was not until the 1860s, with the production of plays by Maria Angélica Ribeiro (1829–1880) that women playwrights saw their works staged under their own names in Brazil (until then their works may have been staged and/or published under men's names); Ribeiro's *Gabriela* was staged in Rio de Janeiro in 1863, while her abolitionist drama, *Cancros sociais* (Social cancer), was produced in 1865 and published in 1866 (Galante de Souza 1960, 2: 455–56).

The almost complete absence of women from the theaters of colonial Brazil made stage transvestism an accepted practice. With the exception of the Virgin Mary, female roles in Jesuit plays were performed by young indigenous boys. Male-to-female cross-dressing was standard performance convention well into the nineteenth century, both in Rio de Janeiro and in more remote parts of the country. Sanctioned on stage over such a long period of time, transvestism acquired a solid footing in Brazilian theater, becoming an essential component in the musical revues that prevailed in the late nineteenth and early to mid-twentieth centuries (*teatro de revista* and *teatro rebolado*) and creating a special space of its own with the *show de travesti*, or transvestite show, popular in mid- to late-twentieth-century Brazil.[27] As I mentioned earlier, transvestism is central to one of the key phenomena that inform and define Brazilian culture (carnival) and as such has been a highly visible component in contemporary Brazilian society. Cross-dressing artists figure among the most recognized figures in national life and culture, as evidenced by the acclaim of actors such as Rogéria and Eloína and performers such as Roberta Close and Isabelita dos Patins.[28] A good deal of androgyny and gay performativity has come to be accepted and even expected in mainstream entertainment, as represented prominently in the popular personas of singer Ney Matogrosso, carnival choreographer Joãozinho Trinta, and stylist-cum-television personality Clodovil.[29] Such cross-dressing and gender play is however almost exclusively male-to-female. Only relatively recently did female-to-male cross-dressing begin to be visible; outright female-to-male transvestism, however, remains unacceptable in a staunchly male dominated society since, unlike its male-to-female counterpart, female-to-male transvestism upsets the traditional representations of gender in Brazil. What has so far been permissible is a certain measure of gender bending—teasing instances of gender play involving mostly popular entertainers and singers (Araci de Almeida,

Maria Bethânia, Simone, Leci Brandão, Angela Rô Rô, and the late Cássia Eller, among others).

The figure of Madame Satã (João Francisco dos Santos, 1900–1976) deserves particular attention among Brazilian image and gender benders because his assertive individuality and lifestyle affords us an appreciation of how transgression, subalternity, and performance intersect. With his in-your-face attitude, Madame Satã was more emblematic of the *"assumido"* ("out") urban gay male of half a century later than of the more demure homosexual normally associated with the 1930s and 1940s. Through his celebrated adventures (a good number of which have become the stuff of folk legend), Satã marked an epoch in mid-century Rio de Janeiro, transcending the subculture to which he would traditionally have been relegated. As a performing artist, his career included stage appearances as early as 1928 and as late as 1974 (Durst 1985: 59, 71). As a black man, in addition to struggling with the already heavy burden of racial discrimination and poverty in Brazil, Satã subverted stereotypes of black virility and, by challenging other black men to confront their sexuality, provoked serious anxiety in them. Furthermore, as an openly homosexual man who was proud of his orientation, he subverted the idealized image of the *malandro* (rogue or hustler, with a strong implication of masculinity and bravery) of the time; whereas true to the *malandro's* requisite qualities of living in the social interstices and breaking the law (stealing, gambling, pimping, and so on), Satã made no secret of his enjoyment of being anally penetrated. His life sheds light on the degree of cross-class and cross-racial interaction as well as on the consequent tensions arising from the mixing of people of unequal economic means and social station in twentieth-century Brazil. The devilish attributes denoted in his assumed name bespeak perceptions of race and evil in Brazilian society, which he of course exploited to his own advantage, building on his already dangerous mystique—due in part to his impressive knife-wielding talents and the murder of a policeman for which he was sentenced to sixteen years in prison. Like Jean Genet, with whom he had much in common, Satã profited in strange ways from his crimes, both real and fictional. His stays in jail contributed to his tough-guy image and seemingly remarkable survival skills and helped to increase his stature in the eyes of his peers and enemies alike.

The performative nature of Satã's life could be read as a critique of traditional gendered behavior in Brazil. This is apparent in his sometimes exaggeratedly macho behavior and his close ties with the underworld of crime, on the one hand, and his patently camp ways and enjoyment of homosexuality, on the other. Satã's ability to combine macho bravado and uninhibited campiness reveals much about cultural definitions of masculinity in Brazil. As stories about Satã's feats circulated in Rio's Lapa (a red-light district where bohemians, artists, intellectuals, prostitutes, drag queens, and crime figures freely mixed), with each raconteur adding embellishments, Satã's penchant for new exploits only seemed to increase—as did his performative adeptness. Madame Satã's behavior challenged Brazil's rigid hetero-dominant sexual system and affirmed the multiplicity of gender identities assumed by Brazilian men. Because of this, his life has become an inspiration for men who have sex with other men as they negotiate their way through an often hostile society.[30]

Theater afforded male homosexual artists in turn-of-the-century Brazil certain necessary elements for representing their own perceived difference. Yet with few exceptions, internalized homophobia prevailed, and drama was oblique and artificial. Gifted playwrights, actors, directors, and set designers sometimes rendered the strategies of concealment that many male homosexuals used in their lives into richly layered artistic practices. For the playwright—João do Rio (Paulo Barreto, 1881–1921) being the preeminent name here—wit and paradox became more important than sincerity, since sincerity meant self-acceptance (which could mean the end of one's career) and self-exposure (which could mean the end of one's life).

A latecomer to the uneasily imported, hastily arranged event that was Brazilian modernism, the theater approached sexual difference with more suspicion than the turn-of-the-century scene. Chapter 2, "Modernist and Neorealist Backtracking,"[31] pays close attention to the two major exponents of Brazilian modernist theater, Nelson Rodrigues and Oswald de Andrade, and the preeminent name in neorealist theater, Plínio Marcos (1935–1999). The three playwrights, all heterosexual white males, included gay and lesbian characters in their theater as mouthpieces for some of the new ideas they wanted to pioneer on the Brazilian stage (Freudianism in the case of Nelson, marxism for Oswald, and a kind of social theater of cruelty for Marcos). However, in their theaters, homosexuality is repositioned in relation to an ideal, if flawed, heterosexuality, thus undermining, albeit for different reason, the movements to which the authors subscribed.

Barely able to go beyond the naturalist notion that same-sex affection was a symptom of a social pathology that spelled doom for those who indulged in it (a notion crystallized by Adolfo Caminha [1867–1897] in *Bom crioulo* [1895]), Nelson Rodrigues authored a theater where transgressive sexuality connotes depravity, social disintegration, and collapsed personalities, with the expected outcome of disgrace and ruin. Although credited with renovating the Brazilian stage, rescuing it from the stagnation of poor imitations of *revistas* and comedies of manners in which it had been trapped for decades, Nelson could not overcome his own male heterosexual anxieties and the set of prejudices handed down to him by religion and social class. For Oswald, sexual transgression seemed to signal moral weakness and capitalist decadence, reflecting a marxist view or, more aptly put, the curiously personal brand of marxism that Oswald seems to have adapted to his needs (with watered-down notions of orthodox marxism coexisting with his aforementioned ideas of "cultural anthropophagy" and a not inconsiderable dash of *deboche*, a term best translated as a mischievous attitude or impish nature). Oswald seems to favor the facile interpretation of homosexuality critiqued by Sedgwick and Butler, a reading that traditionally casts it in terms of "inversion." Thus, in his theater Oswald preferred to relegate gay men to the *teatro de revista* chorus lines and other inconsequential roles marked by hyperbolic affectation, thus reinforcing the longstanding stereotypes of the gay experience as highly dramatic or theatrical and of gay individuals as sensitive, witty, tasteful, and always displaying a great sense of timing and repartee, but ultimately expendable, if not pathetic, creatures.

In subsequent years, Oswald's depiction of homosexuals only reinforced the general inability of the Brazilian left, its claims to progressivism notwithstanding, to contend with homosexuality.[32] Major names in the Brazilian theater of the 1950s and 1960s, playwrights of the stature of Dias Gomes (1922–1993), Gianfrancesco Guarnieri and Augusto Boal (b. 1931), failed to question these prejudices, and even the much respected Teatro de Arena de São Paulo, with which the latter two names were closely connected, succumbed to patriarchal prejudices and—ironically for a group fighting the forces of oppression overtaking the country—perpetuated repressive attitudes toward and thinking about a minority group. For example, Boal and Guarnieri's *Arena conta Zumbi* (1965; Arena tells the story of Zumbi), the group's biggest success, includes a scene in which the enemy, in this case a Dutch platoon attempting to destroy Palmares, is represented through a stereotypical portrayal of gay men. In Trevisan's report (1986: 113), openly gay actors were prevented from joining Arena in the 1960s, a claim corroborated by Guarnieri in an interview published in the Rio de Janeiro weekly *O Pasquim* in 1981. Arena's stagings, Guarnieri (1981: 9) explained defensively to the editors of the key counterculture journal, called for a "masculine performance" in which speech and body language were "unambiguous" and void of affectation; such criteria led Arena to ban those they suspected might be gay. In a 1977 interview with David George (1995b: 51–58), another Arena member, set designer Flávio Império, discussed at length the climate of homophobia at Arena. Conversely, with Oficina (see chapters 2 and 3), another major group of the 1960s and 1970s, transgression—of all stripes, including homosexual—was at center stage, not just as political contestation as in the case of Arena. Oficina was created and is directed by José Celso Martinez Correa (b. 1937), better known in Brazil as Zé Celso, for whom, as Mariângela Alves de Lima (1992: 1–2) has stated, transgression is the defining poetics. Zé Celso, who is openly gay, was seen by many in the late 1960s and early 1970s as the *enfant terrible* of Brazilian theater; even today, although not as often or as strongly, the frontal nudity, sexual situations, and general homoeroticism in his stagings shock certain audiences.

The work of Plínio Marcos, a member of the generation that followed Nelson's and Oswald's, is also considered in chapter 2. Although he kept his distance from the more engaged protest theater favored by Boal, Guarnieri, and others, Marcos is equally political and, in his depictions of an underclass trapped in crass, violent exploitation, and extreme disaffection, as powerful in his protest. Marcos's plays speak eloquently about how the self-destructive behavior of the oppressed reveals the ampler societal forces that dictate it. But even Marcos, the champion of what Trevisan (1986: 124) termed the "disgraced pariahs" of the Brazilian theater of the 1960s and 1970s, did not take his representation of gays and lesbians beyond personages both pathetic and depraved. In the 1960s, Marcos wrote a number of plays that include gay characters (such as Veludo, in *Navalha na carne* [prem. 1967, publ. 1968, Razor in the flesh]) or depict homosocial relations (for instance, those of Paco and Tonho in *Dois perdidos numa noite suja* [prem. 1966, publ. 1979; Two men lost in a dirty night]) and explore issues of violence and power, including homosexual rape (*Barrela* [written 1957, publ. 1976, prem. 1979; Male gang rape]). As victims of a system that mercilessly rejects the financially deprived, these characters have learned to rely on violence as their only leverage. Their personal interactions are thus marked by physical aggression, and vulgarity and abrasiveness drive the dialogue. As members of self-contained communities with their own inflexible mores and rules, they have learned to beleaguer those around them with an abundant use of foul language.

Marcos, more than any other recent Brazilian playwright, may have had the most serious problems with the censors. His works were banned so frequently and so consistently that he came to regard the impediment as insurmountable and stopped writing for a long period. However, following the easing of military rule in the late 1970s, his two best and—to the censors—most offensive plays were published in 1979, *Dois perdidos numa noite suja* and *Navalha na carne* (*Navalha* had been released in an earlier, 1968 edition but that version was confiscated shortly after publication). Marcos wrote a few minor plays in the 1970s and, by staying out of the political limelight, managed to evade imprisonment or exile. In his next major play, the 1985 *Madame Blavatsky*, Marcos chose to keep his distance from social theater and from the Brazilian experience itself. Also, much to everyone's surprise, Marcos avoided the use of foul language in his new play. This is of course very ironic, because when he finally had the chance to use offensive language and freely write on the plight of the oppressed, Marcos chose not to. Marcos returned to social activism in the late 1980s as he became involved in AIDS education and prevention, especially in prisons. This experience formed the basis for his next major play, *A mancha roxa* (The purple stain), which is examined in chapter 4.

Nelson, Oswald, and Marcos are playwrights whose immense iconic stature in Brazilian culture calls for frequent reinterpretation. What I intend to argue here is that the theater of these men, although sporting a veneer of modernity and tolerance, harked back to a period that vilified difference and thus excluded most signs of the fluid nature of gender identification in Brazil. The harm caused by their exclusionary practices in fact continued into the next generation of dramatists, and it was not until the 1970s that a new approach to the representation of gays and lesbians began to appear on the Brazilian stage. Still, when examined in terms of transgression and gay representation, the plays discussed in chapter 2 (Oswald's *O rei da vela* [publ. 1937; perf. 1967; The candle baron], Nelson's *Album de família* [publ. 1946; perf. 1967, A family's portrait album], *Beijo no asfalto*, and *Toda nudez será castigada* [perf. 1965; publ. 1966; *All Nudity Shall Be Punished*], as well as Marcos's works mentioned above)—all of which are generally considered to be among the best Brazilian theater ever produced—lend themselves to new readings.

Chapter 2 also aims to locate homoeroticism[33] as well as hints of, allusions to, and mixed signals about suppressed gayness in the Brazilian theater of the first decades of the twentieth century. If we discount Nelson's, Oswald's, and Marcos's representations, gays and lesbians were virtually absent from the Brazilian theater of the period. No other group was so systematically silenced from the mainstream Brazilian stage, an ironic state of affairs in light of the large number of gay and lesbian theater professionals at the time. In *Reading the Body Politic,* Amy Kaminsky (1993: 25) highlights the political ramifications of physical presence, where presence "declares the existence of the individual not as a coherent psychological subject, but rather as a potent political subject." Such a claim is made possible by the physicality of the body, its tangibility, its corporeality, even, and especially, "in the face of erasure and silencing" when "some dominant force deliberately denies it." Kaminsky illustrates her argument with the Latin American practice of honoring victims of repression by calling out their names as if taking roll, with those in attendance responding, "*presente!*" This affirmation of presence is "at once embodied and represented, individual and historical" (24–25). The dichotomy presence/absence is particularly relevant in the case of theater. Absence becomes conspicuous on the stage—taking on new signation, "dramatized" as it were by its very nature. Performativity demands the double corporeality of an actor's body engaged in the activation of a represented other. With the body not present, esthetic exigency and political statement combine to forge a formidable testimony of erasure. In the case of Brazilian theater, the "presence in absence" of gay men and lesbians up until the 1970s provides a backdrop onto which those absent are made present in the abiding action of their successors.

A related matter is that of speaking for others. Linda Alcoff (1991–92) identifies two problems in speaking for other people. First, the speaker's social location (or social identity) can serve either to certify or disallow one's speech; and second, "the practice of privileged persons speaking for or on behalf of less privileged persons has actually resulted . . . in increasing or reinforcing the oppression of the group spoken for" (6–7). To return to the more immediate concerns of chapter 2, consideration must be given to the dangers involved in heterosexual playwrights such as Nelson, Oswald, or Marcos attempting to speak for gay men and lesbians, as they do in the plays mentioned above. Feminist criticism is again pertinent in this regard. The warning issued by Hélène Cixous (1990: 143) in one of her many texts on Clarice Lispector states the challenge succinctly: "Our problem, when we want to write, speak, evoke the Other, is how not to do it from ourselves." Cynthia Duncan (1994–95: 18), in her examination of women writers' attempts to challenge traditional discursive practices, remarks on the importance of their works, as "they examine the limits that have been imposed on language, literature and, by extension, women in general, and call attention to the inconsistencies and injustices inherent in a system that has sought to exclude them on the basis of their gender." Unlike the authors Duncan writes about, the playwrights examined in chapter 2 speak in the voice of the Other while they reinforce stereotypes and reinscribe hierarchies, strengthening as a result the limits imposed on gay men and lesbians. As biased representations of transgression, their plays promote prejudices and perpetuate exclusion. These authors are thus ironically privileged in several respects; they are allowed to speak while the oppressed themselves are not, and their name recognition and visibility, if not necessarily their artistic prestige, increase as their plays are read and performed.

Also involved here is the issue of men writing the feminine. Before we even consider them as heterosexual male playwrights representing lesbians, Nelson, Oswald, and Marcos need to be seen as male playwrights representing women,[34] privileged exercisers of the male gaze in a society in which men are active and women passive and in a theater in which female characters are traditionally portrayed as fragile, weak, and dependent in their sexual roles. As for the audience reception, the gaze is encoded with "culturally determined components of male sexual desire, perceiving 'woman' as a sexual object" (Case: 1998: 118). Because traditionally the subject has been the male subject, with whom the audience would be expected to identify, this extended situation thwarts the potential for women to emerge as subjects rather than as objects (121). This appropriation does more than merely disregard the existing mobility of gendered and sexual behaviors in the bisexual segments of the population—it fails to take into account even the less fluid woman-focused sexual interest in lesbians.

The problem is aggravated when one considers issues of production and distribution. If, as was the case in Brazilian theater and film of the period under discussion, the audience is made up of and controlled by ruling groups, not only do women remain unable to escape the role of objects but those who are being spoken for are pushed further to the margins. Writing about speaking as an act of resistance, bell hooks (1998: 14) alerts us to how "appropriation of the marginal voice threatens the very core of self-determination and free self-expression for exploited and oppressed peoples." If the dominant elites retain control of the means of cultural production and dissemination, she concludes, "it becomes easy to speak about what that group wants to hear, to describe and define experience in a language compatible with existing images and ways of knowing, constructed within social frameworks that reinforce domination" (14).

The seriousness of the problem became apparent to me as I searched in vain for lesbian-authored plays of the period.[35] The invisibility of lesbians in the Brazilian theater—as published or performed playwrights, as characters, directors, or major actors—reflects the invisibility of lesbians in the Brazilian society of the time.[36] This situation is not dissimilar, I believe, to the relatively small numbers of women writers and playwrights. Writing on this fact, Hélène Cixous (in her essay, "The Laugh of the Medusa," commented on in Case [1998: 128]) relates the paucity of women writers to the cultural assimilation of women's bodies by the dominant male system of desire and representation. Ignoring and attempting to erase the existence of lesbians (and gay men), the heterosexist imperative extends its control to the stages and screens, maintaining in the process a hegemonic position.

The aforementioned paradigm of attraction to and rejection of the experience of the different and the disenfranchised prevails throughout the history of Brazilian theater, yet only recently, as chapter 3 ("Beyond Evasiveness") attempts to show with regard to the representation of homosexuality, has it been questioned with any measure of success. Attempts to disrupt this pattern did occur in the colonial era and during the nineteenth century but for the most part met with failure, even in those cases when they originated within the educated elite, as, for example, in the case of the brilliant, caustic theater of Qorpo-Santo (José Joaquim de Campos Leão, 1829–1883) in the second half of the nineteenth century.

Living in provincial isolation in Rio Grande do Sul, apparently oblivious to the theatrical scene of the nation's capital, Qorpo-Santo occupies a unique place in the history of Brazilian drama. Although he spent most of his adult life fighting a misguided judicial system that accused him of mental illness, Qorpo-Santo still managed to leave seventeen extant plays composed during the various all-too-brief periods of tranquility he enjoyed in 1866. Largely ignored by theater directors, critics, and historians until the mid 1960s, Qorpo-Santo was nevertheless the theatrical genius that, had his plays been produced, might have raised Brazilian drama to theretofore unknown heights.

Qorpo-Santo's plays are short satires populated by characters who often bear such odd names as Rapivalho, Miguelítico, Impertinente, Truque-truque, Perna de Galinha, and Espertalínio da Porciúncula. His theater as a whole constitutes a wry indictment of his contemporaries, a satirical commentary on the pedantry of the Second Empire, and a truly subversive alternative to the commercially successful and officially sanctioned theater of his time. His transgressiveness, evident at the linguistic level, in the simplified, phonetically accurate spelling he championed and—to the horror and derision of his literate contemporaries—used in his writings, explains the accusations of insanity that dogged his life. Owing to a general disregard for spatial and chronological consistency and the numerous instances of disjunction and irrationality in his works, Qorpo-Santo is rightly seen by most contemporary Brazilian critics as a precursor of the theater of the absurd. These traits are most readily noticeable in his best works, *Mateus, Mateusa* (Male Matthew, female Matthew), *As relações naturais* (Natural relationships), and *Eu sou vida, eu não sou morte* (I am life, not death) written, respectively, on 12, 14, and 16 May 1866. Qorpo-Santo was also the first Brazilian playwright to portray same-sex couples (Tamanduá and Tatu, the two male spouses in *A separação de dois esposos* [The separation of the husbands])[37] and to allow actors and directors latitude in the staging of his plays. Scorned by contemporary publishers and perhaps sensing that future generations would be more likely to understand and value his art, Qorpo-Santo printed his own works in a small press he purchased for that purpose. One of his projects was a multivolume *Enciclopédia*, the fourth installment of which includes the texts of the seventeen plays. The now extremely rare volumes illustrate his peculiar notions about spelling as well as other idiosyncrasies.

His isolation coupled with the scorn with which he was treated by his contemporaries left Qorpo-Santo with no imitators or followers. In contrast to Martins Pena, the best-known Brazilian dramatist of the nineteenth century and popularizer of the *comédia de costumes* who enjoyed enormous success during and after his brief life, Qorpo-Santo remained virtually unknown for more than half a century after his death, and the first staging of his plays did not take place until 1966, one hundred years after they were written (Aguiar 1975: 245–50). The Brazilian theater thus remained in the grip of the *comédia de costumes*, which along with its counterpart, the *teatro de revista*, resonated well into the twentieth century. That genre's hold was not even relaxed by such auspicious developments as the opening of new theaters and the advent of younger playwrights and innovative acting companies. In fact, the twentieth century would be almost half over before the conventions of the previous century gave way to the genuine changes introduced by Nelson Rodrigues.

Brazilian theater can boast only two major women playwrights—Leilah Assunção (b. 1943) and Maria Adelaide Amaral (b. 1942), whose careers did not begin until the late 1960s and late 1970s, respectively—and no major gay or lesbian dramatist ever risked writing homosexually identified theater. As a consequence, even as we enter a new century, male authors still monopolize dramatizations of women's lives. The best-known treatments of male and female homosexuality in Brazilian theater remain those created by a heterosexual man (Nelson Rodrigues), and in the country's strongest AIDS play so far (Plínio Marcos's *A mancha roxa*), six destitute women prison inmates (among them lesbians and African Brazilians) are portrayed by a white, heterosexual, male playwright whose works are now very much a part of the canon, his early antiestablishment credentials notwithstanding.

A consideration of the half century that follows João do Rio's death in 1921 should throw some light on the reasons the plays viewed by some people as the best treatments of homosexuality in the Brazilian stage of the period were the work of heterosexual playwrights (Nelson and Marcos). To say it was so because they were the *only* plays to deal with the issue would only in part be a facetious claim. Indeed, there were very few dramatic treatments by other heterosexual authors and none (none at least that were performed or published) by openly gay or lesbian playwrights , fearful as they were of retribution, including professional and social ostracism. In 1970, Brazilian theater, still dominated by heterosexual playwrights, presented few multifaceted gay characters.

Throughout that half century, a time many see as the most creative period in all of Brazilian theater, the notion of the homosexual as sick, twisted, perverted, and perverting endured. Even the comparatively permissive 1960s and 1970s (which in urban Brazil coexisted uncomfortably with political repression) contributed to the perpetuation of that image. Still, the fact that a major openly gay or lesbian playwright never appeared during the period is an indication of continuing repression.

While it would be futile to attempt to identify precise turning points or to establish borders between the different situations treated in chapters 2 and 3, it seems safe to say that around the time *Hoje é dia de rock* (It's rock and roll today) by Zé Vicente (José Vicente de Paula, b. 1945) was first performed, in 1971, things were beginning to change. With a keen understanding of the younger urban generation and the new values it espoused, Vicente saw his play—a lyrical paean to love and peace built around images drawn from myth and reality, both Brazilian and foreign—achieve near cult status across the nation. Both *Hoje é dia de rock* and José Wilker's *A China é azul* (prem. 1972; China is blue) were staged by the Rio de Janeiro group Teatro Ipanema (led by Rubens Correa and Ivan de Albuquerque and named after the theater where they performed), to which a large number of fans and followers gravitated.[38]

Another clear marker of change in the early 1970s was the appearance in 1972 of the group Dzi Croquettes, led by Lennie Dale, an American choreographer and dancer who lived in Brazil for a number of years. What was novel about the group's undeniably camp dance, song, and text was the fact that, unlike the drag shows popular in the theater district of Rio de Janeiro (Cinelândia and Praça Tiradentes), the Croquettes were "baritone-voiced men decorated with glitter and make-up [who] projected male virility yet wore feminine accoutrements. . . . [Their] camp humor inverted all standards of normative sexual roles, upsetting traditional gender markings and representations of masculinity" (Green 1999: 257). Trevisan (1986: 119) provides a colorful description of the group:

> Mustachioed and bearded men appeared in women's clothes and false eyelashes, wearing football stockings with high-heeled shoes and brassieres over hairy chests. Neither men nor women—or rather exaggerated men *and* women—they danced and told double-edged jokes in an attempt to break through the noose of repression which censorship and the police drew round the slightest deviation from what was permissible in the period of the dictatorship.

The Croquettes had enormous popularity and influence during their existence as a group. But their appeal could be felt long after their demise, in shows ranging from music concerts to plays and also in the social arena, in such areas as fashion and youth behavior (reflecting their promotion of drug use and sexual experimentation). In James Green's apt summation (1999: 257), the success of Dzi Croquettes reflected the existence of "a broad social acceptance among middle-class audiences for provocative portrayals of gender roles and identities."

The stamp of the Croquettes is seen in another significant instance of the importation into Brazil of the "gender-fucking" vogue of early 1970s San Francisco, London, and Amsterdam. Ney Matogrosso burst onto the scene in 1973 as lead singer of the ground-breaking band *Secos e Molhados*.

Going on a solo career in 1975, Ney was the first major Brazilian singer to speak openly about his homosexuality.[39] His shows, like those of the Dzi Croquettes, always a magnet for gay men, lesbians, and bisexuals, also attracted a large number of open-minded heterosexuals who were intrigued by the singer's falsetto voice and his shows' daring originality. A master of ambiguity, Ney brought to his performances a theatricality seldom seen before in Brazilian music halls, with blocking and choreography combining with visual components (lighting, make-up, wardrobe, and accessories) to create a striking celebration of androgyny.[40]

A final and fascinating example of Croquettes' influence is the appearance in Recife of a group that is best defined as a trashy version of the Rio group. A product of the interplay of pervasive poverty and the arrival of an inadequately understood and poorly adapted "modernity" to a chronically underdeveloped region, Vivencial Diversiones was the rage in Northeast Brazil from 1979 to 1981, although it had started in 1974 and did not fold until 1984 (Lima 2000: 5). In Trevisan's apt description (1986: 131), Vivencial was

> almost all adolescent, illiterate and very much on the fringes of delinquency. . . . The group began to vomit its deliria onto the stage, sometimes pirating texts, sometimes inventing with their love of obscenity . . . [and] with a component of radical outlawry which came from life onto the stage. . . . With Vivencial Dimensiones being gay was an inflammatory element of subversive invention.

That Vivencial remained a regional phenomenon illustrates the perpetuation of the virtual monopoly that Rio de Janeiro and São Paulo have always had over theater in Brazil, making it very difficult for any playwright, director, actor, or group who refuses to move there to achieve national prominence. Vivencial did nevertheless create an original and riveting esthetics of rubbish for their performances in the seedy space where they performed in Ilha do Maruim, a slum located in the outskirts of Recife. Growing out of a youth church group (Igreja do Amparo), Vivencial was later directed by Guilherme Coelho, who inspired a talented cast (which included Pernalonga [Roberto de França], Alfredo Neto, Miguel Angelo, Ivonete Melo, and Suzana Costa, among others) and set designer Beto Diniz to stage such outstanding examples of "the theater of trash" as cultural agitator Jomard Muniz de Britto's *Nos abismos da Pernambucália* (In the abyss of Pernambucoland). The group's inventiveness and improvisational skills informs Jomard's work as well as many of their other productions, including *Repúblicas independentes, darling* (Independent republics, darling), a radical new reading of the Recife-centered, nineteenth-century nationalistic uprising Confederação do Equador. In addition, ambiguity nuanced their dramatic sketches, outrageous narratives, and parodic versions of such plays as Jean Genet's *As criadas* (*The Maids*), the paragon of the transgressive canon. As with the Croquettes and Secos e Molhados, with Vivencial ambiguity took center stage and left its mark on the cultural map of 1970s Brazil.

The 1970s and, following the repeal of Ato Institucional Número 5 in 1979, the early 1980s ushered in the somewhat freer atmosphere that made possible the appearance of the openly gay playwrights whose works are examined in chapter 3. Fernando Melo (b. 1945) gained notoriety with the 1973 premiere of his *Greta Garbo, quem diria, acabou no Irajá* (Who would ever guess that Greta Garbo would end up in Irajá) (the text was published in 1974), as did Paulo César Coutinho with *A noite do meu bem* (prem. 1977; A night made for my love), Fauzi Arap with *O amor do não* (prem. 1977; Contrarian love), Zeno Wilde (1947–1998) and Wanderley Bragança with *Blue jeans* (prem. 1980), Aguinaldo Silva (b. 1944) and Doc Comparato (b. 1949) with *As tias* (prem. 1981; Old queens), and Herbert Daniel with *As três moças do sabonete Araxá* (publ. 1984; The three young women in the Araxá soap bar poster).[41] A number of these plays, however, focused on neurotic, unhappy, self-hating older homosexuals or those who gravitated to them; this development should be seen at least in part in light of the impact of *Os rapazes da banda*, the Brazilian staging of Matt Crowley's *The Boys in the Band* (1967), which opened in Rio de Janeiro in 1971.[42]

Market demand for this kind of theater increased as the process of gay assimilation into the mainstream culture continued. The quantity, if not necessarily the quality, of these plays grew throughout the 1970s and 1980s. By the early to mid-1990s, the staging of plays by Caio Fernando Abreu (1948–1996) and others facilitated the presentation of unorthodox lifestyles and sexual liaisons in more matter-of-fact ways, enabling unbiased representations of homosexuality to be seen on stage. At that time, more sophisticated spectators (regardless of course of their sexual orientation) were able to react in a manner distinct from that of earlier audiences to the multiplicity of meanings found in plays that presented the experience of gay men and lesbians in Brazil.

I offer as an illustration the 1996–97 theater season in Rio de Janeiro simply because of my firsthand experience as a spectator. Other seasons also included a large number of gay-themed or gay-related plays and could easily be used here. In 1996–97 the sizable number of imports were balanced out by a good representation of original contributions by Brazilian playwrights. Among the autochthonous works were Alcides Nogueira's *Ventania* (Wind storm) and Caio Fernando Abreu's *Pela noite* (Through the night), *Dama da noite*, and *O homem e a mancha* (A man and a stain) (the four works are examined in chapter 4). Among the foreign plays were Bernard Marie Koltès's *Na solidão dos campos de algodão* (Loneliness in the cotton fields)—for which Ricardo Blat was awarded the 1996 Mambembe Prize for best actor—Jean Genet's *Alta vigilância* (Haute surveillance), and a stage version of James Baldwin's *Giovanni's Room* (*Giovanni*, a production dedicated to the memory of Caíque Ferreira, who had starred in a previous staging of the play in 1985 and had died of AIDS complications in 1994). Also part of the 1996–97 season was the staging, by the celebrated if controversial director Gerald Thomas, of Heiner Müller's *Quartett* (1980) with the central characters (Marchioness Merteuil and Viscount Valmont—as in Choderlos de Laclos's play on which it is based) played by actors Ney Latarroca and Edilson Botelho. Thomas has announced his plans to stage an adaptation of Alberto Guzik's AIDS-themed novelistic treatment of a gay love story in 1980s São Paulo, *Risco de vida* (1996, Life risk); Guzik's first play, *Um deus cruel*, (prem. 1997; A cruel god) features a bisexual character, an actor called Pedro, who catches the HIV virus from a male hustler. Two other major players in contemporary Brazilian theater, Ulysses Cruz and Sérgio Britto, both based in Rio de Janeiro, have also added their contributions. In March of 1997, director Cruz staged *O melhor do homem*, the Brazilian version of Carlota Zimmermann's play *The Best Part of a Man*, which focuses on the relationship of two jailed men, Skyler (played by Milhem Cortaz), incarcerated for raping his sister, and Dean (played by Rubens Caribé), a sensitive HIV-positive hustler who spends his time devising games that he hopes will lead his cellmate to kill him. And actor and director Sérgio Britto announced his staging of *Os corações a ponto de explodir* (Hearts on the verge of bursting), a Brazilian adaptation of Puerto Rican Edwin Sánchez's play about gay life on old-time 42nd Street in New York (transposed to Rio de Janeiro's downtown Lapa area of Madame Satã fame).

A strong measure of how safe it has become for commercial theater to embrace gay themes is the staging of Maria Adelaide Amaral's play, *Para sempre* (Forever), which brought together the pivotal figures of Amaral, one of the most distinguished playwrights of the postdictatorship era, and Paulo Autran, widely considered the best actor in mainstream Brazilian theater of the second half of the twentieth century. Now in his late seventies and still at the peak of his talent, Autran is in a position to lend his considerable prestige to the validation of a homoerotic theater in Brazil.[43] Autran gave a supremely confident performance in the role of Max, an older homosexual who finds himself torn between his sexual attraction to his lover Tonio and his rejection of the younger man's intellectual limitations.

Gay characters and/or references to homosexuality also occur in other plays staged in that same season, among them Miguel Fallabela's *Louro, alto, solteiro ... procura* (Tall blond single male in search of ...) and *Todo mundo sabe que todo mundo sabe* (Everybody knows that everybody knows), and Guilherme Karam's *Karamba: Confissões de um ator maduro* (Karamba: Confessions of a mature actor). Also noteworthy are the gay-nuanced performances of two major actors, Italo Rossi and Marco Nanini, in Molière's *O doente imaginário* (*The Imaginary Invalid*) and *O burguês ridículo* (*The Bourgeois Gentleman*), respectively; the theatricality and gay sensibility in Ney Matogrosso's show at the large mainstream music hall Canecão; and the long-running drag performances and male striptease shows by Laura de Vison and Eloína's *Os leopardos* (The leopards), both of which have become cult phenomena.

This impressive roster did not go unnoticed in the general press[44] and occasioned some discussion among critics concerning the significance of the phenomenon. By now homosexuality is hardly a novel subject in Brazilian theater; therefore, these works have raised few eyebrows, at least among a big-city public.[45] What sets this period apart from past ones is the convergence of several factors that seem to point simultaneously to the advent of a commercially successful "assimilated" homoerotic theater[46] and the continued presence of a more creative, perhaps more genuine, kind of homosexual dramatic expression in Brazil. Most of these plays ran for several weeks in commercial venues and attracted relatively large audiences of gays and heterosexuals alike. In the case of *Giovanni*, the avid public packing the Teatro da Praia seems to have been to a large extent heterosexual and female, drawn mostly by the scenes of full nudity involving *telenovela* heartthrobs Carmo della Vechia and Edson Fieschi; the box-office success of *Giovanni* is as good as any illustration of how commercial theater has become ancillary to television. Still, what matters here is not so much the size of the audiences or the relative audacity of some of the scenes but the fact that it has become not only safe but even desirable for professional actors to be associated with gay themes. In a not-too-distant past, Brazilian actors shied away from such roles and productions, either as a personal decision aimed at protecting their careers or as a result of pressure from or even downright prohibition by their employers (in the case of Fieschi and della Vechia, the employer is the all-powerful, and once gay-averse Globo Television). The audiences at the other plays (at least when I attended) were also mixed, with a visible gay and lesbian component.

Openly transgressive contemporary theater oriented toward Brazil's gay community is to be found not in commercial venues and plays created around big box-office drawing names but in groups concerned with issues like HIV and AIDS. As I attempt to show in chapter 4 ("AIDS, Subalternity, and the Brazilian Stage"), theater has helped to cast light on the ways a late-twentieth-century peripheral society dominated by inequity and violence represents its confrontations with difference. The several paradigms around which the chapter is constructed illustrate the diverse approaches Brazilian playwrights have taken as they react to a very real crisis—a health crisis to be sure, but also a community crisis and a grievous crisis of representation.

In Brazil, as in much of the world, AIDS is the fittest metaphor of our time, linking sex, race, class, politics, and the perception the Other. Of central importance to a study of the representation of AIDS in a politically and economically subaltern society are some broad issues that bear directly on the theater.[47] The first of such questions is if and how AIDS in Brazil has complicated the cultural process of determining who is entitled to speak for whom in a time of crisis. Two of the plays discussed in chapter 4 cast light on this issue. Are HIV-negative playwrights, for example Plínio Marcos, the author of *A mancha roxa*, "competent" to understand the situation and compose meaningful works? Did he and other HIV-negative playwrights who produce artistic responses to AIDS take on a patina of otherness by virtue of being associated with the disease? But, one may also ask, can HIV-positive dramatists (as the members of the Oficina de Teatro Expressionista, who collectively write their plays) detach themselves sufficiently from the problem to contribute cogent responses? Does seropositivity affect the strategies and discourses used by a playwright to deflect, consciously or not, diverse antagonistic forces[48] and find a forum for his or her works? While it may not be possible to formulate categorical answers to these questions, the fact remains that the audiences who attend a show of *Cabaret prevenção* (Cabaret prevention) (the work I am positing is antipodal to Marcos's mainstream play) are different from those who went to see *A mancha roxa*.

A related issue is that of theatrical allegorizations of AIDS in Brazil. This entails examining how such treatments are received by the public and critics.[49] Luis Alberto de Abreu's *O livro de Jó* (The book of Job), also examined in chapter 4, while strictly speaking not a translation into Portuguese, is in many ways a foreign text, as it incorporates long passages from the Book of Job; still, the audience's familiarity with the story if not with the text itself bespeaks its "nativeness." Full of pathos and Dantean scenes, Abreu's allegorical approach to the biblical material strives to challenge the fear of blood, contagion, and, by implication, difference, in a society numbed by denial. The play does not perpetuate the dominant constructions of AIDS and it avoids the trap of opposing good to evil, which is almost inevitable in allegorical portrayals of the condition. *O livro de Jó* also affords us an opportunity to ask new questions concerning the relationship between catharsis and entertainment. What, for example, are the implications of presenting a ruthless epidemic in what is essentially the domain of escapism and fantasy, and in what ways might the allegorizing of AIDS occlude catharsis? These are some aspects of the burden of representation inherited by Abreu's recasting of the story of Job in a time of crisis.

Of key importance to the study of representations of AIDS in Brazilian theater is the possible impact the disease may have had on a culture, such as Brazil's, of "celebratory sexuality." As Richard Parker (1991) has suggested in *Bodies, Pleasures, and Passions*, the issue of celebratory sexuality is fundamental in establishing a national mythology and self-definition of Brazil. An examination of different approaches to the representation of sexuality in AIDS-era Brazilian theater would try to detect differences in the ways risk and sexuality play out. Have manifestations of exuberant, "careless" sexuality been checked in the mainstream theater following the appearance of AIDS, with nonprofessional groups remaining, as one would expect, free to experiment and take chances? As the evidence available so far from the commercial theater is mixed, with examples of restraint as well as of open sexuality, conclusive remarks would be premature at this point.

Regardless of the different groups' approaches to stage sexuality, one must ask whether gay-oriented theater in Brazil has become or will become inseparable from AIDS, as was the case for most of the 1980s and early

1990s in the United States—so much so that David Román and Alberto Sandoval could offer this succinct characterization in 1995: "The context of AIDS now informs all productions of gay male representation regardless of the actual content of the representation" (562). In the case of the United States and Great Britain, Román and Sandoval's statement is no longer accurate, as recent film and television productions such as *Broken Hearts Club* and *Queer as Folk*, where AIDS is not even mentioned, attest.[50] In the Brazilian case, as in most if not all of the third world, the issue is likely to remain unresolved for some time.[51] Hesitation with regard to this and related questions may have deprived the Brazilian theater of the articulations of some of its most talented voices, people who could have joined the debate but have so far opted to wait on the sidelines. Some of these playwrights evade moral and artistic responsibility, fearing not so much the stigma associated with writing about the condition but, mindful of posterity and theater history, the charge of what Sábato Magaldi (1989: 19) has termed "oportunismo dramatúrgico, a receber o castigo do esquecimento" [theatrical opportunism being punished with oblivion] once the disease becomes manageable and is out of the spotlight. I have little doubt that the quality of most of the works examined in chapter 4 should sufficiently allay Magaldi's reservations. These dramatic explorations are grouped into six different paradigms that I believe encapsulate the different approaches Brazilian playwrights have taken to the representation of AIDS: the neorealist paradigm, the neoexpressionist paradigm, the collective theater paradigm, the allegorical paradigm, the evocative paradigm, and the postmodern paradigm.

The long march of Brazilian gays and lesbians from near-invisibility and demeaning stereotypes to respected membership in the extended family of the theater world parallels their bumpy ride in social history, one punctuated by derision, rejection, and violence. But as a new millennium starts, the cultural schemata and inculcated notions behind Renato Gaúcho's statements in *Veja* magazine seem less cataclysmic as more people begin to critically examine the constructs he typifies. In addition, as the hidden history of homosexuality in Brazil is gradually revealed, the legacy of millions of lives becomes visible and more readily available to those who wish to learn about it. And if things begin to look less gloomy, especially as the Brazilian Congress—thanks in large measure to the leadership of former congresswoman and current mayor of São Paulo Martha Suplicy—prepares to vote on a homosexual union bill, the formation of a gay identity and community remains a problem, mostly because homosexuality in Brazil is not defined as a matter of identity politics. As a consequence, there are still few signs of a mass movement forming around the issue, although at the local level one can see lively manifestations of gay life.[52] As a partial consequence of the absence of a political identity among homosexuals in Brazil, the level of violent acts against homosexuals remains very high in a society that condones the use of violence as it confronts difference, with hundreds of murders and other heinous crimes still unchecked and their perpetrators largely unpunished, as documented in Luiz Mott's 1996 work *Epidemic of Hate*.[53]

The following chapters of *Tentative Transgressions: Homosexuality, AIDS, and the Theater in Brazil* examine the representations sketched above, their intricacies and their relevance. The issues explored in a number of these plays problematize identity, at least before assimilation catches up with them in its endless quest to consume (cannibalize) the most relevant parts of an entire subculture. Thus, it is only a matter of time until a subversive[54] intervention like *Dama da noite*, the Dzi Croquettes, Vivencial Diversiones, or Laura de Vison's performances begins to attract the attention of the mainstream middle-class public. But before that happens, new ways to express human substance are put forth and magical instances of a truly poetic vision are shared with members of that community. In the final analysis, these plays help us better understand the impact of a subaltern context on the meaning of transgression and the importance of the work of gay-oriented men and women who, taking advantage of gaps and fissures in the normative barriers, have given us a theater that, retrocessions notwithstanding, undercuts the dominant ideology of identity in Brazil.

chapter 2

Modernist and Neorealist Backtracking

By investigating heterosexual representations of homosexuality in the theater of Brazilian modernism, this chapter explores the different ways homosexuality was occluded in a key period of Brazilian culture and questions the extent to which playwrights like Oswald de Andrade and Nelson Rodrigues were ready or qualified to serve as critics of their own repressive historic moment. A reconsideration of their theater ushers in new questions and suggests ways of inscribing gayness onto the era. As we interrogate the aesthetic of lack—the turning of a blind eye—that seems to define the "official" theater of this period, two points are readily evident. First, these playwrights were writing at a time when the system of power in Brazil functioned and sustained itself partly by means of its repression of deviance. And second, whereas sexuality has played a key role in shaping the reputation of these playwrights, very little has been written on the interrelations of their works for the stage and the political and ideological energies that shaped the trajectories of these and other Brazilian modernists.[1]

As modernism gained control of the intellectual territory in 1920s Brazil, certain public figures and cultural manifestations that either had prefigured the movement or that shared certain features and interests were overshadowed. Prominent among such figures and manifestations were the prolific writer, playwright, and journalist João do Rio and the Luso-Brazilian version of revue, or *teatro de revista.*

Performing Decadence, Rio-style

The first openly homosexual prominent man of letters in Brazilian literature, João do Rio embraced the idea of decadence and set out to live it, with considerable relish, in the cafés, bars, and streets of turn-of-the-century Rio de Janeiro.[2] Through his demeanor, clothes, and general self-promotion, he presented belle-époque Brazilian society with a lifestyle performance like none seen before.[3] Had João do Rio lived to witness the first years of Brazilian modernism (he died the year before São Paulo's Week of Modern Art, held in February 1922 and considered the country's official initiation with the artistic movement) he may well have joined the group of poets, musicians, and painters who formed the first modernist nucleus. We can only speculate as to whether he would have been welcomed by that group but I believe it safe to say that most exponents of modernism would have been far from effusive.[4] Although João do Rio was older than most of the participants (he was thirty-nine when he died), age should not have hindered his participation; Graça Aranha, one of the leaders of the first phase, was in his fifties at the time of the Week, while Manuel Bandeira, another major modernist, was not much younger than João do Rio. Nor would his dandyism alone have been enough for the modernists to shun him. At the outset, Brazilian modernism used a large number of shock tactics to call attention to itself and its ideas. Of the early modernists, Oswald de Andrade may have had the keenest sense of the importance of such tactics, carefully planning his every public appearance and statement to stun the middle class and intellectual establishment out of their morose smugness. Of all the modernists, it was Oswald who perhaps came closest to appreciating João do Rio's importance. In a review of do Rio's *Eva*, which had a brief run in São Paulo in July of 1915, Oswald wrote favorably of João do Rio's theater (Rodrigues 1996: 180). Oswald had the piece published in *O Pirralho*,[5] a journal he had founded in São Paulo in the early part of the second decade of the twentieth century. *O Pirralho* (published weekly between 1911 and 1917) was one of several harbingers of modernism in Brazil, and Oswald made sure that in his review he stressed the excellence of *Eva* as a symbolist play. Oswald and João do Rio had met some years earlier during Oswald's then frequent trips to Rio de Janeiro; by 1911 the two playwrights were members of the infamous bohemian group led by the charismatic and controversial Emílio de Menezes (1866–1918) (Fonseca 1990: 50).

While some intersections can be detected in the life and art of João do

Rio and one of Brazilian modernism's most influential members, other modernists either did not know João do Rio personally or were wary of any association with the flamboyant *carioca*. Almost universally accepted as the intellectual leader of the movement, Mário de Andrade (1893–1945) either knew personally and/or corresponded with anyone who was anyone in Brazilian art and culture in the first decades of the twentieth century. Conspicuous for his absence among Mário's acquaintances is João do Rio. When João do Rio died, Mário had been frequenting artistic and literary circles for at least a decade; what is more, both men had visited each other's hometowns but apparently never met. As active Brazilian intellectuals in the second decade of the twentieth century, it is almost inconceivable that they did not know, or at the very least, know about one another. I would argue that such a silence must be the result of a deliberate decision on the part of Mário de Andrade. As he fought to keep his own homosexuality secret, it would make sense for Mário to choose not to be associated with those who, like João do Rio, made little secret of their homosexuality. Protected by the social climate of his lifetime and by a coterie of dedicated friends and admirers for decades after his death, Mário's "public secret" was not mentioned in writing until the 1990s.[6] As of this writing, a biography of Mário de Andrade has yet to be published, an astounding and glaring gap in Brazilian literary history but attributable in part to his directive that the massive collection of his personal papers remain locked for half a century after his death. Even after that date, his family, friends, and literary executors have resisted public access to the papers.

João do Rio was no stranger to rejection. Influential intellectuals and public figures of every sexual persuasion shunned association with the obese, effeminate mixed-race eccentric.[7] "Moral grounds," the Brazilian Academy of Letters claimed in twice rejecting João do Rio's candidacy, choosing minor figures instead. It was not until his third attempt that the persistent João do Rio was accepted into the powerful organization, and there are strong indications that he was successful only because this vote came after the death of the Academy's founder and president-for-life, the great novelist Machado de Assis (1839–1908) (Rodrigues 1996: 59).

Schooled in the tough streets of Rio de Janeiro, where he would wander night and day (the writer described himself as a consummate flaneur), João do Rio was a privileged witness to the radical changes—and considerable social strife—taking place in his hometown.[8] João do Rio's impressions and fictionalizations of what he saw were recorded in a series of *crônicas* published first in the daily press and later collected in his books. He was of two minds about such changes, which consisted for the most part in the demolition of vast areas with narrow streets and rundown colonial townhouses and other buildings used as tenement houses in downtown Rio de Janeiro. Even entire hills were leveled as Mayor Pereira Passos and President Rodrigues Alves conducted their massive urban renewal and public health campaign to transform Brazil's capital into a showcase of European architecture and public works, a smaller scale version of the reforms Mayor Haussman had conducted in Paris a few decades earlier.[9] On the one hand, João do Rio seems to have supported the architectural renovation on the grounds that he thought it made Rio look more like his adored Paris, and yet he was concerned about the social repercussions of such physical changes, since the demolition of entire neighborhoods effaced or at least seriously threatened the very lifestyles that had exerted such a pull on him and that he so vividly described in such books as *A alma encantadora das ruas* (1908). As Teresa Meade (1997: 41) points out, one of the distinctive characteristics of old Rio de Janeiro was "the relative democracy of its popular culture, in spite of the extreme inequalities that divided social groups and classes. . . . The physical overlap of these vastly unequal social strata was striking." According to Meade, the consequences of the renewal project were devastating to this unique form of social coexistence:

> It was this overlap—this relative democracy of shared raucous entertainment, all-night cabarets, and, during carnival, the wild pranks, or *entrudos*, and street dances—that the renovations would destroy. By the end of the first decade of the twentieth century, almost all of the cabarets and bars where the popular classes occasionally rubbed shoulders with the elite in Lapa and Catete fell under the ax of Mayor Pereira Passos's renovations. Thus the campaign against decadence and vice, which particularly targeted the amusements of the urban poor, had as a by-product the regulation and transformation of the cultural values of the middle and upper classes as well, particularly the men. (43)

As a man, and as a member of the middle class and of the intellectual elite, João do Rio was directly affected by the campaign against decadence and vice. The locales that inspired many of his *crônicas* and where he picked up lower-class men were quickly disappearing. Still, João do Rio chose not to fight the changes. He depended on the upper classes and the political and intellectual elites for the furthering of his career as a journalist and the continued publication of his books. He faced enough antagonism as it was and decided he could not afford the new enmities that would result should he participate in the movement against the renewal campaign. Thus, while he had misgivings about the disappearance of some of the habits and traditions distinctive of the older neighborhoods, for the most part João do Rio accepted the changes without protest. As the years went by, he became even less concerned about the social and cultural outcome of the massive urban renewal. In his later career, as Jeffrey Needell (1987: 225) argues in *A Tropical Belle Époque*, João do Rio, like Coelho Neto (1864–1934) and other premodernists, "generally spoke only to their era's elite: indeed, they helped to elaborate those expensive fantasies of theirs." Drawing on a contemporary of João do Rio, the memorialist Gilberto Amado (1887–1969), Needell remarks on the concerns that eventually came to govern the trajectory of João do Rio's writings, concerns that were "far indeed from the social critiques and the dives and *favelas* which had drawn the journalist as a youth." Needell concludes, "Increasingly, then, Paulo Barreto [João do Rio] fostered the milieu from which much elite culture drew substance and form" (209).

Although it was conflicted at its core due to its being simultaneously a foreign importation and a movement seriously interested in the indigenous elements of Brazilian culture, modernism, especially in its first phase, sided with the imported notions of development and progress, and thus welcomed the kind of transformations taking place in the larger cities. It was likewise conflicted about the predominance of serious art over a current that valued humor and irreverence; the latter streak, while quite strong in the early years of the movement, fizzled out as time went by and the movement grew stodgy.[10] Some initial shock at their ideas notwithstanding, the modernists were quickly accepted by Brazilian elites and officialdom; their smooth transition into general acceptance is illustrated by the ease with which an establishment poet such as Manuel Bandeira (to cite only one name) could switch from symbolism to modernism, or the number of modernists (including Mário de Andrade, Carlos Drummond de Andrade, and Heitor Villa-Lobos) who had enormous prestige or held high-ranking positions during the Vargas regime (1930–1945).

João do Rio could see his plays produced only if they conformed to the expectations of "official" theater, and these expectations, which hardly changed with the advent of modernism, did not include a serious treatment of homosexuality. Stage works written with a blatant homosexual content would not only have been shunned by producers and playhouses but put paid to his journalistic and literary career. The most daring the cultural and theatrical establishment could accept in premodernist Brazil was a harmless exploration of the reversal of gender roles such as that attempted by the prolific Coelho Neto in *O patinho torto, ou os mistérios do sexo* (1924, The ugly duckling, or the mysteries of sex). The play is a farce, with some clever turns in plot (beginning with a young woman who is engaged but who one day discovers that she is a man and whose family then tries to arrange his engagement with his ex-fiancé's sister) but serious flaws in its structure and argument. Coelho Neto was too much of a traditionalist to offer a truly provocative treatment of sexual ambiguity and gender roles; to do so he would have had to venture into territory he was unprepared for and risk being accused of supporting the liberals, especially with regard to women's rights.[11]

Nor did the association of João do Rio with the most widely known homosexual men of letters of the time, including the French writer Jean Lorrain (Alexandre Martin Duval, 1855–1906) and, especially, Oscar Wilde (1854–1900) facilitate his acceptance by the modernists, who for the most part abhorred these writers, particularly the author of *Salome.* For the young Brazilian modernists, being modern meant rejecting decadence.[12] João do Rio's fascination with Wilde could only invite rebuff by the new group. He carefully cultivated a connection with the Irish author, worshipping Wilde's aesthetic decadence down to particulars like diction, gestures, tastes, and attire. He championed the writings of Oscar Wilde in Brazil, lecturing on him, writing about his ideas in his *crônicas* for the daily press, and translating a number of Wilde's works, including *Salome* and *The Picture of Dorian Gray.*[13] As part of his account of Brazilian modernism's attitude toward Wilde, Gentil Luiz de Faria (1988) has documented numerous negative references to Wilde (and to João do Rio), whose name and works received a hostile reception from some notable modernists (Menotti del Picchia [1892–1943] called for the killing of Wilde) and even premodernists who, like the otherwise enlightened Lima Barreto (1881–1922), used strong language to express their distaste for Wilde (Faria 1988: 211–19).[14] So close was the association between the figures of Wilde and João do Rio that the latter's name was almost inevitably included—explicitly or implicitly—in this kind of denunciation of Oscar Wilde in Brazil.

João do Rio's works, like those of Wilde and Lorrain, are distinguished more by a homosexual sensibility that informs the narrative than by actual homosexual characters or plot details. Ambiguity assumes a central place in the texts of all three writers, resulting in added nuance and complexity.

Richer overtones develop and, significantly, alternative meanings of sexuality are created without, however, issuing the kinds of overt challenges that most readers would find too daunting. What Michael Gillespie has written of Whitman and Wilde pertains, I believe, to João do Rio as well. Both Whitman and Wilde, Gillespie (1996: 2–3) states, "use their cultural milieus to delineate their writings, yet both resist the prescriptive forces in traditional, linear, interpretive approaches. To this end, [their works] incessantly emphasize the diversity of imaginative expression that can still occur within broadly structured societal limits." While the artist's creative individuality is extolled by these authors, they take pains to preserve the complex relationship between the individual and society. Still, however subtly and timidly (by our standards, at least), transgression occurs here as homoerotic desire is modulated in the closet of representation[15] that shaped most of their lives and careers.

Despite the homoerotic content of a few of his *crônicas* and short stories,[16] the majority of João do Rio's writings have a heterosexual focus, and his plays are no exception. In them, however, and in distinction to the prose, the guiding voice has a homosexual sensibility and instances of homosociality and same-sex desire are not altogether absent. Furthermore, the overt heterosexual content of a printed playscript does not fully convey the possibilities afforded by a performance of the same text. As Joseph A. Boone (1998: 15) notes, in the context of any potential analysis of homosexuality as heterosexuality's inevitable other, "all the component instincts, chameleon desires, embedded identities, and fantasies that make up the vastly complex realm of sexuality in general" can be brought out by a director and cast who engage with the play as an artifact that affords contemporary audiences an opportunity to peer at the psychosexual vagaries of an author's time.

This quasi-archaeological endeavor is a consequence of a cultural atmosphere that has generated the closet of representation alluded to above. Such milieus favor the "mainstreaming" of homosexual artists or the "salvaging" of their works for the canon, where they are discussed without mention of their authors' orientation or sexuality. This happens because of the nature of such works; in them, homosexuality is not manifest, for their authors have observed, at least to a degree, the decorum of the dominant culture's rules of representation.[17]

Such a critique of canon formation leads to an investigation into questions of cultural production in twentieth-century Brazil. Not long after modernism became hegemonic in Brazilian culture, modernist critics moved to put their stamp on the national canon. They allowed the inclusion of a larger number of women (though the increase was far from dramatic) but made no visible attempt to include those, like the financially deprived or the openly homosexual, who were traditionally bypassed by the system that regulated the modes and means of artistic production. In Brazil, as elsewhere, some distinctions applied. For example, male homosexual writers had access to literary production due to their gender privileges; however, such entitlements were enjoyed on the condition that they abide by the rules of representation. Writers whose work might validate their experience as homosexual men and women were automatically excluded. Modernism could thus accept João do Rio only if he was placed in the type of tradition that "erases the homosexual while praising his text" (Thomas Yingling qtd. in Piontek 1992: 134).

A Truly Gay Tradition

The other locus of investigation in an archaeology of premodernist homosexual theater in Brazil is the *teatro de revista* tradition. The realist *teatro de casaca* (frock theater, for the dark, heavy clothes actors tended to wear on stage) or *teatro de tese* (thesis plays) gave way in the second half of the nineteenth century to the hugely popular format of song, dance, and light comedy that became known as *teatro ligeiro* or *teatro de revista*. Tired of the thesis play, theatergoers now demanded to be entertained rather than preached at and edified. The impact and permanence of the *revista* genre were such that the Brazilian theater completely bypassed the naturalist period then prevalent in other parts of the world.

The *teatro ligeiro* evolved from a number of sources, including the Brazilian *comédia de costumes*, English *music hall*, Italian *burletta*, American *vaudeville*, French *cabaret* and *can-can*, parodies of foreign dramas, and the *revistas de ano*, or satirical sketches of the previous year's most important events. A Portuguese import, the *revista de ano* had made its debut on the Brazilian stage in 1860 with *As surpresas do senhor José da Piedade* by a little known public employee named Justino de Figueiredo Novais (1829–1877), but it would be two more decades until the mode really met with success. Parodies of Offenbach's *operettas* were also enormously popular, particularly those staged by the director Jacinto Heller (1834–1909) and the actor Correia Vasques (1839–1892). By the late 1870s, theatrical activity had shifted from the stately houses of previous decades to a number of more informal spaces, located mostly in the nation's capital and bearing such names as Alcazar (the most successful of them all) and Varietés. In keeping with the turn-of-the-century fascination with all things Parisian, many actors and especially actresses were either French-born, French-speaking, or made dubious claims to a French origin.

The most important name associated with the *teatro de revista* is undoubtedly that of Artur Azevedo (1855–1908), who was to become one of the most beloved figures in the history of Brazilian theater. Although he was also a prolific author of light verse, short stories, and newspaper columns, Azevedo is revered for his indefatigable work on behalf of a national theater and for the faithful reproduction of an era in some two hundred original plays as well as translations, adaptations, and parodies of foreign dramatic works.

Equally important as social records are two series of contributions to Rio de Janeiro's daily newspapers, "O ano que passa" and "Teatro a vapor," which Azevedo devised as an alternative to exorbitant production costs: the former are *cenas ilustradas,* or drawings of dramatic scenes, published in *O País* from February to November 1907, in lieu of the *revista de ano* for that year; the latter are 105 humorous vignettes or comedies (named "Teatro a vapor" [steam-powered theater] because of their rapidly sketched, quick-paced short scenes), which he published almost every week in *O Século,* from 1906 till 1908 (Moser 1976: 23–26).

Among the *revistas* of Azevedo's sole authorship, *O tribofe* (1892, The big cheat) deserves critical scrutiny not only for its intrinsic merit but also because Azevedo, with the assistance of three competent musicians—Nicolino Milano, Assis Pacheco, and Luiz Moreira—rewrote some of its scenes into his masterpiece, *A capital federal* (The federal capital, 1897), perhaps the most popular Brazilian play of all time and the first Brazilian play ever to be performed abroad (Lisbon, 1906) (Gonçalves 1975, 1: 330). Better than any other play of the period, *A capital federal* reflects a compact that seemed to exist between the practitioners of the *teatro de revista* and their public. Its enormous success speaks of a commonly held wide-eyed fascination for the telltale tokens of civilization (fashionable stores, fine restaurants, comfortable hotels, race tracks, and so on) that were beginning to appear in the capital city of the young republic.

Although it was not the first play to focus on the illusory charms of the nation's capital (José de Alencar's *O Rio de Janeiro: Verso e reverso* [1857] readily comes to mind), Azevedo's work captured so well the spirit of the city that it remains (even after the countless imitations that have followed) the unsurpassed dramatic portrayal of the former capital city. Its vibrant scenes, credible characters, perfect pace, and delicious verbal wit combine with the lively music to form a cohesive unit rightfully seen as the climax of Brazil's *teatro de revista.*

The influence of the *teatro de revista* and its close relative, the *comédia de costumes*, resonated well into the twentieth century.[18] The genre's hold was too tight to be relaxed even by such developments as the opening of major new theaters (imposing municipal theaters opened in Rio de Janeiro and São Paulo in 1909 and 1911, respectively) and the advent of younger playwrights and innovative acting companies. In fact, the twentieth century would be almost half over before the conventions of the previous century gave way to genuine changes.

Long before explicit pornography became widely available in Brazil, *revista* productions at Praça Tiradentes and elsewhere displayed a fair amount of raciness, double entendres, campiness and other signs easily decoded by homosexual members of the audience. Even before the female *revista* stars were largely replaced by transvestites in the 1960s, there was considerable erotic appeal in the revues for homosexuals who could fantasize about being, or being with, the men who courted the gloriously beautiful and marvelously dressed and bejeweled female star. To this homoerotic climate were added carnivalizing elements (the mocking of social convention, authority figures, and popular festivals, for example) and the cannibalizing of news and other genres to produce a general feeling of *deboche* and carefree cheerfulness.

Instrumental in the formation of this general ambiance and in keeping with the fast pace was the figure of the *compadre* or *compère* (sometimes combined with the figure of the *cabaretier* and sometimes appearing in pairs), who exercised several functions. In Neyde Veneziano's explanation (1991: 117), the *compadre* is

> aglutinador, apresentador, comentarista, dançarino, cantor, bufão, contador de piadas, . . . atravessa a revista de ponta a ponta como a costurar os diversos quadros, cristalizando a dinâmica do pacto com a platéia, característica própria do teatro popular.
>
> [the one who makes it all gel, presenter, commentator, dancer, singer, buffoon, teller of jokes, . . . he is seen from beginning to end as if stitching together the various scenes, cementing the dynamic pact with the audience, which is a characteristic of popular theater].

Often performed by the foremost comic actor in the company, the *compadre* had to be able to quickly improvise gestures, puns, and suggestive comments to the audience. It is a common though undocumented belief among students of gay and lesbian culture in Brazil that often the *compadre* was a gay man who would interact on one level with the mostly heterosexual audience who would not necessarily know or care about the man's orientation and on another level with both the other homosexuals on stage (male dancers and other actors) and those in the audience who were "in the know."

This sense of complicity between actors and dancers on stage and homosexual elements in the audience was essential for the long-term gay devotion to the genre. Although concerned more with the general traits of the genre, Roberto Ruiz (1988) offers some comments that are quite pertinent here. Speaking of the essential importance of a strong rapport between *compadre* and public at a time when ambiguity was mandated by the prevailing notions of decorum and social convention, Ruiz states, in the beginning of his groundbreaking book on the history of the *teatro de revista* in Brazil:

> . . . o teatro de revista deve incidir sobre o que se pensa naquele exato momento da história. Ou sobre *como* se pensa: o teatro de revista é um teatro de *cumplicidade perversa*, é teatro de perversão, . . . de reflexão perversa acerca do mundo, pacto entre as partes para falar o que se sabe, mas que está no limite da lei. (9)
>
> [. . . *teatro de revista* must focus on *what* people think at a precise moment in history. Or rather, on *how* people think. For *teatro de revista* is a theater of *perverse complicity*, a theater of perversion, . . . of perverse reflection about the world, a pact between the various sides to tell what one knows, even if it borders on the illicit.]

In this text, Ruiz uses "perversão" not as a moral judgment but in the word's other meaning, as the adulteration or subversion of an existing or intended message or goal. In this "*teatro de cumplicidade perversa,*" as in a silent pact, homosexual men in the cast and in the audience are joined as accomplices as they manage to communicate with each other, surreptitiously connect with others like themselves, and enjoy themselves and the general cheer while all along flirting with the illicit.

To call the *teatro de revista* tradition and the theater and cultural interventions of João do Rio queer sites in turn-of-the-century Brazil might seem an exaggeration. They are nevertheless important manifestations of a sensibility that held out in the face of considerable repression and that opened the way for the more openly gay theater of the second half of the twentieth century.

As important manifestations of a certain cultural inflection, *teatro de revista* and João do Rio may be seen, to quote from Boone (1998: 14), as illustrations of a "protogay production of an alternative modernist practice that encodes many of the precepts of contemporary queer theory." By suggesting alternative interpretations of the stage representations in which they were involved, these practices questioned the validity and exposed the tenuousness of key sexual constructs then prevalent in Brazil. The endurance of the near-mythical quality of these interventions stresses the need for a reexamination of the sexual politics of Brazilian modernism. As it bypassed these preexisting queer sites, the movement sought to provide the theater with a new image, one the modernists considered less frivolous and more attuned to their notions of progress and contemporary society.

In rejecting a theater of homosexual suggestion and ambiguity, Brazilian modernism was spurning one of the most expressive metaphors of the turn-of-the-century imaginary—the mask. Modernism stressed the removal of masks and its works often framed the truthfulness of the individual in contradistinction to the falsehood of the community. Again following Wilde and Lorrain, João do Rio undertook a process of masking, that is, making provocative use of the mask in different manifestations, challenging others (and himself) to confront issues of physical appearance, sexuality, and identity (through, for instance, the various names and pseudonyms he used throughout his life). Concurrent with such a rejection on the part of modernism was the absence within the movement of dramatists who could offer truly new, provocative uses of the mask, by questioning and surpassing those contributed by João do Rio. Equally absent were playwrights with the drive, determination, and strong voice to write and fight for the staging of works with a clear homosexual identity. Lacking that type of play, the theater of Brazilian modernism proceeded to view homosexuality solely through the eyes of heterosexual playwrights who used it as a convenient example in their stage explorations of the political and economic ills that afflicted Brazil. As it canonized these playwrights, modernism translated such a lack into a vividly felt presence. Self-identifying homosexual playwrights were ignored and well-adjusted, "normal" homosexual characters were nonexistent in heterosexual-written plays, or, to apply Larry Gross's phrase

(1991: 26), they were "symbolically annihilated"; Henning Bech (1997: 234n. 111) stresses the "symbolic" aspect of the "annihilation," that is to say, the absence produced by it as well as its implications.

Very Present Absences

With reference to women writers in Latin American literature, Amy Kaminsky (1993), as discussed in chapter 1, has written eloquently on the "presence of absence"; she stresses the importance of the effect of a text, leading to "the reader's recognition of the text as a form of practice, connected to existing ideological formations in a combination of resistance and complicity" (26). I believe we can safely substitute terms like "spectator" and "play" for "reader" and "text" and extrapolate this thinking to the context of Brazilian modernist theater. Visibility alone, while important, is not enough to promote change and fill in this lacuna. In order to adequately reflect the life experiences of homosexuals in early-twentieth-century Brazil, modernist theater would have needed to welcome homosexually identified texts and authors. Audiences would then be given the opportunity to interact with a body of texts and a group of playwrights that, as a kind of tradition-in-the-making, would have assisted in resisting any attempts at "annihilation."

In the context of Brazilian modernist theater, the "presence of absence" is nowhere more strongly felt than in the depiction of the lesbian experience. No self-identified major lesbian playwright is to be found in that period or in the entire history of the Brazilian theater, and I know of no play that focuses exclusively on lesbian relationships. What we have instead are lesbian characters in secondary roles in the plays of modernist dramatists like Oswald de Andrade and Nelson Rodrigues. Inclusion of such characters in their plays was almost inevitable as the playwrights sought to illustrate with formulaic examples the imported ideas (simplifications of marxism, Freudianism, Jungianism) they were exploring in their dramas.

Before we look at lesbians in the theater of Brazilian modernism, we need to consider the overall presence of women playwrights in that period. Women playwrights are noted for their absence in Brazilian modernist theater and Brazilian theater in general, and the leading figures (Leilah Assunção, Consuelo de Castro, Maria Adelaide Amaral) began their careers only in the 1960s and 1970s. In this respect Brazilian literature and theater are no different from that of the rest of Latin America. If, as Amy

Kaminsky (1993: 27) points out, the names of a few women authors appear in the official histories, it is because these were truly exceptional writers. For them, "absence is a complex and burdened notion. It is a Pandora's box of meaning, containing silence and invisibility, censorship and self-censorship, disappearance and exile." Kaminsky next alludes to French feminism's notions of "the feminine" as lack and of "woman" as an empty space, "a grammatical marker that makes the presence of the masculine possible"; in this line of thought, the feminine then becomes "the embodiment of absence." Adapting again from Kaminsky, I will use the trope of "woman-as-absence" to signify the dearth of women playwrights and lesbian characters in Brazilian theater. This trope naturalizes the absence of women from literary history and conceals the material practices that account for the lack of women's names in the literary canon. It tends to make the existence of embodied women irrelevant and renders the absence of women a non-issue. In so doing, it traps the woman writer in an untenable situation, one in which she cannot be fully absorbed into phallic presence—that presence that is visible, takes space, enters, asserts, demands. Nor, as a usurper of language, can she be relegated to vaginal silence, dark, emptiness, the no-place that the masculine intrudes upon to make his presence meaningful (28). Woman-as-absence is emptiness, its mathematical equivalent being zero, "the place marker empty in and of itself, but crucial for any complex calculation" (28). In Brazilian theater, lesbians are not there, but at the same time they are. The negation of their presence points to a desire to erase them precisely for their importance. Their absence, in other words, signals a crucial presence.

Performance, insists Annette Wannamaker (2001: 81), "is an especially productive site in which to create memory out of absence." Wannamaker is drawing on the work of Peggy Phelan (1993: 146), whose notion of performance becoming itself through disappearance corroborates Kaminsky's work. The rationale that accounts for "presence in absence" also approximates the notion of "absent homosexuality" proposed by the Danish critic Henning Bech. For Bech (1997: 39), "absent homosexuality" is a particular type of homosexuality, the most common in modern societies, which is characterized by being "something which is everywhere and no place at all, something everyone wants and doesn't want, something everyone knows about and knows nothing of." Among the signs one should pay attention to when trying to identify absent homosexuality are "conspicuous absences" and "a dialectics between presence and absence, knowing and ignoring, desire and denial" (38–39), since "the most absolute absence of even the smallest and most ambiguous suggestion of homosexuality should be seen as an indication of its presence" (64). The cultural urge to suppress it in fact reveals a hidden and essential importance. Indeed, it adds to our responsibility as readers and critics as we approach these plays.

Lesbian playwrights and lesbian-identified characters being absent, heterosexual playwrights enter the resultant empty space. Modernists such as Oswald de Andrade and Nelson Rodrigues and neorealists such as Plínio Marcos make their theater visible by means of its phallic presence and thus represent lesbians in whatever way best suits their goals. Thus, in the theater of Oswald de Andrade, lesbians are there at the same time they are not. Their presence is negated through a kind of sleight of hand that controls the dialectics between presence and absence. For example, the cast of characters for his best-known play, *O rei da vela* (The candle baron),[19] announces a character called Heloísa de Lesbos; nevertheless, throughout the play she is identified simply as Heloísa and behaves like a heterosexual woman who is engaged to be married to Abelardo, the uncouth candle baron and loan shark who is planning to marry into the old aristocracy, essentially in exchange for his financial rescue of the bankrupt family. Abelardo, in turn, is indebted to the American banker, Mr. Jones, and does not seem to care that his fiancée and Mr. Jones appear *"em franca camaradagem sexual"* (Andrade 1976: 87) (in openly sexual camaraderie). Heloísa's initial identification is thus quickly withdrawn from the printed text and an absent lesbianism takes over, despite the fact that in one scene she wears a man's suit (77). Another character, Heloísa's sister Joana, is identified throughout the play with the masculine version of her name, João, the script's "cast of characters" being the only instance she is named with the feminine form; hence, while the reader of the printed text is aware of the two versions of her name, the spectator is not, unless a printed program is provided. Denying Joana/João the use of a woman's name reinforces the stereotypical view of the lesbian as masculine. In addition, although Joana/João often behaves like a stereotypical dyke, we know that at one point she had a boyfriend called Miguelão (Big Mike), who was stolen from her by her brother, Totó (98), and that she had resorted to prostitution before Abelardo's money came to the rescue (99).[20] Such contradictions are underscored by her behavior in the play[21] and by the addition of the epithet *"dos Divãs"* (of the divans) to her name. With this new name, "João dos Divãs," the woman is clearly associated with mental disease or behavior problems; in Brazil the term "divan" had been recently linked to mental disorder when the play was written in 1933, a time when mental illness was still strongly stigmatized.[22] The character's eating away of her fingernails is emphasized nearly every time she appears, as if further markers of her neurotic behavior were needed. On the other hand, Mr. Jones, the American banker, is at one point accused of being a lesbian man, because he seems to be attracted to masculine women (95). A female homosexual who is being forced into a heterosexual marriage and her sister, a lesbian who is not allowed to use a woman's name—these are empty spaces, sites of the conspicuous absence of homosexuality in a society where its absence signals a crucial presence. At the same time the two women are never called lesbians, a man is the only person in the play to be so identified. Incongruence and the occasion for a *bon mot* thus prevail over embodiment of presence and assertion of homosexual identity.

The embodiment of absence is also found in the theater of Nelson Rodrigues, where lesbian characters are members of several of the dysfunctional families illustrative of the overall decay he detected at the core of the Brazilian bourgeoisie. Nelson and his theater were for most of his life the object of social disparagement and political censorship, not just for his pitiless exposure of the hypocrisy and corruption at the center of the most sacred of social institutions but also because he embodied, as Monica Pimenta Velloso (1996: 91) puts it, "*a versão* noir *da nossa modernidade (que se queria dourada)*" (the *noir* version of our modernity [which believed itself to be golden]) and because his work was a kind of theater that was at first not deemed serious art.

In Nelson's plays, as in Oswald's, lesbians are present but at the same time are denied a presence. We know, for example, that Ivonete, the widow in the farce *Viúva porém honesta* (A widow, but an honest one) had had only one affectionate relationship prior to her marriage, and we are told that that relationship was with another woman, Luci (Rodrigues 1981–90, 1: 242, 246). But we never get to see Luci, and Ivonete, forced by her father, the evil media magnate Dr. J. B. de Albuquerque Guimarães, to marry a sordid queen called "Dorothy Dalton," is prevented from living her life as a lesbian. Farce conventions allow for several turns in the plot, including the quick death, followed by the prompt resurrection, of Ivonete's pro forma husband, which saves her from a widow's lonely existence and reaffirms the peculiar belief in a wife's right to infidelity while her husband is alive, but never after his death.

A very different situation is presented in *Album de família* (A family photo album), one of Nelson's imposing "mythical plays." Still, for all the differences from the farcical treatment seen in *Viúva porém honesta*,

Itala Nandi as Heloísa de Lesbos in Oswald de Andrade's *O rei da vela.* Directed by José Celso Martinez Correa. Teatro Oficina, São Paulo, 1967. Photograph by Derly Marques. Arquivo Multimeios/Divisão de Pesquisas. Centro Cultural São Paulo.

fifteen-year-old Glória, too, is denied a life as a lesbian. Her affair with a boarding-school classmate named Teresa occasions the expulsion from school of the two young women and the return home of Glória. Perhaps because Nelson wished to depict a primordial situation in which the members of the family stand for ideas he had recently absorbed from second-hand exposure to Freud and Jung, the playwright associates the family only remotely with an identifiable time and place (there are vague references to the farm being located in Minas Gerais, a state with a key role in Brazilian history and mythology). Glória comes home to face the patriarch, Jonas, a domineering father who makes no secret of his sexual attraction to her, an attraction he sublimates by making love to a number of virgin girls his daughter's age. Glória, who hates and is hated by her mother, reciprocates her father's love, seeing Jonas's face in lieu of Christ's at church and confessing to one of her brothers that every time she kissed Teresa at school she had been thinking of her father.[23] Jonas's

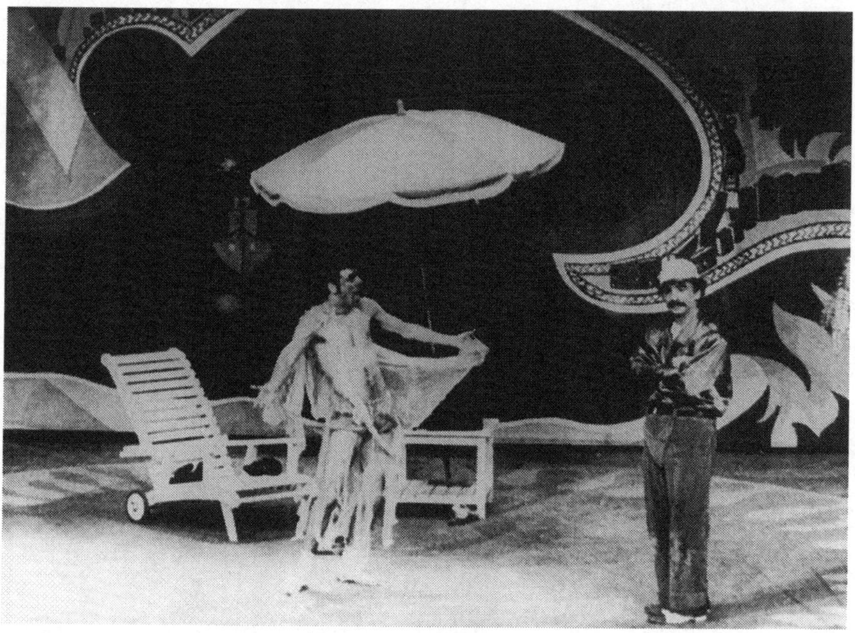

Edgard Gurgel as Totó Fruta de Conde and Renato Borghi as Abelardo I in Oswald de Andrade's *O rei da vela*. Directed by José Celso Martinez Correa. Teatro Oficina, São Paulo, 1967. Photograph by Fredi Kleeman. Arquivo Multimeios/Divisão de Pesquisas. Centro Cultural São Paulo.

sons, Guilherme and Edmundo, hate their father and fantasize about killing him, a reference to the murder of the primeval father so that the primitive horde could gain their freedom (Jonas is eventually killed by his wife, Senhorinha). Both sons compete with their father for the love of the women in the family, with Guilherme desiring Glória (whom he ultimately kills in a desperate attempt to keep her from Jonas) while Edmundo desires Senhorinha, who is his mother and Jonas's wife. Both Guilherme and Edmundo commit suicide. A third son, Nonô, roams the property naked and howling like an animal at night, having lost his sanity after having sex with his mother one day when he was a teenager. In *Album de família* and throughout his theater, Nelson's perfect command of the language of his medium accounts for a striking combination of poetry and vulgarity in his portrayal of a violently prejudiced patriarchal society, exposing in the process—with a mixture of fascination and disgust—all manner of sexual repression, perversion, and taboos.

Upholding Inversion, Staging Submission

Homosexual men in the theaters of Oswald de Andrade and Nelson Rodrigues seem to exist mostly for the purpose of embodying the then-prevalent notion of sexual inversion, which upheld the idea of an essential heterosexual desire. In this simplified view, homosexuals were seen as men who behave like women, caricatured, for instance, as delicate or distraught.[24] Like Totó Fruta-do-Conde (Fruity Totó) in *O rei da vela*, they are mostly flamboyant or pathetic queens evoking feebleness and repulsiveness. Along with his sisters Heloísa and Joana/João, Totó is meant as an illustration of the moral decadence fostered by the savage capitalism that foreign interests have imposed on Brazil.[25] At one point, Totó, who has the habit of trying—sometimes successfully—to rob women of their male lovers, sets his eyes on Mr. Jones, who seems to be interested in Heloísa, until Totó is informed that the American banker is really interested in his own chauffeur. But for most of the time Totó eats sweets and pines away after losing his lover, Godofredo. This exchange between Totó and his mother gives a sense of the character:

> TOTÓ: (*Aparece à direita, com uma vara de pescar e um saco de bombons na mão, absorto e pesaroso.*) Eu sou uma fracassada!
> CESARINA: Meu filhinho, venha cá. Benzinho do meu coração!
> TOTÓ: Não quero. (*Bate o pé.*) Não quero. Me deixe!

Giulia Gam as Glória and Ciça Carvalho as Teresa in Nelson Rodrigues's *Album de família. Nelson 2 Rodrigues.* Directed by Antunes Filho. Teatro SESC/Anchieta, São Paulo, 1984. Photographs by João Caldas. Arquivo Multimeios/Divisão de Pesquisas. Centro Cultural São Paulo.

CESARINA: Mas venha aqui, Totó. Venha conversar com sua mãezinha! Há quanto tempo você não me beija?
TOTÓ: Não quero, não quero, não quero! (Andrade 1976: 91)

[TOTÓ: (*Coming in from the right, holding a fishing rod and a bag of candy, self-absorbed and sorrowful.*) I am a scorned woman!
CESARINA: My little boy, come here. Darling of my heart!
TOTÓ: I won't (*stamping his feet*). I don't want to. Leave me alone!
CESARINA: But Totó, come here. Come and talk to your sweet mother. You haven't kissed me for the longest time.
TOTÓ: I don't want to. I don't want to. I don't want to.]

The problem with this kind of representation is, of course, that it inevitably produces stock figures: targets of humor, agents of evil, emblems of loneliness. Instead of multidimensional characters, homosexual men in these plays slip into the shackles of caricature.

Totó Fruta-do-Conde, stamping his feet and throwing tantrums, is not too different from other stock figures in other plays by Nelson Rodrigues—such as "Dorothy Dalton"[26] in *Viúva porém honesta* and two brothel employees, Odésio in *Toda nudez será castigada* (*All Nudity Shall Be Punished*) and "Pola Negri" in *Perdoa-me por me traíres*. These effeminate stock figures began to appear with more frequency a few years before Oswald and Nelson's debuts as dramatists. An earlier example is Alfredinho, in *Adão, Eva, e outros membros da família* (Adam, Eve, and other members of the family, 1927) by Alvaro Moreyra (1888–1964), a friend of Oswald de Andrade's and fellow Communist Party member.[27] The following exchange between the characters Mulher (Woman) and Um (One) evokes, through the use of diminutives and other linguistic markers, an Alfredinho (Little Alfredo) who is spoiled, rich, frail, and effeminate.:

MULHER (*vem de dentro*): O Alfredinho. Não pôde vir. Está gripado.
UM: Ah, o Alfredinho. É todo em diminutivos esse mocinho. O Alfredinho da baratinha, que já teve um Fordzinho . . . aquelezinho. . . .
MULHER (*protesta, com doçura*): Tão bonzinho! Tão meu amiguinho! (Moreyra 1990: 108–109)

[WOMAN (*coming from inside the house*) That was Little Alfredo [on the phone]. He can't come. He has a cold.
ONE: Ah, that little Alfredo. Everything about that young man comes in small sizes. Little Alfredo who has a little roadster, who used to have a little Ford . . . that little one. . . .
WOMAN (*protesting, sweetly*) He is such a sweetie! Such a dear little friend of mine!]

Although created later than the modernist characters, Plínio Marcos's Veludo (Velvet) in *Navalha na carne* is a neorealist counterpart of Totó, Dorothy, Alfredinho and several others. He lisps, refers to himself in the feminine and stamps his feet. There are, however, significant differences. Veludo is a lower-class queen who works as a janitor in a filthy brothel where he picks up survival skills that include lying, stealing, and never trusting anyone. More importantly, Veludo displays a trait the other three do not: he can be tough. In the scene in which Veludo's sometimes friend Neusa Sueli and her pimp, Vado, accuse the gay man of stealing their money, the janitor slyly drops an insult (*"galinha velha"* [old hen]) (Marcos 1984: 29) which Vado later borrows to taunt the woman. Veludo thus provokes a serious fight between Neusa and the pimp (leading in fact to their breakup) and shows himself to be as competent an inflictor of violence as Vado. Veludo also holds his own in a charged-up, homoerotic interaction in which he first begs an unwilling Vado to share a joint with him, only to decline the offer when Vado finally relents and extends it to him. Vado then beats Veludo repeatedly, insisting now that Veludo smoke with him. The janitor aggravates Vado by not resisting the beating and even asking for more, claiming he was getting off on being hit. Veludo adamantly continues to refuse to smoke the joint with Vado, infuriating the pimp, who feels demoralized by his failure to force Veludo to do what he wants (26–32). In order to obtain gratification, the janitor invites verbal and physical abuse from a partner who does not become aware of the nature of his role until the elaborate ritual is well under way (Prado 1987: 217). More significantly, Veludo's *escrachamento* (campy affectation) succeeds in deflating Vado's attempts to manipulate him. Vado then realizes that the macho pose he has been trying to strike has taken a serious blow and he begins to wonder if in the end, having been ensnared in Veludo's ambiguous game, he has served less as an agent of injury than of pleasure.

His cunning notwithstanding, Veludo still presents many of the neurotic traits of his predecessors and is far from the workaday gay man that would appear on the Brazilian stage in the 1970s.[28] As a scorned *bicha* working a despised job in a filthy environment, Veludo is as close to the lowest rung as one can be in Brazilian society, and as such, he can be seen as a foil to another male homosexual working in the same type of milieu in another Marcos play, but in different conditions. In *O abajur lilás* (The lavender lampshade) another Marcos play that was banned for many years before it could be staged and published in 1975, Giro also works in a

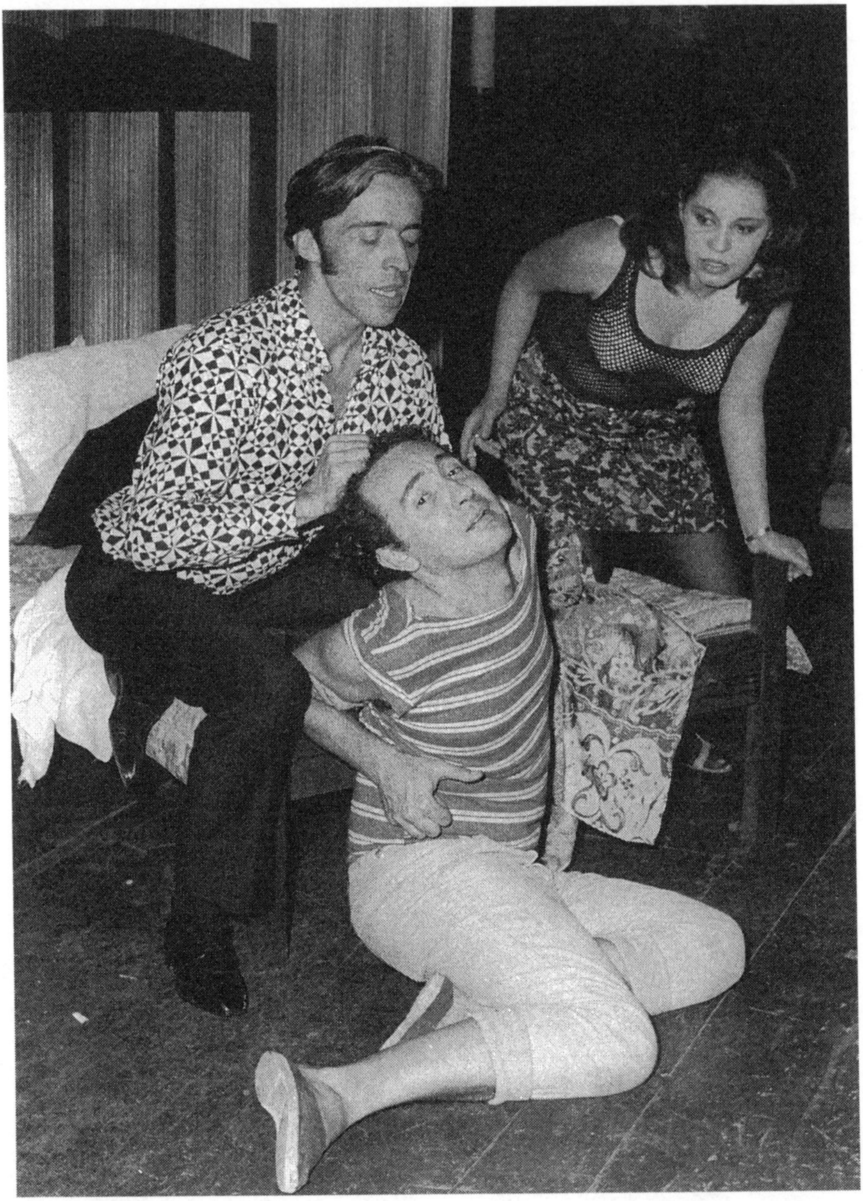

Paulo Vilaça as Vado, Sérgio Mamberti as Veludo, and Ruthnea de Moraes as Neusa Sueli in Plínio Marcos's *Navalha na carne.* Directed by Jairo Arco e Flexa. Teatro Ruth Escobar, São Paulo, 1967. Photograph by Derly Marques. Arquivo Multimeios/Divisão de Pesquisas. Centro Cultural São Paulo.

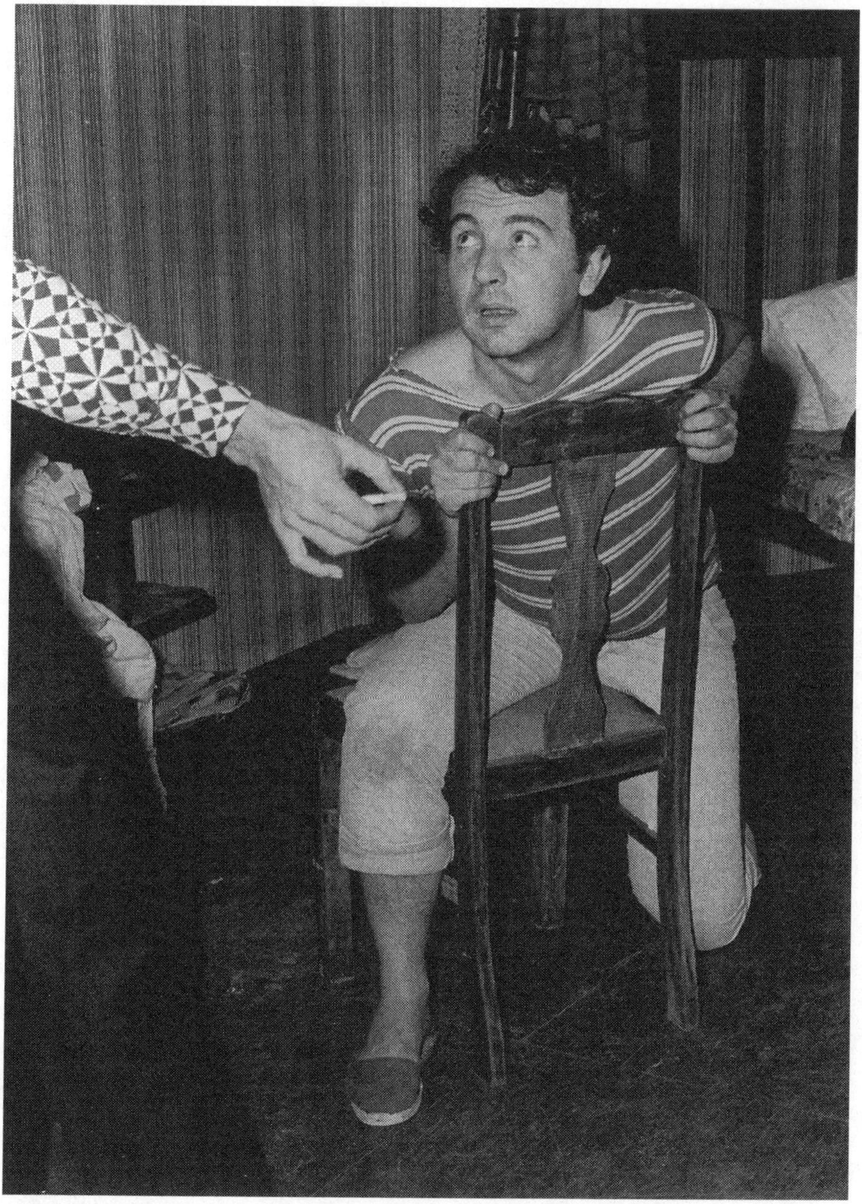

Vado (Paulo Vilaça) entices Veludo (Sérgio Mamberti) with a joint in Plínio Marcos's *Navalha na carne.* Directed by Jairo Arco e Flexa. Teatro Ruth Escobar, São Paulo, 1967. Photograph by Derly Marques. Arquivo Multimeios/Divisão de Pesquisas. Centro Cultural São Paulo.

brothel, but he seems to control it. In order to hold such a position, Giro depends on a brutal associate, Osvaldo, whose job it is to keep the sex workers terrified of the two men. The role of the victimizer is here split into two components, Giro, who plans and directs the victimization, and the heterosexual Osvaldo, who executes Giro's threats and follows his commands. This "compound" victimizer endeavors to neutralize potential attacks against its two vulnerable flanks, Giro's homosexuality and Osvaldo's impotence. In the state of affairs depicted in *O abajur lilás*, the former is compensated for by a relative accumulation of capital and the latter by physical brutality. While in a power struggle each of these traits alone would tend to increase a contender's vulnerability, together the two attributes combine, ironically, as a source of strength. Still, with regard to the depiction of homosexuality, we have here a gay man who needs the assistance of a brute if he is going to be in control of the business. Without the support from the heterosexual Osvaldo, it is implied, Giro would not be in a position to wield power.

Early modernist playwrights also used male homosexuality as a means to attack fascism and fascist sympathizers in Brazil. As Joan Scott (1986: 1073) has remarked, the symbolic realms of gender roles and sexual behavior are major venues for political rivals to dispute the legitimacy of their adversaries:

> Gender is one of the recurrent references by which political power has been conceived, legitimated, and criticized. It refers to but also establishes the meaning of the male/female opposition. To vindicate political power, the reference must seem sure and fixed, outside human construction, part of the natural or divine order. In that way, the binary opposition and the social process of gender relationships both become part of the meaning of power itself; to question or alter any aspect threatens the entire system.

In Oswald's *O homem e o cavalo*[29] (Men and horses), homosexuality is equated with the worst fears of male heterosexuals, with the fascists embodying the ultimate threat to male heterosexuality when they anally rape the jockeys during the horse races. As a trainer relates to the visiting Icarus and Saint Peter, the gang of uniformed fascists penetrates the jockeys and even, in one case, a horse, in full view of those watching the races. Because that horse turns out to be the winged Pegasus, whom Saint Peter identifies as "the only surviving angel," the fascists are also accused of the indefensible blasphemy of not only assaulting heavenly creatures but of raping the last extant angel. At the time Oswald wrote his play, "the construction of homo-fascism"—to use the title of the first chapter in Andrew Hewitt's *Political Inversions* (1996)—was well under way, with perversion, filth, corruption, and other base traits neatly fusing with fascism in the modernist imaginary. The denunciation of fascism was important to Oswald for reasons both political (he was a member of the Brazilian Communist Party at the time he wrote the play) and artistic, as he always strove to keep up with the European avant-garde, a large segment of which was then either siding against the fascists or wavering between a progressive aesthetic practice and a reactionary political ideology. The association of fascism and homosexuality, a conflation Hewitt studies as an "imaginary construct," presents some clear dangers. For, as Hewitt (1996: 4) explains, "To read fascism through the psychologizing prism of homosexuality is . . . to trivialize its historical reality: that which is invoked to explain the crime (i.e., homosexuality) itself becomes the crime." Moreover, "The identification of proletarian revolution with values of virility and sexual potency leads all too easily to an attribution of homosexuality or effeminacy to the enemy: this observation holds for the communists' homosexualization of the fascist as much as it does for the fascists' effeminization of the Jew" (9–10).

Oswald seemed to be aware that, because fascism resists being represented, the deployment of homosexuality as an allegory of fascism involved risks in theater. He therefore eschewed a strict association, choosing to include in *O rei da vela* another fascist, Perdigoto (brother of Totó, Heloísa, and Joana), a presumed heterosexual but still berated for his amorality and dissipation. The loan shark Abelardo decides to finance a fascist brigade to be organized by Perdigoto, but does so on the condition that it be a rural operation, since the wily Abelardo—aware of his brother-in-law-to-be's inability to live away from the big city—predicts the impracticality of the enterprise. The big city, the metropolis in Foucault's interpretation, is the bastion of totalizing power; the urban topographies inhabited by its anonymous and alienated dwellers further the creation of a distorted expression—a fascist expression—of individuality and modernity. In the shifting entity constituted by a then rapidly growing middle class, Perdigoto and his kind—backed by guileful financiers—aimed to affect the political layout through intense nationalism, vows of patriotic fervor, and a belief in the regenerative possibilities of violence for man and society; they also advanced a misconstrual of such notions as personal sacrifice, discipline, and self-control. In his portrayal of Perdigoto as lazy, dishonest, and dissolute in *O rei da vela*, however, Oswald subverts all of these notions, taking special care to undermine the fascist glorification of modern masculinity.[30]

The cultural and political anxieties of authority explored by the Perdigotos and Totós of the day also drew the attention of Oswald and his then-wife Pagu, whose contempt for lesbianism and male homosexuality—in Oswald's theater, in Pagu's 1933 novel *Parque industrial* (published in a 1993 translation as *Industrial Park*) and in their writings for *O homem do povo*[31]—were a part not only of the Left's homosexualization of fascism but also of a more generalized critique of exploitative sexuality. Pagu and Oswald were writing as intellectuals who were close to the party leadership and who capitulated to, or believed they were repeating, relevant beliefs of those they thought they were writing for—the *povo*, the masses, the rank and file of the party. Writing in *Political Inversions* about the attempt to associate fascism with the petite bourgeoisie and homosexuality, Andrew Hewitt (1996: 9) offers these remarks about the political infighting on the Left during the 1930s:

> There has always been in "progressive" political thought a dichotomy between party leadership and the rank and file on the question of homosexuality. Far from being a theoretical abstraction in leftist ideology, the conflation of homosexuality and fascism seems to have marked an opportunistic capitulation of theory in the face of popular sentiment.

It is worth noting here that in the first volume of his autobiography (titled *Um homem sem profissão: Sob as ordens de mamãe* [1974, A man without a profession: At mama's service]), which covers the first thirty years of his life, Oswald makes at least four references to homosexual sex, including anal penetration. In the memoirs, written long after his marxist years, at a time when he no longer had to worry about toeing the party line on homosexuality, Oswald is free to make some very revealing disclosures about his own homosexual inclinations. In only one of these occasions was he a direct participant, as a child involved in what is described succinctly as "*um brinquedo sexual frustrado, com um menino, junto a um monte de areia*" (frustrated sexual playing with a boy, next to a pile of sand) (Andrade 1974: 9). The other references to homosexual sex clearly mention anal penetration. In one of them—the only passage in the volume where he resorts to poetry to narrate an event—Oswald (29) tells of a young cousin playing bottom to an unidentified top during one of the *festas juninas* (the folk and religious festivals held in the month of June). In another, more detailed, passage, Oswald relates his teenage relationship with his school chums, including Adolfo, "*o melhor aluno da turma, que diziam vestir roupas vindas da Inglaterra . . . que revelavam grossas e perfeitas pernas morenas*" (the best student in the class . . . said to wear clothing imported from England . . . which revealed thick, perfect, dark thighs). Oswald confesses his own surprise at falling in love with Adolfo and his "*nádegas redondas e plasticamente perfeitas . . . sob calças colantes e curtas*" (round, perfectly constructed buttocks . . . under skin-tight shorts) and he laments the fact that "*os gabirus da classe*" (the butt-fuckers of the class), Ponzini the Italian boy, Lúcio Veiga, and Oswald himself, never succeeded in seducing Adolfo. Another beautiful classmate, Francisco de Paula, was more receptive to Oswald's advances but never let Oswald have his way with him. Ponzini was vastly more successful than Oswald, seducing not only Francisco but several others, a triumph the jealous Oswald attributes to Ponzini's family money and lavish spending. Oswald does not miss the opportunity to blame capitalism for the moral corruption of his generation ("*Era a mentalidade bancária que irrompia em nossa moral, quebrando valores que supúnhamos eternos*" [the profiteering mentality sabotaged our morals, shattering values we thought were eternal]) and closes with an envious remark on Ponzini ("*Detinha tudo em suas mãos—a cola, a cumplicidade e o reto dos colegas bonitos*" [he had everything—our beautiful classmates' exams to copy from, their rectums, and their complicity]) (40–42).

Oswald's apparent capitulation to popular sentiment and Communist Party thinking regarding homosexuality in the 1930s, did not, curiously, exempt him from allegiance to the old order. As the Brazilian critic Iná Camargo Costa (1996) points out in her provocative book *A hora do teatro épico no Brasil* (A time for an epic theater in Brazil), Oswald's reproof of the old aristocracy—his very own social class—is shaky at best. In *O rei da vela*, she points out, the playwright does not just shield Colonel Belarmino and Dona Cesarina (parents of Heloísa et al.) from "*choques didáticos com a realidade*" (didactic clashes with reality)—the reality of their financial debacle and of how their children are coping with it. In his portrayal of male and female homosexuality, Oswald "*não vai às últimas*" (does not go all out) (163) in attacking the Belarmino children because of who they were. Rather than approaching the issue in terms of class loyalty, I prefer to read Oswald's representation of homosexuality in his theater as a serious attempt to deny homosexuality a presence by giving it only the empty spaces and zero markers that form an embodiment of absence.[32]

Male rape in a prison environment is another means of associating homosexuality with violence in the modernist and neorealist theater of Brazil. In the modern period, rape has served different thinkers and currents of thought in diverse figurative approaches to the nature of power. It has been the most enduring paradigmatic trope for colonial relations; it also figures prominently as an abiding metaphor for the imposition of power of man over woman and, less frequently, of man over man. In the latter case, rape is more about emasculating another male than about possessing his body or being one with his body. Anal rape is then used as an instrument of feminization, a process whereby a man is delegitimized, discredited, or disempowered. As Richard Trexler (1995) argues in *Sex and Conquest*, the degradation visited upon male victims of sexual violence is much more than the fact of being penetrated by another man; for those born into a "world of penetrative penality" (7), in Spanish and Portuguese colonial Latin America as well as in the same region today, the true violence lies in being made into a woman by receiving the same kind of sexual punishment a woman would. What repels males in such a world is "less sodomy *per se* than the assumption of the 'female' role . . . with all its submissive associations to force and conquest. . . . The abomination . . . [is] submission" (171). The theatrical representation of such a forced sexual act presents the stage director with important decisions: whether or not to depict it on stage, to depict it realistically, or to present only a limited or figurative scene. Male rape in prison not only introduces the risks that normally attend the staging of violent acts but also challenges the audience's prejudices against homosexuals, anal sex, and prison inmates in general.[33]

Two cases in point are Nelson's *Toda nudez será castigada* and Plínio Marcos's *Barrela*. One of Nelson's later works, *Toda nudez será castigada*[34] revisits several of the playwright's favored themes—incest, prostitution, infidelity, false morality, the meaning of obscenity, and chastity as inseparable from depravity. Homosexuality also figures in the larger canvas of moral corruption Nelson has drawn. Close scrutiny of the play reveals how Serginho's prison experience and his rape by fellow prisoner Ladrão Boliviano (Bolivian Thief), as well as his and other people's reaction to it, are central to the play's attack on family hypocrisy. As the darling of his three elderly maiden aunts, the teenager is portrayed not only as pure but as the embodiment of an exalted form of chastity; repulsed by any hint of obscenity, Serginho will not undress in front of anyone, including his doctor. With his distorted notion of purity, he is convinced of his right to demand that, like himself, others abstain from sex or even from the thought of it. Because of the incestuous and homosexual attraction Serginho feels for his widowed father, Herculano,[35] the young man demands a vow of chastity from his father and chides him for having an affair with a prostitute named Geni and thus betraying the memory of his dead mother. When Herculano fails to mind Serginho's demands, the young man first forces his father to marry Geni and then seduces her, not because he is attracted to the woman but as a way of exacting vengeance from his father. In sleeping with his stepmother, Serginho is symbolically sleeping with the father he lusts after. But the hypocrisy of the family and society depicted in the play keeps Serginho's homosexuality from ever being admitted: in one of Herculano's conversations with the family doctor, repressed homosexuality is not even mentioned as a likely source of the young man's problems; when Serginho ultimately runs away with another man—none other than his rapist Bolivian Thief, his three spinster

Enio Gonçalves as Serginho and Cleide Yáconis as Geni in Nelson Rodrigues's *Toda nudez será castigada.* Directed by Zbigniew Ziembinski. Teatro Serrador, Rio de Janeiro, 1965. Photograph by Carlos. Arquivo Multimeios/Divisão de Pesquisas. Centro Cultural São Paulo.

aunts insist their nephew has gone on an extended vacation by himself; and Geni prefers to kill herself rather than face the true sexuality of the young man with whom she has fallen in love.

Serginho's elopement with the very man who raped him in prison—a development some critics decry as an element of melodrama, a "surprise ending," is in fact subtly presaged in the drama. The danger here is not of melodrama but the implication that the victim enjoyed being raped and in fact has fallen in love with his rapist. Moreover, one is left with the impression that it was the Bolivian Thief who showed Serginho his true sexuality and freed him from a world of inhibitions and irrational preoccupations. By play's end all nudity—the uninhibited expression of one's sexuality—has indeed been punished, except that of Serginho. And that is so, by implication, because Serginho was saved by his rapist.[36] This idea of redemption through male rape is summed up by the trusted family doctor, who examines Serginho following the rape; as the physician tells Herculano, "*Pois essa monstruosidade foi o ponto de partida para todo um processo de vida.... De ressurreição*" (Rodrigues 1981–90, 4: 230) ("This whole calamity is the point of departure for a whole new way of living.... A resurrection" [Rodrigues 1998: 188]). The fact that the perpetrator of the rape remains anonymous and is never seen on stage (we are told, though, that he is "*Um sujeito dos seus 33 anos, imundo, mas bonito*" [Rodrigues 1981–90, 4: 221; "About thirty-three. Filthy. Handsome." Rodrigues 1998: 179]) adds an aura of divine mystery to the violent act. In addition, the fact that he is a foreigner who speaks Spanish ("*língua de namorado, de amante*" [Rodrigues 1981–90, 4: 225; "the language of love. Of lovers." Rodrigues 1998: 183]) may impart a poetic touch to a situation that would be merely criminal had the victimizer been Brazilian and identifiable, as Sábato Magaldi (1990: 39) speculates in his introduction to the play. Although unseen and unknown, the character is of tremendous consequence not only because, for better or worse, he serves as the catalyst for change in Serginho but also because his actions lead directly to Geni's suicide.

In *Barrela* the centrality of rape is inescapable and salvation is nowhere to be found. Plínio Marcos's suffocating play is suffused with violence and male competition, for the imposition of power is overwhelming in this exclusively male space.[37] With the six prisoners in constant search of a chance to feminize—that is, deprive of power—a fellow inmate, the prison cell becomes the site for a *barrela* ("male gang rape" in prison parlance, as Marcos [1976: 6] tells us in his introduction to the play). The tension in this short play gradually works up to the climactic anal rape, with two of the six cellmates, Portuga and Tirica, as the focus of the action. The men initially target Portuga in retaliation for his having awakened his companions with screams related to a nightmare. Portuga, however, finds a quick escape when he identifies Tirica as a more suitable choice for rape because of some information he was able to unearth about an earlier rape during Tirica's time in the reformatory. Led by Portuga, the men begin to taunt Tirica, with occasional interventions by Bereco, the *xerife,* or leader of the group, and Louco—the self-described insane companion whose sanity is nevertheless very much unimpaired and who keeps yelling *"Enraba ele! Enraba!"* (Fuck his ass! Fuck his ass!). Tirica reacts strongly to the suggestion, threatening to kill Portuga once the other man falls asleep, and the veritable dance of aggravation and retaliation continues for some time. Foremost among the provocations is the use of the feminine form of address as well as traditional put-downs of gays, such as *boneca* (doll) and *bichona* (which might be rendered into something like "queen mother" in English). Just as important here are gestures, body movements, and posture as well as the reduced distance between bodies, employed as a way to intimidate an opponent.[38] The stage directions suggest the intensity of such interactions (see, for example, 16–17, 43–45) as the tension rises between Portuga and Tirica. The confrontation is interrupted at its peak by the arrival of a seventh cellmate, the recently arrested Garoto (Kid). As the six prisoners size up the latest arrival, it becomes clear that the good-looking young man, who is their social better, is suddenly the perfect victim. Garoto is terrified as he realizes their intentions. Aware that Garoto's father will soon obtain his release, the men act quickly and rape him; Bereco the leader (called Pachorra in an earlier draft of the play) is the only one who does not participate in the forced sex act. Tirica, however, is unable to have an erection and therefore cannot penetrate the young man. This causes the other men, led by Portuga, to jeer Tirica for not being "enough of a man." Portuga then resumes his taunting of Tirica, which quickly leads to the denouement, with Tirica fatally stabbing Portuga with a sharpened fork handle.

While Tirica's failed performance with a male sexual partner would seem to more logically confirm his heterosexuality—his being "very much a man"—in the world of *Barrela* it is seen as confirmation of his homosexuality (56–57), homosexuality in such a milieu being understood as encompassing only those who prefer a passive role in male sex while those, such as the other inmates, who penetrate another male are considered heterosexuals. The desire to force another male into submission through the humiliation of anal sex thus becomes the litmus test for manliness; failure to be the penetrator signals inferiority and feminization. While Bereco's decision to stay out of the rape could cast doubt on his virility and thus ultimately weaken his hold over the other inmates, the men ultimately opt not to confront Bereco, for fear of retaliation. There are earlier indications, however, that they are only waiting for a chance to band together against Bereco, and with Portuga dead and his assassin, Tirica, removed from the cell, the power dynamics of this group appear on the verge of radical change as the play ends.

Although for reasons different from those in *Toda nudez*, the anal rape in *Barrela* also casts that act of violence as an empowering experience. Unlike Nelson's play, however, Marcos's work requires a realistic staging of the moment in which power is gained or maintained through the forceful

Plínio Marcos, *Barrela*. Directed by Plínio Marcos and Renato Consorte. Teatro TAIB, Bom Retiro, São Paulo, 1980. Thanah Correa (Portuga), Carlos Costa (Pinto Mole), Bené Silva (Bereco), Francisco Milani (Tirica), Antônio Leite (Fumaça), Adelino Rodrigues, (Laranjeiro), and Paco Sánchez (Mudinho). Photograph by Ruth Amorim Toledo. Arquivo Multimeios/Divisão de Pesquisas. Centro Cultural São Paulo.

submission or disempowerment of another male. The realistic presentation of the rape scene, quite aside from the fact that it led to the banning of *Barrela* for many years, actually detracts from the impact of the play. The violence is too obvious, too crude, too predictable, and the spectator as a consequence is struck by the anticlimactic quality of the scene.

Written in 1957, *Barrela* was Marcos's first play.[39] Banned from a National Student Theater Festival in Santos in 1959, it faced the ire of the censors from the very beginning. Had it not been for the intercession of Paschoal Carlos Magno (1906–1980)—creator of the student theater festivals, one of the greatest promoters of the theater Brazil has ever had, and then chief of staff for President Juscelino Kubitschek—*Barrela* would not have been staged at the festival. Despite the amount of critical praise and public interest,[40] only one performance was permitted at the festival (with Marcos himself directing) and another twenty-one years went by until permission was given for a second staging of the play.[41] Attempts were made in the 1960s and 1970s to stage the play, all in vain; most noteworthy among such attempts was that of the group Teatro Jovem in Rio de Janeiro in 1968,[42] who were not informed of the censors' negative decision until opening night, as well as another staging in São Paulo in 1969, directed by Alberto d'Aversa, where the ensemble was again kept in the dark about the negative decision until the play was ready to open. As the censors of the military dictatorship that took over the government in 1964 became more intolerant, outright prohibition was slowly dropped in favor of this more sophisticated tactic. The censorship bureau would approve the submitted text, allow rehearsals, let the company incur sometimes considerable debt to produce the play, and then, on opening night, hours or even minutes before curtain time, word would come to the theater that the play was unacceptable. This kind of action caused the financial ruin in 1973 of the producers of Chico Buarque and Ruy Guerra's *Calabar: O elogio da traição*, reputedly the most expensive production in Brazilian theater as of that date.

Barrela was labeled a "subversive" text and Marcos a "communist" author, two of the labels used in the 1960s to disqualify anyone perceived as different and rebellious. He was shunned by producers and theaters afraid of economic and political damage and it was not until 1966 that he managed to see another of his plays, *Dois perdidos numa noite suja*, staged. A possible result of Pagu's influence on Marcos's reading, the play, as Marcos readily admits, is based on a short story by Alberto Moravia entitled "The Terror of Rome" and published in *Roman Tales*. *Dois perdidos numa noite suja* premiered in late 1966 at an alternative space, a bar called Ponto de Encontro, located in Galeria Metrópole, then a busy nighttime gay cruising area in downtown São Paulo. The production, directed by Benjamin Cattan and featuring Ademir Rocha and Marcos himself as Tonho and Paco, was later moved to Teatro de Arena, perhaps the epicenter of cultural resistance to the military regime at that time.

The plays of this period in which homosexuality is conspicuously, insistently, absent are precisely the ones in which it is most present. Works such as *Dois perdidos* and Nelson's *Beijo no asfalto*—in all likelihood the two most potent works on homosexuality by modernist and neorealist playwrights—insist on concealing homosexuality, yet manage to engage with it in a manner that goes beyond the censorious, exclusionary implications of previous representations. While the latter fail to present a coherent, neutral treatment, these two works, although not immune to the homophobia and machismo of the period, allow new channels of inquiry into their import and relevance.

Dois perdidos, like *Barrela*, *Navalha na carne*, and other early plays by Plínio Marcos, depicts an underworld where each individual, victimized by an uncaring system, oppresses others who are just as disenfranchised as he. In *Dois perdidos*, Paco's ruling preoccupation is to find himself a flute that would allow him to make a modest living playing for tips at bars, while Tonho's is to get hold of a good pair of shoes that would improve his chances of finding a decent job. Paco eventually persuades the reluctant Tonho to cooperate in an armed robbery. Both before and after the hold-up, the two men angrily try to outwit each other, engaging in violent verbal and nonverbal rituals of control and submission.

Paco, who as the action unfolds is identified as the physically weaker—that is, the more feminine member of the pair—launches a relentless verbal assault on Tonho in order to mask his own vulnerability and his dependence on his roommate. He is shocked when Tonho announces his intention to leave and resorts to physical violence in an effort to prevent his roommate's departure. As he begins to fathom the meaning of Tonho's departure, Paco attempts to convince his companion of the validity of a relationship that Paco himself had tried to undermine (78–79).

Jealous of Tonho's quiet, unassuming good looks, Paco brags about nonexistent girlfriends (the text subtly suggests that Paco has never had a relationship with a woman and hints that his nice pair of shoes was earned in exchange for sex with men) and torments Tonho with a series of references to the exploitation imposed on Tonho at his job, unloading truckloads of goods at the local market. Paco embellishes the story to include a relationship in which Tonho plays the sexually submissive role to a dominant Negrão, who is the leader of the market workers. Calling Tonho "a Boneca do Negrão" (the Big Black Guy's Doll), Paco prances around the dingy room, tauntingly referring to Tonho with feminine adjectives and pronouns. The tension reaches a climax when Tonho answers his roommate's relentless provocations with an explosion of fury that ends with his brutal murder of Paco. Before shooting Paco execution style, Tonho forces him at gunpoint to put on an earring and walk around the room swinging his hips (91–92), making Paco play the feminized role, like a grotesque Boneca do Negrão, and asserting his own newly gained power. But in the end, Tonho is unable to free himself from Paco, and his survival as an individual is doubtful. When he exits, dancing and playing the harmonica as Paco used to, Tonho can no longer revert to his former demeanor or speech pattern. Brandishing Paco's gun and renaming himself after Paco's self-chosen epithet—"*Eu sou Tonho Maluco, o Perigoso*" (93) (*I'm Crazy Tony, the Dangerous One*)—he is doomed to embark alone on a violent path that is likely to eventually lead to his own elimination.

The violent dance the two characters perform reveals the fissures that attend the production of Brazilian masculinity. The intense homoeroticism teases out the complexly encoded fears and anxieties that Paco and Tonho harbor. Because it is a two-male-character play, *Dois perdidos* illustrates a broad variety of issues in male–male relations. First, it is a strong reminder of the extent to which aggressiveness in homosocial relations is pervaded with scarcely contained desire. And it shows how such relations can often be reduced to a single question, "Who is in charge?" This question, as we know, is a gendered one, for who is in control determines who will accrue the privileges of cultural masculinity. If one of the pair does not self-identify as a woman or a feminized male, then he must be made to do so.

As in *Dois perdidos*, there is no overt homosexual act, character, or relationship in *Beijo no asfalto*. Still, the play constitutes in many ways an intense discussion of the nature of homosexuality, and at least one critic considers Nelson's work "a profoundly didactic playtext" (Lockhart 1994: 151).[43] In *Beijo no asfalto,* a dying man lying on the pavement in a busy Rio de Janeiro thoroughfare begs a total stranger to kiss him on the mouth before he draws his last breath. Arandir, the protagonist, obliges. This simple act of charity for a dying human being might be considered a noble gesture, one with strong links to warrior culture in the West (for example, British soldiers dying on the battlefield—most famously, Lord Nelson—would demand a final, mouth-to-mouth kiss from their fellows before passing into the next world).

Yet any fleeting sense of understanding on the part of those who witness the kiss gives way to vehement denunciation. Public hysteria follows the sensationalistic reports that completely distort the gesture of solidarity, and Arandir's "worthiness" becomes the focus of discussion for a group of people (obvious representatives of society as a whole) intent on degrading the Other who is perceived to have transgressed. The kiss sets the media, the police, Arandir's in-laws, and much of the community into a collective act of what Judith Butler (1999: xii) calls gender policing, of enforcing heterosexual behavior. However, as Melissa Lockhart (1994: 152) puts it, "The true perversion is not the kiss but rather the vision of the dominant ideology reflected in the piece." The social and individual consequences of his act of piety prove overwhelming for Arandir and his wife, Selminha, who are caught in a maelstrom of criticism, challenges to his masculinity (i.e., heterosexuality), and the consequent rupture of their marriage.

Unlike the ending of *Toda nudez*, the surprise revelation at the end of *Beijo no asfalto* has not been sufficiently intimated, nor is it infused with convincing dramatic vigor. The melodramatic revelation that Aprígio, Arandir's father-in-law, is in love with him and kills him detracts from the impact of the play; not even the episode of homosexual panic experienced by Aprígio when his daughter Dália confronts him about what she assumed was her father's incestuous love for her sister diffuses the impending melodrama.

Aprígio, Arandir's father-in-law, is represented as a staunchly heterosexual man, a *pater familias* with some very conservative ideas. Yet as the action unfolds, we learn that he not only has incestuous feelings for his daughter but that he lusts after her husband—whom he ultimately murders. Insufficiently intimated, the melodramatic ending diminishes the value of what is otherwise a very strong drama. Even more unfortunate is the way Aprígio is characterized in the play, for, as Lockhart (1994: 153) points out, "His homosexuality demonstrates that for some, coming out of the closet or acknowledging one's sexual inclinations that extend beyond the parameters of those sanctioned under patriarchy can only lead to death." Still, and in fairness to Nelson, one can argue that it was Aprígio's closeted life—not his sudden coming-out at the end—that led to violence. In other words, this alternative reading would suggest that the violent acts committed by Aprígio at the end of the play would not have occurred had he been honest about his feelings and—going against great odds—lived a transparent life as an adjusted homosexual. Of course it is to Nelson's credit that a case can be made for his representation of Arandir as a denunciation of the prejudice and homophobia of a sensationalist press and mindless public. On the other hand, such praise for the playwright is cut short as we realize that to everyone around the protagonist and even to Arandir himself, a relationship between him and the man or any man seems utterly unthinkable. For, as Lockhart (1994: 156) states at the conclusion of her article, Nelson "also reveals his *own* adhesion to the norm by tying the 'humanity' and 'purity' of the kiss to Arandir's perceived heterosexuality. *Beijo no asfalto* would have truly been a remarkable play had it presented the notion that homosexuality is not incompatible with such 'positive' attributes."

Serious flaws such as this one place *Beijo no asfalto* just this side of being a great play, but they do not completely undermine its claim to being, along with Marcos's *Dois perdidos*, the best dramatic treatments

Marcos Oliveira as Arandir and Washington Lasmar as Aprígio in Nelson Rodrigues's *Beijo no asfalto. Nelson Rodrigues, o eterno retorno.* Directed by Antunes Filho. Teatro São Pedro, São Paulo, 1981. Photograph by Ruth Amorim Toledo. Arquivo Multimeios/Divisão de Pesquisas. Centro Cultural São Paulo.

of homosexuality that Brazilian modernism and neorealism had to offer. Both plays addressed for the first time in Brazilian theater the issue of death as the ultimate moment of revelation of homosexual feelings and contrasted Tonho's anger and Aprígio's outburst to Paco's despair and Arandir's supreme humanitarian gesture. But most importantly, the two plays portrayed the heterosexual imperative as an arbitrary ideological limit, helping to redress the compulsory heterosexuality that is normative in Brazilian and other Latin American cultures. As we ponder the manifold questions posed by Nelson's and Marcos's dramas, the extent to which homosexuality in these cultures is invested with violence, a kind of violence that can only issue from the intervention of repressive segments that are intent on effacing it, becomes clear. When denied or occluded—as *Beijo no asfalto* and *Dois perdidos numa noite suja* show, homosexuality is, ironically, at its most conspicuous.

Offering the heterosexual members of the audience the opportunity to think of themselves as upholders of normality, the plays of Oswald de Andrade, Nelson Rodrigues, and Plínio Marcos also allow gay and lesbian spectators to challenge the authenticity of the practices and markers put forth in these plays. To apply to the issue at hand what Paul Julian Smith (1992: 11) writes in the introduction of his book on race and gender in Spanish and Spanish American narrative, these playwrights' representations of homosexuality are in fact "a paradigmatic case of the 'othering'" of homosexuals; what they do is in fact little more than "the old pathologizing of the other," for (and here Smith is quoting Isaac Julien and Kobena Mercer) their works tend "to reinforce . . . the perceived otherness and marginality of the subject itself" (16).

In spite of their limitations with regard to homosexuality, the plays of Oswald de Andrade, Nelson Rodrigues, and Plínio Marcos pushed the limits of Brazil's toleration for representations of transgression. Transgression, in Foucauldian terms, is the interrogation of boundaries, a realm where "what is in question is the limit rather than the identity of a culture" (Stallybrass and White 1986: 200). One needs to approach these playwrights reminded of the error in identifying a tentative representation of transgression with political progressiveness. For they, Oswald and Nelson in particular, were products of a staid bourgeoisie, and as bourgeois artists they produced a kind of theater in which transgression was an instrument to shatter identity boundaries. In this respect, their theater relates to a situation remarked upon by Stallybrass and White (1986: 200) with respect to the writings of Foucault and Kristeva, in which bourgeois writing uses transgression to smash "the rigidities of its own identity by projecting itself into the forbidden territories of precisely those excluded in its own political formation." In both cases (those of Oswald and Nelson), and finally in Marcos as well, a flawed representation of homosexuality contrasts with a body of works—the plays examined in chapter 3—that, as essential critiques of the very posture that supported the legitimation of modernist ambitions and cultural domination, is considered key for an understanding of twentieth-century Brazil.

In part because of their representations of homosexuality, the three playwrights were victims of ruthless censorship through most of their careers. Their unfortunate treatment at the hands of the censors—military and otherwise—does not however clear them of a failure to problematize homosexuality. This shortcoming is serious enough—certainly at their more homophobic moments—to exemplify, in an almost classical manner, the derailing of the myth that representing homosexuality on stage is a manner of proselytizing in its behalf.

The case of Nelson Rodrigues is made even more complex by his cozy relationship with the military regime in the 1960s and 1970s. He was execrated by most of Brazil's intelligentsia, straight and gay, for his staunch defense of the dictatorship (even as they censored his plays and sentenced his own son, Nelson Rodrigues Filho, to death for vaguely defined "terrorist acts"). With the return to democracy in 1985, Nelson, who had died in 1980, was quickly rehabilitated by his admirers, including some of the most important names in Brazilian theater in the second half of the twentieth century, most notably Sábato Magaldi and Antunes Filho. As modernism continued to press—late in the century as it was—for hegemony in drama and elsewhere in Brazilian art, Nelson was dutifully canonized in the 1980s and 1990s, just as Oswald had been in the 1960s and 1970s.[44] With both authors championed as virtual national commodities, we can turn—ironically—to Nelson himself as he warned against all forms of unanimity, in his famous adage, "*Toda unanimidade é burra*" (All unanimity is stupid).[45]

What Might Have Been: A Coda

Homosexual playwrights and others who could have countered the image that had been crystallized in the theater of these authors chose, or were socially coerced, to remain silent in this respect. A case in point is Lúcio Cardoso (1912–1968). An up-and-coming writer and dramatist who lived as openly gay as was possible in 1930s through the 1950s Rio de Janeiro, Lúcio was in a position to move beyond such representations as those seen in the plays examined above. However, in response to contingencies beyond the purely personal, Lúcio skirted the issue altogether in his theater. As a result, his plays have an air of diffuse affectation about them. Critics thus tend to speak dismissively of Lúcio Cardoso, and other playwrights seem to regard him with a kind of condescending affection.

Perhaps the most fascinating aspect of Lúcio's theater is his association with the important African-Brazilian group, Teatro Experimental do Negro. The ensemble, generally referred to in Brazil as TEN, was active from 1944 to 1957.[46] Writing plays for an all-black ensemble, Lúcio had to contend with more than just the racial element. African-Brazilian theater practitioners of the period tended to reflect the notion then held by some black males that homosexuality is a symptom of a decadent white society and a threat to masculinity; interestingly enough, though, this macho stance conveniently ignores the strong presence of male homosexuals in the Afro-Brazilian spirit possession practices of *candomblé*. As time went by, some TEN associates seemed to grow more homophobic as their isolation and radicalism increased. Feeling he could not accentuate differences any further without risking total alienation from the group, Lúcio again evaded homosexuality, and so his plays for TEN also strike the spectator as remote and unfamiliar. He discontinued his association with the group and dedicated more and more time to his novels, having spent many years writing his masterpiece, *A crônica da casa assassinada* (Chronicle of a fallen dynasty), published in 1959. Three years later Lúcio had a first stroke that left him paralyzed and depressed; a second and more massive one killed him in 1968, by which time Oswald's canonization was well under way, Nelson's reputation was already considerable, and Marcos's career was beginning to take off.

chapter 3

Beyond Evasiveness

Seeking to apply the theories of transgression discussed in the introductory materials, this chapter situates the performative and transgressive aspects of theatrical practice in the historical context of a dramatic milieu that saw significant changes in the second half of the twentieth century. In the politically repressive but artistically vibrant period extending from the late 1960s to the early 1980s, the homosexual camp finally secured a cultural stronghold from which to counter one of the defining traits of Brazilian drama since its inception; theater in Brazil had always been a matter of contrary and exclusionary representations, with the colonizer representing the colonized, the catechizer the catechized, the children of the landholding slave owners the slaves. Throughout the formative period of Brazilian society, those in power showed little concern for whether or how the country's disenfranchised were being represented on stage or otherwise. In the late 1960s and early 1970s, Brazilian theater seemed to be producing, for the first time in its history, a wave of more authentic and relevant depictions of sexual difference and dissidence. That such changes were occurring as Brazilian theater lived one of its most electrifying periods is hardly surprising; what is surprising is that all of this was taking place at a time of harsh political repression with serious limitations to freedom of expression and civil rights in general.

By that time, a key feature of the representation of homosexual transgression in the Brazilian theater—namely, its cautious nature, its tentativeness—was beginning to be seriously questioned. Western society had by then accepted the emergence of transgression as central to the modern experience of otherness. As recent advances in mass communications made it possible for Brazil's then-expanding middle class to be quickly aware of the latest developments in European and North American art and culture, timid and—worse—prejudiced portrayals of transgression began to give way to braver depictions that challenged the censorship apparatus put in place by the military. Such recently secured space allowed for a more honest exploration—if not a true crossing—of difference and its barriers, and the range of new possibilities opened up by younger playwrights made possible a freer theatrical investigation of the patterns that make up the framework of experience in modern Brazil. Still, this breakthrough was tempered by the fact that a number of these productions succumbed to the tensions and contradictions encountered along the perilous course of pursuing a market without losing their transgressive edge. Resisting hegemonic practices while fending off increasingly alluring calls to cooptation proved too exacting for a number of these productions, and as a result much of their transgressive punch was lost.

To a large extent these shortcomings are related to the inability to problematize the heterosexual–homosexual duality, the *atividade–passividade* opposition described in the first chapter. Failing to transcend the misguided dichotomies described by Richard Parker and others, these more facile plays (notably *Greta Garbo* and *As tias*) fall short of real innovation and contribute instead to the perpetuation of old stereotypes. The more successful of these works, on the other hand, are those that explore the ambigusexuality in Brazilian culture. As explained in the introductory chapter, Rommel Mendès-Leite's notion of ambigusexuality (1993: 279–80n. 3) is rooted in an understanding of sexuality as a culturally and historically defined manifestation that "begins with the symbolisation of physiological data . . . transmitted by the process which leads to socialisation." Ambigusexuality, for Mendès-Leite, is detected at three different levels—role, interpretation, performance—linking the social actor or sexual individual to her or his character; the diversity of these three positions is directly dependent on the fluidity of social roles in a given society. The fluidity of homosocial relations is particularly well represented in the works of dramatists such as Zé Vicente, Naum Alves de Sousa, and Mauro Rasi, who have offered innovative theatrical manipulations of the ambiguous sexual inflections in the everyday performances of social actors in Brazil.

The Coming of Zé Vicente

Performing ambigusexuality entailed the staging of an exploration of the constitution of homoerotic desire, resorting to a duplicity that often welcomes an element of risk. Zé Vicente's play *O assalto* (1969, Assault) is a suitable place to begin examining this element of risk. But first, it is important to note that two productions mentioned in the first chapter, *Hoje é dia de rock* (also by Zé Vicente) and *A China é azul* (by José Wilker), which premiered in 1971 and 1972, respectively, helped to open the way for a climate of tolerance toward drug use and sexual diversity among middle- and upper-class youth; and this, in turn, facilitated the acceptance of the gay-themed plays staged in subsequent years. In addition, as I indicated as part of the introductory material, the general climate of experimentation prevalent in urban Brazil welcomed the appearance and success in the early 1970s of gay-friendly celebrations like the Banda de Ipanema and so-called androgynous groups like Dzi Croquettes and Secos e Molhados.[1]

Just as the theatergoing public was becoming more acquainted with the performative nature and gender-bending explorations of these groups a new same-sex oriented theater was gaining a voice of its own, and the careers of openly gay playwrights such as Fernando Melo, Aguinaldo Silva, and others were set to take off. I am not pinning these playwrights' importance on their sexuality; the trap of collapsing identity and legitimacy is by now easier to avoid than in past decades. In this respect, and substituting sexual orientation for racial identity, I adapt and paraphrase Paul J. Smith's comments, in *Representing the Other* (1992: 15), on Isaac Julien and Kobena Mercer: a playwright's sexual identity "should neither guarantee its value nor pre-empt critical analysis"; what is important, rather, is to explore "the intersections of differences," particularly in relation to sexuality and to examine "how the texts . . . negotiate elusive and potent myths." A number of these younger playwrights were openly gay but others identified themselves as heterosexual. Regardless of sexual orientation, their works are relevant because of the "intersections of differences" they explore and the new sensibility they attempted to infuse—with varying degrees of success—their works with.

The relatively freer atmosphere had previously enabled Zé Vicente to stage his homoerotic work *O assalto* in 1969. With Plínio Marcos's *Dois perdidos numa noite suja* (see chapter 2), *O assalto* is the most successful Brazilian representative of the two-male-character play that was very much in vogue in the Western theater of the period. Locating the action in an extreme, often absurd, milieu these plays depict the intense and sometimes brutal relations of two individuals who, for all the differences between them, are complementary selves and therefore cannot exist apart from each other. Vicente's theatrical exploration of the destructiveness that seems to constitute an inextricable part of these relationships attracted large audiences drawn to the theater by the highly charged, and for that time, daring performances of Rubens Correa and Ivan de Albuquerque of Teatro Ipanema fame (in the Rio de Janeiro production) and Francisco Cuoco and Paulo César Peréio (in São Paulo), both stagings under the direction of Fauzi Arap.

Because, as George Woodyard (1969: 186) has written, the two-character play is "a technique which permits closer examination, not of motivation and psychological development, but of the irrationality of the frustrated and desperate human animal," some of these works are not readily identified with the theater of social and political commitment that dominated the late 1960s and 1970s in Latin America. Still, even nominally noncommitted plays can be given a political reading, as is the case of *O assalto*. Zé Vicente's play is contestatory in the sense of opposing the dictatorship (as an obvious example, the motto for the bank one of the two characters has come to hate is the same *Ordem e Progresso* [Order and Progress] the military borrowed from the Brazilian flag for their national unity propaganda), but more to my point here, it is also political in its revolutionary homoeroticism.

Zé Vicente depicts homoeroticism and homosexual desire without the affectation and overtones of disease, perversion, and social disintegration seen in the plays of Oswald de Andrade, Nelson Rodrigues, and Plínio Marcos. To be sure, *O assalto* has an exalted and even, at times, surreal mood, but it also includes some lyrical touches and signs of genuine affection. That it ends violently is almost to be expected, given the overall climate of repression against most forms of dissidence, homosexuality included.

Zé Vicente used the title of *O assalto* to suggest the violence that pervades the homoerotic interaction between the two men. The title, as well as subtitles of the play's two acts—"Primeiro assalto" and "Segundo assalto"—explore the ambiguities of the different meanings of the Portuguese noun *"assalto":* assault, holdup, charge, storm, or, in the sense of boxing, round. But for all their violent confrontations, the men are inseparable, as their complementary names (which allude to Victor Hugo) indicate. Vítor is a bank clerk[2] who, having quit his job earlier that day, stays after hours to exact retribution on the institution he feels has taken away all meaning and vitality from his existence; and Hugo is the janitor who, while performing the evening cleaning rounds, encounters Vítor in an empty office. It becomes evident that this was no chance encounter, for Vítor had planned to confess his desire for Hugo. Vítor's impassioned declaration is redolent of notions of the double, or *doppelganger*, then very much in vogue, and it is novel for its statement of desire for another man. Becoming one with the beloved is expressed here through the most essential fluids of maleness (sperm) and life itself (blood). To the age-old notion of two heterosexual lovers cutting their skin in order to physically mix their bloods into an indistinguishable new stream, Vicente counters the image of two men being united as their sperm merges following not a ceremonial blood-vessel cutting but sexual arousal culminating in ejaculation and combination of their bodily fluids. In addition, Vítor's speech brings to mind the obvious association between being one with the object of one's affection and the desire to sexually penetrate the beloved's body. Being inside the other's body allows for Vítor's "knowledge" of the loved one, provides a feeling of being in total unison with his male partner, and constitutes the ultimate merging with the other.

The notion of two lovers becoming one as the sexual act is consummated is stressed further when bank clerk and janitor swap clothes at the end of the first act. Still, as if to prolong a courtship minuet, Hugo continues to resist Vítor's advances, which only adds more ardor to Vítor's pursuit. Dressed in Vítor's clothes but holding out against his lover's pleas, Hugo rejects on social grounds the dual entity envisioned by Vítor. Vítor then resorts to a series of acts of verbal and nonverbal violence[3] that still fail to elicit a commensurate reaction from Hugo. With Vítor too impatient or selfish to understand what seems to be an implied preference on Hugo's part for a prolonged foreplay with sadomasochistic overtones, the violence reaches a crescendo that is finally interrupted when a terrified Hugo, no longer willing to encourage Vítor's aggression, sets off the alarm and screams for help.

A passing exchange early in the play announces the bonding of the two men. Referring to the time in the evening when their shifts overlap, the men allude allegorically to their transitory connection:

VARREDOR: *É a hora que eu entro.*
VÍTOR: *É a hora que eu saio.* (Vicente 1970: 47)

[JANITOR: That's when I clock in.
VÍTOR: That's when I clock out.]

This is not an isolated occurrence in the play; throughout *O assalto* there is an intricate interplay of references to being inside and out, entering and exiting, forcing exits and barring entrances, which culminates in one brief moment of contact. Toward the end, Vítor and Hugo's difficult union is signaled nonverbally as "*os dois ficam de costas, . . . como verso e reverso um do outro*" (61) [the two men stand back to back, . . . as if they were the front and the back of each other], reflecting resentment and admiration, disdaining yet yearning for what the other either has or stands for.

For all its innovation, *O assalto* does not go beyond one of the most serious drawbacks of the mid-twentieth century two-character play. I am thinking here of the double-bind situation in which the two men[4] constantly assault each other, verbally as well as physically; and when the brutality of their interaction drives the pair apart, the surviving member is left to experience the extent of his dependence on a departed companion.

The staging of *O assalto* in 1969 received considerable press attention, favorable reviews, and important awards (including the coveted Molière Prize), but it also attracted the ire of individuals and groups linked to the military and the Catholic Church. Zé Vicente was no stranger to right-wing wrath; the conservative outcry occasioned by the stagings of *O assalto* and *Hoje é dia de rock* had been preceded by the shrill backlash that followed his first play, *Santidade* (1968, Holiness), which was banned after General Arthur da Costa e Silva went on national television to denounce Zé Vicente's work. The denunciation by the country's military ruler triggered a violent campaign against the theater, with paramilitary groups attacking actors and theatergoers perceived as "subversive"; this culminated with a vicious assault by the Comando de Caça aos Comunistas (the Communist Hunters' Command) on the São Paulo theater where Chico Buarque's *Roda viva* (1968) was being staged and bombings of Teatro Opinião in Rio and Teatro Gil Vicente in Porto Alegre later that same year (Michalski 1985: 34).

While the assaults were triggered neither by the participation of gay artists nor the homoeroticism in some of the plays, there seemed to exist a link between the more liberal sexual atmosphere these works were believed to embrace and the increase of institutionalized violence against the theater vanguard of the time. Perhaps more than any other play of the period, *O assalto* was the target of such violent outbursts. When the play was restaged in April of 1970 at Teatro Paiol in São Paulo (starring Vítor Neri and Luis Serra) and later that year went on national tour, members of the cast were arrested on several occasions on vague charges of "subversion," fueled for the most part by the connection some people made between the title of the play (which can mean a bank robbery) and the robberies left wing terrorists were carrying out in order to finance armed resistance to the military regime (Schoenbach 1972: 70). But those arrested were also charged with behavior deemed "lewd and immoral" and counter to "Christian values," code language long used in Brazil in reference to proponents of homosexuality.[5]

Strong reactions to representations of homosexuality such as those encountered by different casts and productions of *O assalto* could be read as substantiation of the work as the *peça terrível* (a theatrical enfant terrible) Vicente had dreamed of writing in his adolescence. Reminiscing in a text published in *Arte em revista* in 1981 about the early stages of his career, Vicente writes of his desire to reveal "*a hipocrisia social de uma forma tão impiedosa que conseguisse ao menos a indignação das pessoas*" (social hypocrisy in such an impious manner that it would awaken, if nothing else, public indignation). In its early drafts, the play that would eventually become *O assalto* depicted "*despudoradamente*" (shamelessly), as Vicente puts it, the marital life of a gay male couple who were unapologetic about who they were. Their transgressiveness was compounded by the fact that both men took advantage of their "*marginalidade*" (outcast status) to make fun of average people. One of the two men is of particular interest here due to the changes Vicente made in the text as he went along. Because the early drafts, perhaps lost, are unavailable to researchers, a study of the development of the character that would later be called Hugo cannot be undertaken at this point. But as Vicente tells us in the same essay, that character was "*um místico exacerbado*" (an intense mystic) who somehow made prostitution one of his articles of faith, convinced as he was that it was through prostitution that he would eventually reach God. Despite its "*limitação naturalista*" (naturalist limitations), Vicente continues, the play managed to elicit the "*indignação*" (indignation) he had initially sought but in which, by the time the work premiered, he was ironically no longer interested. Still, he concludes his recollection of the composition of *O assalto* with the statement,

> *Pra mim significava um trunfo. Eu tinha descoberto um caminho imprevisto e tão rico que só me faltava então conquistar. . . . [N]ão fiz a menor questão de esconder o meu deslumbramento.* (Vicente 1981: 76)
>
> [To me the play was an ace in the hole. I had come upon a path so unexpected and so rich and all I had to do was take it. . . . I didn't even try to hide my dazzlement.]

Just a few years down the road, disillusionment and guilt would supersede the joy Vicente felt at the start of his career. The transformation he underwent was radical, profound, and to this day continues to baffle his former associates.

A brief consideration of the changes in Zé Vicente's life before and after the huge successes of *O assalto* and *Hoje é dia de rock* (which won Vicente a second Molière) serves to illustrate the circumstances attending the intersections of difference in Brazilian theater and culture in the second half of the twentieth century. As he wrote in his 1984 autobiography, *Os reis da terra* (The rulers of the land), Vicente had a profoundly Catholic upbringing in the small town of Ventania[6] in rural, traditional Minas Gerais and was a seminarian for several of his formative years before leaving his family and their conservative values for São Paulo, Rio de Janeiro, Paris, and London, a long sojourn complete with drugs and free love. Vicente's tortured search for inner truth culminated years later with a series of visions in which Jesus Christ, God the Father, and the Virgin Mary reportedly spoke to him.[7] Vicente thereafter renounced all his early plays (which he terms *"teatro de juventude"* [youthful theater]) and began work on a religious trilogy, his *"teatro adulto"* (adult theater) (Vicente 1984: 7).[8]

Although Vicente writes of his close association with several men who were openly gay, he only mentions homosexuality once in the entire book, in a passage where, subsequent to his conversion, he bemoans in a long catalog the *"infinita rede de pecados"* (endless tissue of sin) found in the *"cidades do Mal"* (cities of Evil) (289). Nor are the references to heterosexual sex frequent, one important exception being his tormented relationship with Ana Maria, the woman with whom he lost his virginity (148–51) and to whom he would later return (although he thought she was "vulgar and obscene") only to be rejected by her. Bisexuality is never mentioned in the book, and the several periods when the author (who does not self-identify as gay) shared quarters with gay roommates are paid little attention; and finally, instances of homoeroticism are nowhere to be found in the book, not even in situations that are traditionally conducive to homosociality, such as life in a Catholic seminary. Vicente's religious convictions and his reasons to evade the subject must of course be respected. Still, the biographical background I am providing needs to be considered—even if only as a foil to what we know about *O assalto* and its impact in the late 1960s—because it facilitates our understanding of how homoeroticism and homosexual difference and transgression are perceived and represented in the period under consideration. Attitudes toward sexuality often change and so do its representations, even in the writings and plays of the same author. As the life and theater of Zé Vicente show, the intersection of such feelings and attitudes with portrayals of difference can be very revealing on the stage and elsewhere.

Greta Talks

Intersections of difference are approached in a distinct manner in Fernando Melo's *Greta Garbo, quem diria, acabou no Irajá*. The masculine, intense pair in *O assalto* is replaced by a seemingly traditional *bicha* and *bofe* dichotomy echoing heterosexual gender roles, and the lyrical homoeroticism of Zé Vicente's work gives way to a fast-paced exchange of catty yak controlled by Pedro, the effeminate male nurse who escapes his drab life by fantasizing about being Greta Garbo. Still, the two works converge in some important ways, for just as Vítor sets out to seduce Hugo and is in control of the verbal and nonverbal *assalto* on the janitor, Pedro attempts to seduce Renato. Hugo and Renato play essentially the same role, that of the coy, younger, innocent rube who has moved recently to the big city in search of a better life, only to fall victim to a cunning city slicker who offers financial compensation for sex. The seducer is represented as a more experienced homosexual who is older, lonely, and craves sex and perhaps even, a little love; and in Pedro's case, he is depicted as being sexually *passivo* in relation to the younger, good looking, seemingly naive *ativo* partner.

With Vítor and Pedro having greater economic possibilities than Hugo and Renato, their control over the object of their desire is quickly established. However, as the two plays unfold it becomes clear that Vitor's and Pedro's control of their relationships is not based solely on money. Their ability to wield speech plays a crucial role in gaining and maintaining power, hence Vítor's longer, more elaborate speeches and figurative language are in marked contrast to Hugo's shorter lines and literal expression. In Melo's play, likewise, Pedro has a quick and vicious tongue and is a master of repartee and double entendres, which for the most part escape Renato. Differences intersect further and in even more complex ways in these plays and as a consequence, the *bicha–bofe* dichotomy is problematized. Renato and Hugo, presented as the *ativo* partners and placed lower on the social ladder are however under the control of their *passivo* companions, the smarter and better-off Pedro and Vítor. But it is the dominated one who will in the end take action to terminate the contact (with Hugo activating the alarm in *O assalto*) or the relationship (with Renato leaving Pedro to return to his home town in *Greta Garbo*).

Fernando Melo has been criticized for contributing to gay stereotyping, and there are indeed stereotypical elements in Pedro. Granted, this is a comedy but the humor in a comedy does not have to be built on stereotypes. The fact that it is a comedy, though, places an extra burden on the actors, since for reasons both political and esthetic they must make the characters fully human. The comedic apparatus being so dependent on the rapid-fire one-liners, funny as they are, interferes with deep characterization. The cast of the premiere production did not solve this impossible dilemma but came as close as possible to resolving it.[9] *Greta Garbo* is indeed a problematic play. First, because Pedro's characterization is in the end an imperfect depiction of erotic pleasure as cultural construct while Renato comes across as a heavy-handed illustration of how the game of appearances constitutes an integral component in the formation of a social actor's image. His performance—the third level in Mendès-Leite's notion of ambigusexuality—misreads the social actor's attempt to convince those around him of his adherence to the social model he is expected to follow. Second, although authored by an openly gay playwright, *Greta Garbo* seems to perpetuate the image of a neurotic, pathetic older homosexual man. This kind of character—repressed, affected, laughable—was present in two other crossover megahits of the early 1970s, *Os rapazes da banda* by Matt Crowley (1971; *The Boys in the Band*, 1967) and Jean Poiret's *Gaiola das loucas* (1974; *La cage aux folles*, 1971),[10] both foreign plays translated and adapted for productions staged in the Rio de Janeiro and São Paulo equivalents of Broadway, with unusually large budgets and starring major names. *Greta Garbo* is often thought of as exemplary (in an ironic way) for showing how a play by an openly gay author can be as misguided as the proverbial homosexual-themed work of a prejudiced heterosexual.

Still, in at least two important aspects *Greta Garbo* stands apart from earlier depictions of homosexuals in Brazilian theater. First, the play's stereotyping of the older *bicha* is countered by the subtle transformation Renato seems to have experienced as a result of his association with Pedro. The firm *macho* behavior he affected as we first see him is mostly gone by play's end and as he is getting ready to leave his partner to supposedly return to small-town life in Campos, Renato quietly expresses, if not love for, at least his attachment to Pedro.

The second redeeming aspect of *Greta Garbo* is that it problematizes the *bicha–bofe* association and, consequently, male prostitution. What at first strikes us as a portrayal of a relationship based on the straightforward exchange of sex for money becomes a questioning of exploitation and attachment. Pedro has low self-esteem but he can be tough when he needs to and he understands that power comes from capital accumulation and its ability to function as leverage and as a tool for manipulation. Pedro's awareness shows not only in the way he gradually attains financial control over Renato but also in those moments when he fears that his job, benefits, and upcoming retirement pension might be discontinued by a system that could be particularly harsh with a gay male nurse who has been supplying his lover with drugs from the hospital pharmacy. Renato in turn seems to accept the kept boy arrangement although it poses considerable limitations on the freedom and financial gains he had envisioned attaining as a *michê* (hustler) in the streets of the arts district. His experience in the trade is disputable as it is unclear for how long he had been a hustler before Pedro picked him up that rainy night in downtown Rio de Janeiro. At any rate it is evident that, bored and frustrated with the turn of events, Renato quickly becomes addicted to alcohol and prescription drugs. The only distraction he has are the occasional trysts with Mary, a prostitute at a brothel near the port.

Unlike the (dramatically) more successful introduction of the homosexual Veludo between the heterosexual couple Vado and Neusa in *Navalha na carne*, the mocking of traditional gender roles in *Greta Garbo* is complicated by the arrival of a woman into the space shared by the gay male nurse and his bisexual lover. Mary's appearance in Act II and her continued presence in Act III provoke a change in direction and in all likelihood a blemish to the play, and not just because her entrance breaks the pace of the interaction between Pedro and Renato[11] in Act I nor because there is not enough time to explore her reasons for being a prostitute or Renato's for being attracted to her. Too much negativity is poured on Mary, who is a prostitute, a thief, and a home-breaker; as if that were not enough, too much of the humor derives from the misogynistic tirades Pedro directs at her, her bleached hair, her garish clothes, even her femaleness in asides aimed at audiences who were, in the early 1970s, less sensitive than today's theatergoers to the challenges that sex workers have to face.[12]

Another problem with Melo's work is the insufficient exploration of the intersections of identity and desire around Pedro's identification with movie star Greta Garbo. Other than the couple of occasions when Pedro wonders if Garbo ever had to face the kind of problem he has had to deal with, we do not see Pedro immersed in flights of fancy about or delivering impersonations, monologues, or paeans involving the great actress. The 1973 production attempted to compensate for this deficiency, projecting huge slides of Garbo and her characters on a solid stage backdrop (Oscar 1974: 68), but other stagings have not been so innovative. In any case, the script does not make clear how closely Pedro identifies with the image of Greta Garbo. According to José Esteban Muñoz in *Disidentifications* (1999), queers "disidentify" with normative representations of sexuality, particularly mass-mediated ones, through parodic mimicry. In the introduction to his analysis of minority performance, survival, and activism, Muñoz tells us that disidentification describes "the survival strategies the minority subject practices in order to negotiate a phobic majoritarian public sphere" (4). Pedro's parodic mimicry of the Swedish-born diva gives the vague sense of an inadequate association with Garbo. Pedro starts with an image that has been conditioned by the mass media, if not a star who complies fully with Hollywood expectations of wholesomeness. He settles, rather, on one whose opinions and behavior were suggestive of nonconformity, including, as was widely rumored, in sexual matters. Working, thus, "within and outside the dominant public sphere simultaneously," (Muñoz 1999: 5) Pedro manages to forge a strategy of survival through disidentification with normative representations of sexuality.

The melodrama that has so often been identified as yet another deficiency in *Greta Garbo*'s dramatic craft (mostly because the tone of Act III stands in marked contrast to the high comedy of Acts I and II) is in effect related to Pedro's parodic mimicry. Renato's sudden departure announcement dovetails with Pedro/Greta's penchant for wallowing in the mire. Pedro/Greta's pathetic lamentation fits his recollections (or distortions) of the endings of films such as *Queen Christina* (1933) and *Camille* (1937) in which Greta Garbo played a melancholy woman who sacrifices her happiness for an unattainable love. But the heightened melodrama at play's end does detract from the validity of the two men's mutual dependence. As played by Nestor de Montemar and Mário Gomes (in Rio de Janeiro) and Raul Cortez and Nuno Leal Maia (in São Paulo), Pedro and Renato kiss right before curtain and with much more passion than the stage directions call for. If their ardent, final full-on-the-lips kiss[13] is any indication of their attachment to each other, why then are Pedro and Renato parting? And though Renato is now ready to kiss another man (even if only in the anonymity of a working class apartment somewhere in a big city), he may not be able to cope with the consequences of living as an openly gay man in Campos or anywhere else. Finally, his abrupt departure from Pedro's home raises questions about the honesty of his announced intention to return to the repressive small-town environment he had fled, and as the play closes we are left to wonder if he has in fact overcome his sexual identity crisis. If Renato has not surmounted that crisis, then he is leaving because he is unable to face the fact of his homosexuality and engage in a serious, long-standing monogamous relationship with another man. Unable to confront his true identity, Renato is probably going to return to hustling downtown—a move that would correspond to the interpretation phase, in Mendès-Leite's scheme—where he can escape reality and brag about a heterosexual identity that is not his own.

The vibrant dialogue, many cheerful scenes and rollicking humor gave *Greta Garbo* a militantly pro-gay stand it never set out to have and one which, three decades later, we find difficult to understand. But the sheer fact that it was staged and that it passed the censors in one of the darkest periods of the military dictatorship amounted to a significant statement concerning the visibility of gay men in urban Brazil, even if we take into account the fact that it was cleared by the censors because of its apparently frivolous nature. Be that as it may, the production was jubilantly received by the gay and gay-friendly segments of the large audiences that flocked to see it. Its success emboldened Fernando Melo to pursue a playwriting career where same-sex love figures prominently. Homosexuality takes center-stage in at least two of his other works, *A pequena tragédia de Vera Maria de Jesus, a Condessa da Lapa* (The minor tragedy of the Countess of the Red-Light District) and *Tá boa, santa?* (You okay, hon?). The former is set in a jail and explores the complicated liaison between the good-looking bandit Jorge and his drag queen cellmate Vera Maria; their affair is thwarted by the sadistic jailor, a closeted homosexual who is sexually aroused by his frequent torture sessions of Jorge.[14] *Tá boa, santa?* returns with considerably less success to the formula that had worked so well for Melo in *Greta Garbo*: an older queen named Ananias (played, in the 1984 production, by Nestor de Montemar, who had the title role in the first staging of *Greta Garbo*) takes in a good-looking younger man, Marcos, who claims to be heterosexual but is soon under Ananias's spell, and a woman, Ananias's former wife Zulmira, who steps in to make things difficult for the gay couple and like Mary, in *Greta Garbo*, bears the brunt of a good deal of misogynistic attacks even more out of place in 1984 than the tirades against Mary in 1973.

Lourdes's Four Aunties

The image of the older queen was revisited a few years later in Aguinaldo Silva and Doc Comparato's *As tias* (1981). The lone aging *bicha* in *Greta Garbo* is replaced in Silva and Comparato's work by no less than four desperate middle aged men. Unlike Pedro who works hard at the hospital to meet his financial obligations in Melo's play, these four *tias* (literally aunts but also old queens) are presented as stay-at-home neurotics supported by a mysterious benefactor, Maria de Lourdes, to whom they refer as their adopted "*sobrinha*" (niece) in an obvious play with the literal meaning of *tia*. Although able-bodied and mostly sane, the four men are so content with the situation of utter dependence they find themselves in that panic strikes when Maria de Lourdes arrives for her annual visit and promptly announces that a financial emergency has forced her to discontinue the arrangement. Fighting to keep the status quo of a bucolic life in a comfortable house in the mountains outside Rio de Janeiro, the four men waste no time reminding Maria de Lourdes of the import of her indebtedness to each one of them. In addition, the welcoming the foursome have prepared for this year's visit is a surprise guessing game, with each man performing a scene that recreates a crucial sexual experience from his past. Maria de Lourdes then announces that the author of the skit she favors will be allowed to stay in the house. The new rules intensify the catty attitudes of distrust and suspicion that have emerged with the men's long-term cohabitation.

As the four men scramble to please their guardian angel, Maria de Lourdes's chauffeur suddenly assumes a key role in the unfurling events. Young and good looking, the anonymous *motorista* (driver) becomes the object of the *tias*' desire the instant they lay eyes on him. But fully aware of his striking appearance, the young man keeps a detached demeanor calculated to assist in his attacks on the four men. For Floro, Arlindo, Juarez, and Macedo, it is not just open season against each other any more; now they must contend with a new opponent and one whose tactics include the promise of seduction. Although more menacing than Hugo in *O assalto* and Renato in *Greta Garbo*, the chauffeur shares with them the quality of an enticing figure who either precipitates a crisis or is an important participant in one such moment in the life of an older gay man (the actor playing the chauffeur also plays the sexual partner in each of the skits). This type of character—a mysterious, good-looking young man who chances into the life of the protagonist or protagonists and prompts a sexual identity crisis—was popular in Western film in the 1960s and 1970s, the paragon of which is Pasolini's *Teorema* (1968). In that film, the character played by Terence Stamp leads the members of a bourgeois family to yield to desires they had been repressing or of which they were until then unaware. Also from 1968, Mark Rydell's film version of D. H. Lawrence's novella *The Fox* focuses on the disruption in the marital routine of a lesbian couple (Sandy Dennis and Anne Heywood) that is provoked by the appearance of a gorgeous young man (Keir Dullea).

Bisexuality is a common trait in these spoiler figures, and the chauffeur is no exception. Not unlike Hugo and Renato before him, the chauffeur is a man who self-identifies as heterosexual and yet indicates a willingness to enter a homosexual liaison for monetary gain. This type of character is often an instigator of change but also of destruction. That is the direction the play seems to be heading in until the ritualistic elements are revealed toward the end.

Whether or not the flaws in *As tias* stem from its being a coauthorship, Aguinaldo Silva and Doc Comparato have a dramatic voice that is more compelling for its idiosyncrasy than for its staging efficacy; the situation portrayed and its peculiarities are more likely to stay with us than the action or the conflicts themselves. Much of the problem is related to the hodgepodge of notions and influences (realist theater, existentialism, theater of the absurd, game and ritual theater) that went into the making of this play. Another large part of the deficiencies lies in character delineation. To be sure, an initial effort was made to distinguish between the four recipients of Maria de Lourdes's largesse: Floro is presented as affected and always on the brink of a nervous breakdown; Arlindo is mired in self-pity, Macedo in a peculiar state of abnegation; and Juarez, who used to teach History, is now a drunk who has to confront his pedophilia. Beyond that, however, and the fact that each of them helped Maria de Lourdes in some obscure way in the past, we are told very little about them; in the end the four men are not readily distinguishable from each other and remain for us not individuals but the collective group the title suggests.

Maria de Lourdes, too, is problematic, first because her character is insufficiently developed. Given the secondary nature of their roles, Maria de Lourdes, Mary in *Greta Garbo,* and other women in this type of play receive only scant authorial attention. In the case of *As tias,* the spectator's empathy is taken for granted since what we know about Maria de Lourdes's link to these four men is not enough to explain the strong attachment. Even for the second half of the twentieth century, Maria de

Lourdes is unusual, though, in that she is strong enough to be in control of the men (the four *tias* and the driver). She is just as unconvincing in the way she wields power, in all likelihood because of authorial concerns about possible accusations of misogyny, something Aguinaldo Silva (1981: 12) acknowledges in his foreword to the play. The playwrights tried to minimize the problem by having the chauffeur identify Maria de Lourdes with a masculine ethos. Initially he watches quietly as Maria de Lourdes responds to the four *tias's* accusations of ungratefulness and betrayal but when she places herself in a feminine role (*"Filha, mãe, amante"* [Daughter, mother, lover]) and as the iconic female figure idolized by a stereotypical gay man (*"ideal, distante, impossível de tocar"* [ideal, distant, impossible to reach]), the chauffeur contradicts her: *"Mulher ideal? Engano seu: você é um homem. Você é o homem desta casa"* (99) (An ideal woman? You're wrong: you are a man. You are the man in this house). The chauffeur's accusation is undercut by another element in the plot which in fact returns Maria de Lourdes to a subaltern status. For, if indeed a monetary crisis has arisen (we never know exactly what the problem is), then Maria de Lourdes, for all her alleged masculine modus operandi, has also been brought to her knees by a financial establishment controlled by men.

A power struggle then develops between Maria de Lourdes and the driver and in an apparent reversal of fortune the four *tias* are placed in a situation where they will decide the outcome of the contest. In a nod to the 1960s and 1970s game and ritual trend in Western theater, there is a strong hint that this is not the first time this situation is played out in the house (102). The four *tias* and Maria de Lourdes proceed with the annual ritual, with the men holding the chauffeur down while she stabs him. Soon thereafter Maria de Lourdes and her four protégés engage in mutual reassurances that all is well; perpetuation of the patronage is guaranteed, with monthly checks being sent to the *tias*, who will continue to live in the house and spend their time preparing for next year's visit. Another, final, twist in the plot places the play squarely in the game and ritual tradition. Not only is the chauffeur alive and well but his papers identify him as the young man with whom Floro had earlier enacted his sexual fantasy skit. As the play ends, the *tias* plan for more game playing in the future, when the young man is ready to participate again: *"Então,"* says Juarez, *"a gente começa tudo de novo. Inventa uma nova história"* (108) (We'll start all over. We'll make up a new story).

In his foreword to the play Aguinaldo Silva also refers to the impossible nature of the type of love embodied by Maria de Lourdes (and contested by the chauffeur). There can be no love, he says, in a system that condones a situation where one of the partners (as is the case of the *tias*) has no voice (12–13). However, the type of love desired by the four men (hence the chauffeur's seductiveness) is hardly one in which both sides have agency, since the young man—as the skits suggest and his status as ritualistic puppet confirms—is forever to serve the *tias's* every whim.

One is tempted to give in to allegorizing and speak of minorities who submit to a regime of patronage and become defenseless and susceptible to the mesmerizing but spurious symbols of beauty, such as the chauffeur; of how daydreaming about past loves and happier days can be tantamount to stagnation and death; and of how competition for the favors of a tyrant (benevolent though she seems to be) can only generate internecine struggle amongst the victims of repression. Or still, in accordance with the playwrights, who saw fit to preface the published text of their work with a page-long definition of love taken from Brazil's leading dictionary (the *Novo Aurélio*), one could attempt to find in the play possible illustrations of the diverse meanings of love. I am not necessarily arguing against the feasibility or even desirability of such exercises but one still must confront how the negative representation of the four *tias* perpetuated stereotypes and affected the self-esteem of individual spectators and of the political debates around the gay liberation movement then functioning in Brazil.

A last but certainly not unimportant angle here is the ludic element that transgression can contribute to a political critique. The situation described above can be read as parodic of the representation of the older homosexual man in Brazil. With Bataille, and especially his *Inner Experience*, in mind, this approach would run counter to or be subversive of the practices or processes contested by Aguinaldo Silva and Doc Comparato. The notions of power and accomplishment represented in the play are problematized through the *mise en jeu* of their complement, which Joseph Libertson identifies as the concept of identity as integrity. In the context presented to the spectator, the excesses performed by the *tias* and their acolytes visit but do not overcome the attending prohibitions. To quote from Libertson's explication of Bataille's idea of transgression, "the 'problem of possibility' serves as the background for a transgression that 'exceeds without destroying' a profane world of prohibitions" (Libertson 1977: 1012).

For all its flaws and risks, *As tias* was a big box-office draw (although on a smaller scale than *Greta Garbo*), not so much for the stellar cast[15] but because of the visibility it brought gays at the height of gay liberation in Brazil (spearheaded by groups such as SOMOS and journals such as *Lampião da esquina*, of which Aguinaldo Silva was a founding member).[16] At that time, hard as it is for us to understand today, this visibility mattered more than the negative image perpetuated of older gays (a parallel could be drawn with *The Boys in the Band*, which opened two years before Stonewall.)

In addition to playwriting and working as a journalist for mainstream as well as gay-oriented publications, Aguinaldo Silva was also a pioneer in rendering sensitive portrayals of homosexuals in Brazilian fiction (*Primeira carta aos andróginos* [1975; First letter to the androgynous]) and autobiography (*Lábios que beijei* [1992; Lips I have kissed]). Aguinaldo went on to fame as a scriptwriter for film (*A república dos assassinos* [Murderers' republic] based on his 1976 novel of the same title) and television, for which he composed original scripts (*Bandidos da Falange* [Outlaw phalanx] and *A história de Lili Carabina* [The story of Lili Carabina], to name but two) as well as adaptations of literary works (Jorge Amado's *Tenda dos milagres* [*Tent of Miracles*] and *Tieta do Agreste*). And he has been of course a prominent author of *telenovelas* for Rede Globo (*Partido alto* [Contralto], *Pedra sobre pedra* [Heaps of stone], *Fera ferida* [Wounded beast], among many others)[17] some of which have included gay and lesbian characters (see chapter 1).

In addition to *As tias*, Doc Comparato (whose real first name is Luis Felipe) coauthored with Aguinaldo a television miniseries recounting the life of the iconic priest-turned-folk-figure Padre Cícero (Cícero Romão Batista, 1844–1934); the script was later published as a book-length biography (*Padre Cícero* [Father Cícero] [Rio de Janeiro: Record, 1984]). Comparato has been a highly successful television scriptwriter (including of the groundbreaking *Malu mulher* [Malu, a woman], *Plantão de polícia* [Police on duty], and another collaboration with Aguinaldo, *Lampião e Maria Bonita*) while simultaneously pursuing careers in literature (which has won him the prestigious Paraná National Award for Fiction for 1979 in the Short Story category as well as other prizes) and the theater, especially a fascinating exploration of time in a trilogy titled *Prisioneiros do tempo* (Prisoners of time), which comprises *Nostradamus* (1986; 1999), *Michelangelo* (1999), and *Círculo de luzes* (2000; Circle of light).

Gracinha Tropical and Friends

Zeno Wilde[18] and Wanderley Bragança's *Blue jeans*, another coauthorship, is equally problematic, although for different reasons. Male prostitution is a defining element in Wilde and Bragança's play and to a much greater extent than in *O assalto*, *Greta Garbo*, and *As tias*. The playwrights have added a subtitle to their work, *uma peça sórdida* (a sordid play), which suggests societal condemnation of the taboo practice *Blue jeans* tackles. However, while avowedly "sordid," Wilde and Bragança's work invites debate on the limits on the transgressiveness. Testing, as it were, Foucault's description of the relation of transgression to the limits of tolerance while responding to societal hypocrisy, the play compounds the stigma by depicting several of the *michês* (male prostitutes) as under-age sex workers.[19]

Blue jeans draws a picture of four of these boys in an urban reportage style made up of scenes in which they take turns performing interspersed monologues about their lifestyle and relationship to their implied coprotagonist, the Patron. Delivered inside the apartment to which they have been invited by their silent promoter and eventual victim, their speeches include snippets of their past, frustrations, and fantasies. The urge to document and dramatize the plight of poor youths in large cities (thus fulfilling some kind of community service) proves too much for the playwrights, who are lost in sociological issues and end up losing sight of their original goals. In Bataillian terms, the transgressive element thus ceases to be "the adequation of an intentional act and its object under the sign of utility and of its complement, identity" (Libertson 1977: 1012). In *Blue jeans* too, because it forbids what it creates, the *interdit* fails to interrogate the conditions and possibilities of the violation it dramatizes.

Still, *Blue jeans* has some strong points, foremost among them the intelligent treatment of the evils of the closet as portrayed by the Patron.[20] Being in the closet, he does not have a voice, that is, he abdicates agency and therefore invites all kinds of violence against him (from blackmail by the *michês* to discrimination at work and physical aggression by men who are assured of no retribution). Toward the end, when Renguitem is about to kill him, the man still will not call out to his neighbors for help, afraid as he was of their discovery of his sexuality, and his death is thus a kind of punishment for his renunciation of a voice.

In dramatic terms, a silent, unseen character can become an impediment to the flow of the action and may prevent a more thorough exploration of conflict, and Wilde and Bragança's play is not immune to this danger. But the Patron can also be viewed as standing for the spectator, who, in traditional dramatic practice, is a silent addressee with no right to intervene in the action or to acquire agency (as Augusto Boal reminds us in *Theatre of the Oppressed*). Seen in this light, *Blue jeans* could be described as engaged theater, warning spectators of the dangers of a closeted life and urging them to *assumir-se* (come out). Because the boys are—in dramatic and sexual terms—performers (they play a dramatic role on the man's private home stage and provide him with sexual gratification), the Patron acquires a transitory, limited agency as consumer and dispenser of capital. Ironically, in the end he remains eminently *passivo*, both sexually (even when he picks up the transvestite Gracinha Tropical, who penetrates him)[21] and otherwise. Another key component of his silence and passivity is the tape recorder he switches on during the visits, not in all likelihood with an eye to facilitating the work of the prosecution later on but more likely for subsequent mechanical reproduction of the performance. This points to yet another aggravating factor in his passivity, his apparent inability to have an orgasm while the boys are physically in the apartment, preferring instead the delayed and mechanically facilitated pleasure attained through masturbation while listening to the recording.

Because of its realist affiliation, *Blue jeans* focuses on a gritty topic and takes pains to be grounded in "social reality."[22] Accordingly, the play is not an apology for homosexuality nor is it a vehicle for the gay liberation movement of the 1970s. However, its claims to realism fall apart when one considers characterization. The boys are presented in a Manichaean light that strikes one as particularly primary: Renguitem, the incarnation of evil, murders the Patron while Serginho—the only character with a critical view of the situation and the one police consider the prime suspect of the murder—is cast in angelical light. Melodrama also creeps in with every lamentation about fate, society, and the evils of capitalism.

The musical version of the play, developed, staged, and directed by Wolf Maia in 1992, does not resolve the problems that plagued the 1980 original. The removal of the aggressive edge of the Wilde-Bragança text makes it in fact a weaker piece, nor does the addition of music and dancing by Companhia do Lobo improve things. The dancing was acceptable at best and the musical score—with the exception of a couple of new songs Eduardo Dusek composed for the show—was simply a selection of previously released tracks by Caetano Veloso, Cazuza, Titãs, and other well-known composers, groups, and solo performers. According to Maia, the changes were meant to make the play *"mais leve, mais dançante, mais divertido"* (Coutinho 1992) (lighter, more danceable, more fun), an orientation that clashes with the production's other intended goal, the recasting of the work in light of AIDS (see chapter 4).

For the new production, which premiered in Rio de Janeiro's Teatro Galeria in 1992, Wolf Maia, in a financially astute move, selected a group of *telenovela* heart-throbs including Alexandre Frota, Maurício Mattar, Fábio Assunção, Carlos Loffler, and a group of fifteen dancers. After an eleven-month run in Rio de Janeiro, the production moved to São Paulo's Teatro Palladium in 1993 (with Humberto Martins replacing Maurício Mattar) and then went on national tour. The producers' casting choices created the ironic circumstance in which an avowedly heterosexual cast plays an essentially homosexual situation to an audience composed mostly of heterosexual young women. These women, joined by a good number of gay men, were treated to what amounts to an excellent illustration of the changes AIDS had by then effected in Brazil, with sexual desire being met by the allure of voyeurism.[23]

With the coauthors' permission, Maia opted for more glamour and a mellow, less aggressive tone, which was evident at different levels, from the deletion of the 1980 subtitle *uma peça sórdida* to the virtual elimination of nakedness in all but one scene (and even then the nonfrontal nudity was featured on a dimmed stage). In press releases and interviews with the media in Rio de Janeiro, São Paulo, and other cities, Maia repeatedly stressed the changes, toning down (the verb *"atenuar"* keeps recurring in the releases) *"os grandes discursos de cunho social"* (heavy social themes) and playing up instead *"a estética física dos atores"* (the actors' physical beauty) (São Paulo press release).

When it first opened in 1980, shortly after the annulment of Institutional Act Number Five but still during the military regime, *Blue jeans* was attacked by conservative forces but, unlike *Hair* eleven years earlier,[24] it was never banned. Its long run,[25] the large number of people who came to see it (whatever their reasons), and even its offspring (for example, Carlinhos Lira's 1981 *Garotos de aluguel* [Boys for hire]) were instrumental in the acceptance of full-frontal male nudity on the Brazilian stage (in heterosexual-themed as well as gay-focused plays), something seen as banal by the mid 1990s.[26] In fairness to Wolf Maia, that male nudity had become shopworn a decade and a half after *Blue jeans* premiered was a factor, though not a major one, in his decision to forego one of the most daring aspects of the original production.

The 1980 and 1992 productions of Wilde and Bragança's play are also a demonstration of lost opportunities. Neither highlighted the role of the least stereotypical of the five characters, the drag queen Gracinha Tropical (thus named for her fascination with a gay icon, singer Gal Costa, whose first name is Maria da Graça or Gracinha, and who once performed in a show titled Gal Tropical). She is also the first teenage transvestite on Brazilian stages, but despite strong performances by Luis Carlos Niño in 1980 and Carlos Loffler in 1992, is not as memorable as her counterpart in Brazilian film, Lilica in Babenco's *Pixote.* In addition, not enough is made of the fact that Gracinha is doubly a performer, both in terms of gender and in the sense of acting for the Patron. Thus, instead of being differentiated from the other *michês*, Gracinha is equated with them through the use of the same name, "Luis Carlos Soares," that each of them uses in their individual monologues. The common name implies that all hustlers are the same and obviously deprives them of any individuality. The problem is compounded by the fact that the printed text (in the dramatis personae, stage directions, and right before their speeches) gives the young men individual names (Marcos, Serginho, Renguitem, Gracinha) but the spectator knows them only as the generic "Luis Carlos Soares."

Had Wilde and Bragança's representation of transgression been less tentative and Gracinha Tropical been made a more complex character, a deeper insight could have been gained of the challenges and realities faced by what is perhaps the least understood and most despised minority group in Brazil. Gracinha and other *travestis* have resorted to prostitution not so much for the money but because "it is one of the only contexts in which they can experience themselves as tantalizing objects of desire and develop a sense of personal worth, self-confidence, and self-esteem" (Kulick 1998: 136). Gracinha could have given dramatic force to a point which was as relevant in 1980 as it is today, that it is the *travestis* who are in their own way waging the political war that the mostly closeted gay Brazil refuses to fight. As Don Kulick (1998: 222–23) puts it, *travestis* are

> Brazil's only truly "out" homosexuals. . . . [They] are radical homosexuals who have more or less single-handedly created a homosexual space in an otherwise rigidly heterosexual Brazil. They note that while the majority of gay men and lesbians in Brazil are still afraid to come out in public and let people know they are homosexuals, *travestis*, at tremendous personal cost, publicly proclaim their homosexuality through their dress and demeanor.

Who's Afraid of Geni?

Geni's transgressiveness in Chico Buarque's 1978 *Opera do malandro* (The Rogue's Opera) is represented in a less tentative light than Gracinha's in

Blue jeans. Geni navigates the murky waters of early 1940s Brazil, a pre-industrial, peripheral nation under Getúlio Vargas's *Estado Novo* dictatorship, with Nazi sympathizers in power but strong pro-Allied public sentiment. To this era Chico Buarque deftly adapted John Gay's *Beggar's Opera* (1728) and Bertolt Brecht and Kurt Weill's *Dreigroschenoper* (1928; *The Threepenny Opera*)[27] and their treatments of, respectively, the moral degradation that accompanied the onset of an industrial economy and the ravages of a nascent multinational capitalism. Paralleling Gay's humorous exposure of all manner of corruption in Imperial Britain and Brecht's sarcastic look at a society so corrupt that crime and deception become the only acceptable behavior, Chico Buarque's musical depicts social change as capital and power is transferred to a new group.[28] In *Opera do malandro*, two warring crime barons, Max Overseas (contraband) and Duran (prostitution) move from an initial antagonism to an alliance that is lucrative to both of them. As in Oswald's *O rei da vela*, marriage plays a key role in such social and financial shifts, and the arrival of modernity is at best incomplete. A new, "modern" way enters the picture but it fails to entirely replace the old order of a society barely half a century past abolition.

Through Geni, Chico Buarque depicts the defilement and scorn Brazilian *travestis* undergo, but his Geni is no shrinking violet. Geni speaks to the resilience of the oppressed,[29] and also to their survival skills, which in her case include a good deal of craftiness, and even, in the end, betrayal of Max Overseas, her employer, protector and the love of her life. Max does not shun Geni's love and company (he even lets her sit on his thigh) but the possibility of a sexual relation between the two, notwithstanding the hint of one having taken place at some point in the past, is not stressed.

In her resilience, Geni is reminiscent of Molina in Manuel Puig's *Beijo da mulher aranha*[30] and of Veludo in *Navalha na carne.* The latter comparison is made more relevant by the fact that in the Rio de Janeiro productions both roles were played by Emiliano Queirós, who bravely incurred the risk of being typecast in gay roles,[31] just as had happened with Edgard Gurgel Aranha, who played Veludo in the São Paulo production of *Navalha na carne* and Totó Fruta de Conde in *O rei da vela,* both in 1967. Geni and Veludo learn that if they are to survive amid an adversarial power structure they must connive and betray like everyone else around them. But more importantly, Geni, like Veludo, also speaks to the legitimation of homosexual pleasure in a heterosexually dominated milieu, an assertiveness reminiscent of Robert Wilson's enthusiasm for transgression's positive, liberating energy. Geni has no qualms about admitting the vast number of lovers she has had and she is proud of their variety in terms of age, race, and social station. She has guaranteed a safe place for herself in Max's inner circle and she often appears next to the object of her desire. Geni is thus in a position to humiliate and hurt those who despise her; she does not hesitate to do so with the hypocritical pimping couple, Duran and his wife Vitória, when they need crucial information about Max and his whereabouts.

While the songs usually follow the general Brechtian precept of stopping the action to allow the spectator to reflect on the message conveyed in a previous scene, at least two of them ("O meu amor" [My loved one] and "Pedaço de mim" [Part of me]) hark back to illusionist theater. However, the romanticism that shapes these two songs is nowhere to be found in "Geni e o Zepelim" (Jenny and the Zeppelin), sung by Geni and the chorus. In it, Geni's positive self-image is countered by the choral refrain,

> *Joga pedra na Geni*
> *Joga bosta na Geni*
> *Ela é feita pra apanhar*
> *Ela é boa de cuspir*
> *Ela dá pra qualquer um*
> *Maldita Geni.* (Buarque de Hollanda 1978: 161–63)
>
> [Throw stones at Jenny
> Throw shit at Jenny
> She is there to be beaten
> and spit on
> She'll let anyone fuck her
> Damn Jenny]

The first two lines above reflect the humiliation and violence *travestis* face on a daily basis. But, undaunted by the chorus's antagonism, Geni sings of her fantasy of the arrival of a very phallic German dirigible whose captain demands her love for one night in exchange for sparing the city. The entire population comes to Geni on their knees begging her to accept the offer. Satisfied with the humiliation and embarrassment of those who used to defile her, Geni, though repulsed by the captain, acquiesces and the man has his way with her. Soon after he and the Zeppelin leave the next day, the populace forget Geni's magnanimous gesture and go back to their old ways. This allegorical comment on the extremes of inclusion and exclusion that transgendered people encounter in Brazil also points to shifts in transgression's registers, that is, the relative status and changing limits of "transgressiveness."

Nor does Geni spare Chaves, the police chief, who was once at the service of the ringleader and later switched loyalty to become an ally of Duran and Vitória in their war against their son-in-law Max (whose real name was more prosaic, Sebastião Pinto). Geni's chance comes when Chaves, also known as Tigrão (Big Tiger), and the Durans try to pry out of her details about Max's involvement with a rebellion and protest march that Duran's prostitutes were organizing. Extorting from them huge amounts of money for smuggled merchandise she sold for Max, Geni humiliates her boss's enemies, forcing them to sit through her cabaret set in which she sings of her many loves. Chaves is not as patient as Max's in-laws and, losing his composure, attacks Geni physically and verbally. The verbal assault seems to hurt Geni more than the physical aggression and consequently she agrees to proceed with the negotiations only after Chaves apologizes. But before he asks for Geni's pardon, Chaves demands to know what exactly Geni is, if not a *veado* (faggot), to which she responds: "Nem veado nem machão. Eu sou plurissexual" (155–56) (I am neither a faggot nor a macho guy. I am plurisexual").[32]

The substitution of a drag queen for Jenny the prostitute in Brecht's play allows for new insights about the fissures in the interplay of the sexual and commercial spheres in early 1940s Brazil. That period was the heyday of the *malandro* celebrated in Buarque's play (one of the key songs in the play is "Homenagem ao malandro" [Homage to the rogue]). As David William Foster (1999: 39) explains in his excellent analysis of the film version of *Opera do malandro* (directed by Ruy Guerra; 1986),

> The *malandro* is viewed fundamentally not as a marginal social phenomenon, an outlaw who functions in the mostly hidden underworld of a social life that would be all the better for his disappearance. Rather, the *malandro* is a foot soldier . . . of the economic system, a highly efficient agent of the interplay of corruption, influence peddling, payoffs, exploitation, and strong-arm control that is the very essence of patriarchal capitalism.

His socioeconomic polymorphism and ability to move freely among different levels of society require a high degree of nimbleness, including in matters sexual, and the "pansexuality" of the *malandro,* as Foster puts it, "is legendary." (44).

As a product of the imperfect transition from the personalist system of pre-modern Brazil to the institutional nature of investment capitalism, the *malandro* is comfortable in the interstices of Brazil's socioeconomic fabric. Thus Max functions as mediator between regulated commerce and unsanctioned practices such as contraband and extortion, on the one hand, and between legally sanctioned sexual behavior (marriage) and disallowed conduct such as frequenting brothels and welcoming the constant company of a drag queen, on the other. A *malandro* in her own way, Geni too negotiates these unsettled social borders, but her gender allows her to go one step further as she parodies and subverts Max's on-again-off-again macho bravado and sensitive nature. Hence the combination in Geni of a campy demeanor and calculated power reminds the Durans and others that, as a close associate of Max's, Geni is not to be brushed aside; as a consequence, they reluctantly approach her—drag-queen trappings and all—with a measure of awe and respect.

Other Voices

More stagings deserve inclusion here than just those male-accented plays that, like *Greta Garbo*, *Blue jeans*, and *Opera do malandro*, drew large audiences and received considerable publicity. Evading half-forgotten figures or works of lesser artistry or impact might deprive us of relevant information and result in an imperfect portrayal of a key period. Such explorations of counternormative sexualities range from the grittiness of Fauzi Arap's *O amor do não* to the lyrical homoeroticism of Paulo Afonso Grisolli's *Não me maltrates, Robinson* (1977; Don't abuse me, Robinson) and Renato Borghi's *O lobo de ray-ban* (1987; A wolf in Ray Ban glasses) to the *homoternurismo*[33] of Mário Prata's *Bésame mucho* (1987; Kiss me passionately) and finally, to the outright comedy of Walcyr Carrasco's *O terceiro beijo* (1984; The third kiss) and Hilton Have's *Desligue o projetor e espie pelo olho mágico* (1987; Turn off the slide projector and check the peephole). A few of these plays warrant more than just a passing mention and I now turn to three of them, Paulo César Coutinho's *A noite do meu bem* (1977), Wilson Sayão's *Como diria Montaigne* (1983; As Montaigne would say), and Herbert Daniel's *As três moças do sabonete Araxá* (1984).

A noite do meu bem is an at times heartbreaking play of damaged lives but is undermined by a convoluted plot and insufficiently developed characters. It is also rife with all manner of clichés, such as the political discourse of the authorial spokesperson, André.[34] As he pursues an impossible monogamous relationship with insensitive, hedonistic Patrick, André issues a succession of pronouncements denouncing philistinism, capitalist exploitation, and internalized homophobia, apparently unaware that he himself partakes of and contributes to these and other problems. André is joined by seven other characters who frequent two supposedly liberated gay zones, a bar and a pre-AIDS-days sauna. Stock figures, these men range from the closeted married Jáder and drag queen Bubi to hustler Lelo and drug addict Serginho. Máximo (the bar owner) and Zorro (his body guard) are clearly identified as the oppressors in Coutinho's sincere (though perhaps a bit too naive) denunciation of oppression within the gay community itself. Even though he is gay, Máximo thwarts the efforts of those who are trying to organize for political representation among the community and he so intensely interferes with the lives of his bar's patrons that a consensus slowly evolves among them to have him killed. As the action unfolds, Manicheism takes over and Máximo becomes wickedness itself. The representation of his murder as the crushing of unmitigated evil is lamentably predictable, one problem among many that the 1999-2000 staging of the play failed to resolve.

Staged in 1995 under the direction of Luiz Arthur Nunes, Wilson Sayão's play focuses on a mother, Irene (Ivone Hoffman), and her three adult children. Well-meaning but confused, the woman, who has the habit of (mis)quoting Montaigne at the most inappropriate moments, tries to rescue her offspring from the pedestrian lives they lead. Each of the work's three sections focuses on Irene's disastrous involvement with one of the children. Parts one and three show Irene's visits to and fights with daughters Nádia (Bianca Byington) and Neusa (Maria Adélia). The most solid of the three parts is the second, in which Irene confronts her only son, Ney (Marcos Breda); some of the strongest, and funniest, moments in the play occur as Irene interacts with her gay son and his lover (Angel Palomero). Although written in the 1970s, *Como diria Montaigne* differs from the other gay-marked plays of the period in that it represents Ney's sexual orientation and lifestyle in a matter-of-fact manner that is more in line with works of the 1990s.

Though never staged, Daniel's *As três moças do sabonete Araxá* deserves attention if for no other reason than because it is exemplary of two separate but related traits of the postdictatorship period. Daniel's work illustrates, first, the disfavor that befell politically engaged plays (note the subtitle, *Um apólogo sobre os anos Médici* [A fable of the years under General Médici])[35] at a time when the theatergoing public had shifted their interest from social issues to the individual. And second, it epitomizes the rebuff faced in the mid to late 1980s and 1990s of the type of gay-accented play the 1970s had glamorized, namely, works that made the homosexual condition ostensive (typically by portraying weak, effeminate men, represented in Daniel's play by the trio Lulu, Tina, and Zebarbosa) but that were nevertheless unable to delve deep into mindsets and relationships.

Looking Ahead

By the late 1960s and early 1970s, it was becoming quite clear that "the liberalization of sexual diversity that has accompanied the modernization of Brazilian life has reconfirmed the central importance of sexuality as somehow a key to the very definition of the self" (Parker 1991: 97). At that time, too, as documented in chapter 1, gay and lesbian characters began appearing in highly influential *telenovelas.* And in the theater, as audiences became more aware of how the stage helps shape our perception of homosexuality, so they came to question the stereotypical, prejudiced representations that characterized most of Brazilian theater up until that point. Other events then happened in quick succession, among them the staging of the plays of the nineteenth-century visionary Qorpo-Santo, one hundred years after he wrote them; as I remarked in chapter 1, Qorpo-Santo's revolutionary theater questioned orthodox sexuality and logical living, and it was in one of his plays, *A separação dos dois esposos,* that homosexual characters first appeared in the theater of Brazil. In his own time, another innovator, modernist Oswald de Andrade, was for all practical purposes unknown as a playwright, like Qorpo-Santo before him, and it was not until the staging of his *O rei da vela* in 1967 (see chapter 2) that the potential of his theater became evident.

To the late 1950s and 1960s Brechtian influence on the Brazilian theater, the late 1960s and 1970s added the theater of the absurd, the notions of Artaud and his theater of cruelty, and—of particular importance to same-sex-focused theater—the plays of Jean Genet. Victor García's superb 1969 staging of *O balcão* (*The balcony*) in São Paulo made a daring use of space to match Genet's abrasive transgressiveness. And the 1966 staging of *As criadas* (*The maids*) in Rio de Janeiro was but the first of numerous Brazilian productions of Genet's incisive exploration of gender and power. Several of these stagings have used an all-male cast to explore the contours of gender alignments in Genet's theater; among the more successful of these efforts were the 1980 collective creation by Vivencial Diversiones in Recife and the 1996 staging by Ricardo Torres in Rio de Janeiro's Teatro dos Grandes Atores. The first all-male stagings of *As criadas* launched a mini-trend, curiously limited to foreign plays, such as Luis Sérgio Person's staging of Jean Anouilh's *Orquestra de senhoritas* (*The Orchestra*) in 1974 and numerous productions of Federico García Lorca's *A casa de Bernarda Alba* (*The House of Bernarda Alba*).

As evasiveness faded away, the number of male-marked works kept growing. In Trevisan's account (1986: 124), "of the 25 plays running in São Paulo in the first half of 1978, 11 dealt directly or indirectly with homosexuality." Trevisan is quick to identify a serious problem with most of these plays. He quotes approvingly Jefferson del Rio's criticism (published in *Folha de São Paulo*, 12 February 1981) of such plays as "conservative and uninteresting," for "when someone appears on stage underlining again and again and again the fact that homosexuals are *people*, we are at the limits of redundancy," and adds his own reservations about the trend, stressing that "gay plays have suffered a complacency that sometimes touches on exhibitionism" in a process that "has been made safe and normalized (as a consumer product) in language if not in theme" (Trevisan 1986: 125). As Trevisan sees it, this risk is not unlike that faced by all marginalized groups as the center turns its attention to them. When that happens to commercial theater portrayals of the gay and lesbian experience, assimilation becomes virtually inevitable, as "the stage space legitimizes those on the fringes of society who expose themselves to generally bourgeois and conservative middle-class audiences . . . [and] the gay boom becomes something new for the system to consume" (125).

Trevisan's reading is not incorrect but it misses a key point made persuasively by Rebecca Schneider in *The Explicit Body in Performance*. Late capitalism, Schneider (1997: 3) writes in her introduction, "appropriates, incorporates, and consumes transgression into fashionable chic at such a rapid pace that the subversive impact of transgression becomes impossible." When it is assimilated into the larger economy, gay-accented theater becomes a commodity. The consequences are felt first at the artistic level, with the risk of these plays becoming a tissue of clichés and uninspired plot lines, such as those Trevisan has catalogued. Schneider, however, catches the political problem that has escaped Trevisan. Although Schneider speaks in general terms, what she finds highly problematic with regard to the avant-garde can be extrapolated to Brazilian theater in the 1970s. For her it is telling and disturbing that "the avant-garde and the option of 'shock' that it championed should die just as women, artists of color, and gay and lesbian artists began to make critically incisive political art under their own gender- , race- , and preference-marked banners" (4).

In my opinion, however, such an option is more likely to disappear when certain artists—Brazilian playwrights and theater people who regardless of sexual orientation stage same-sex themed works—are co-opted by commercial theater. Whenever those individuals and groups who oppose hegemonic structures of power offer at least a degree of resistance to commercial and political assimilation, they retain their ability to give forceful expression to their creative protests against a pervasive homophobic environment. By resisting cooptation, these theater workers preserve at least some of the transgressive bite in their art. That was the case in the 1980s and 1990s with the theater of Naum Alves de Souza (b. 1942), Caio Fernando Abreu (1948–1996), and Mauro Rasi (1951–2003), and, as I will show in the next chapter, that was also the case when the AIDS crisis occasioned a significant overhaul of the representation of homosexuality on the Brazilian stage.

Following the post-1985 return to democratic rule known as the *Nova República,* formerly disenfranchised groups could finally speak freely. In David George's account,

> Removal of barriers erected by ideologues and demagogues . . . allowed myriad forms of theater to flourish, experimentation to run unchecked, and all voices the opportunity to be heard in the marketplace of artistic ideas. . . . Themes once forbidden by censorship or pushed aside by the exigencies of protest against military rule . . . [were] privileged: women's perspectives in directing and playwriting; sexual identity, including gender construction and gay perspectives; psychological issues; the individual in society; religion; and formal experimentation. (George 2000: xvi)

In a very different political climate, with the formidable military enemy out of the picture and censorship no longer the major impediment, post-dictatorship playwrights turned to issues of interest to their generation. The public now expected new ideas and different voices. Attention was diverted to the exciting new work of *encenadores* (stage directors) like Gerald Thomas (b. 1954), performance artists like Denise Stoklos (b. 1950), and groups such as Macunaíma (under the direction of Antunes Filho [b. 1929]) and Ornitorrinco (directed by Cacá Rosset [b. 1954]). It became abundantly clear that the public wanted much more than just the return of those who were, like Boal and Plínio Marcos, more directly affected by censorship, and so these authors' post-*abertura* efforts were poorly received, as were the stagings of previously banned treatments of torture such as João Ribeiro Chaves Neto's *Patética.* Although the new generation of playwrights did not immediately convey their experiences in outstanding contributions to the Brazilian stage, their plays established a major trait of the Brazilian theater in the 1980s, the shift away from political commitment and social protest and toward a more intense interest in examining the individual experience, often returning to childhood and adolescence in search of answers and solace.

As for the homosexual-marked theater, once the so-called "look, Ma, I'm gay" plays were exhausted in the late 1970s and early 1980s, unorthodox sexual liaisons began to be presented as natural variants. Once the collective gay cat was out of the bag and there was nothing shocking about full-frontal male nudity and little left to be said about drag queens and hustlers, the mid to late 1980s and the 1990s began to see works, like those of Naum Alves de Souza and, especially, Caio Fernando Abreu and Mauro Rasi, where transgression was no longer a matter of shock value but rather a measure of an individual's struggle to live his life as he pleased. Theirs is a theater that keeps its distance from both the political commitments of the 1960s and 1970s and the plight of those directly or indirectly afflicted with AIDS. Rather, autobiography, family relations, and artistic values become the centerpieces of lengthy (two of these playwrights have authored trilogies), revealing works with marvelous moments of comedic and dramatic talent.

In Naum Alves de Souza's theater, more than the presence of clearly identifiable homosexual characters,[36] what matters most is the refined sensibility that informs his remarkably perceptive studies of seemingly banal events in equally banal lives. In his plays we see subtle hints of a gay experience—whether in a young schoolboy dealing with repressive classmates and teachers or in an adult man who has chosen to live abroad in order to evade his hypocritical family's disapproval of his homosexuality—as part of a larger picture where other human beings are suffering too, like another schoolboy slowly dying of an incurable disease or an older unmarried sister cruelly abandoned by her siblings.

A aurora da minha vida (prem. 1981; The dawn of my life), perhaps the best of Naum's works to date, reveals the playwright's remarkable sensitivity for the mostly uneventful lives of a large segment of the Brazilian population, represented here through the foibles of a group of school children. In *No Natal a gente vem te buscar* (prem. 1979; We'll come back for you at Christmas), Naum revisits his troubled childhood, and the result is a moving play with several brilliant scenes involving the thwarted hopes and unfulfilled yearnings of a family of Brazilian provincials. In *Um beijo, um abraço, um aperto de mão* (prem. 1984; A kiss, a hug, a handshake), understatement shapes a case of homosexual incest, which is given more evidence in the *versão masculina*, where two brothers share an intense emotional involvement, than in the *versão feminina.* In these male and female versions of the play, which nearly mirror each other, the feelings and actions of the two siblings are played at a nearly mythical level that is reminiscent of such Nelson Rodrigues plays as *Album de família* and *Anjo negro* (Black angel). With *A aurora da minha vida, No Natal a gente vem te buscar*, and *Um beijo, um abraço, um aperto de mão*, Naum has shaped *"um autêntico ciclo memorialista, ao mesmo tempo irônico, sofrido e místico, no qual procura acertar as contas com os fantasmas da sua infância e juventude"* (a genuine cycle of memoirs, by turns ironic, painful, and mystical, in which he attempts to come to terms with the ghosts of his childhood and youth) (Michalski 1985: 86). The poignance of Naum's plays hinges on the idea of wasted opportunities and unconscious cruelties; their sadness comes from the way the playwright alludes to our losses and our unawareness of the significance of the things we love most until they are gone forever. A prize-winning playwright[37] and also an accomplished director and stage settings designer (he was responsible for the superb visual concepts of Antunes Filho's 1978 staging of *Macunaíma*), Naum possesses one of the most distinctive voices in the Brazilian theater today and as such deserves a lot more critical attention than he has so far received.[38]

Mauro Rasi's own trilogy is composed of *A estrela do lar* (1989; Queen of the home), *A cerimônia do adeus* (1987; The farewell ritual), and *Viagem a Forli* (1993; Journey to Forli).[39] In it, as in Naum's, we have "a clear indication that post-dictatorship playwrights have abandoned the 1960s generation's political solemnity while coming to terms with the events which had an impact on that generation" (George 1995a: 189). In the trilogy's portrayals of diverse moments in the adolescence and early adult life of the autobiographical protagonist, the playwright sustains both humor and pathos without trivializing either. In the most successful of the three plays, *A cerimônia do adeus*, we encounter protagonist Juliano (played by Marcos Frota in the Rio de Janeiro production), as a young playwright profoundly dissatisfied with his life in a provincial town in the state of São Paulo and amid a dysfunctional family headed by the proverbial domineering mother and withdrawn father.[40] The theatrics, prolixity, and overblown self-pity of his mother, Aspázia (Yara Amaral), and her sister, Brunilde (Monah Delacy), are offset by a speechless and unseen father, the bedridden Hermes, who is reduced to coughing fits offstage. Juliano finds refuge from this quintessential, stereotypical Freudian scenario in books and authors, especially his beloved Jean-Paul Sartre (Sérgio Britto) and Simone de Beauvoir (Natália Timberg). In a particularly successful touch, Juliano's escape into fiction is dramatized through the materialization of Sartre and de Beauvoir, who are seen by him and the audience as persons and by the other characters as books; the public's empathy with Juliano is thus attained by this bond between protagonist and spectators. The dual reality is matched by a complex handling of time, which alternates between the "present" of Juliano's late adolescence in the 1960s (with references to Che Guevara in Bolivia, etc.) and his interactions with Sartre and de Beauvoir in World War II (in scenes in occupied Paris).

As he matures as a gay man, Juliano must also learn to confront repression, which is represented in different spheres—individual, familial, political—by his fascist cousin Lourenço. Aware of Juliano's mix of fascination for and fear of him, the devious Lourenço uses his good looks to entrap Juliano into a homoerotic relationship, only to torment him later with threats of revealing the liaison. In an attempt to cover up his theft of another boy's expensive watch, Lourenço outs Juliano to Aspázia and exposes his cousin's sexual relationship with a diffident friend, Francisco. An outraged Juliano reacts to this insidiousness with an admission of his sexual orientation and the conviction that he must leave in search of a place where he can be surrounded by art and by others like himself.

The bittersweet drama of this artistic youth is boosted by the force of the dialogue and Rasi's ear for the dialect of that part of Brazil. Much of the humor revolves around Aspázia's philistinism and hypocrisy, for example, when she accuses the French authors of immorality while she herself secretly reads pornographic novels. For all her pettiness and cruelty, for all the problems and considerable pain she causes her son, for all her bombastic outbursts and melodramatic inventions, the mother figure is lovingly portrayed in *A cerimônia do adeus* and, a few years later, in *Pérola* (Pearl).

In *Pérola* (prem. 1995) Rasi uses the real names of his parents and places the mother figure at the center of this piece; she is now the title of the play. Aspázia and Pérola are of course the same woman, the overbearing mother who propels the action as comedy blends with little and not-so-little family tragedies. Old grievances and silly dislikes, failed aspirations and small successes bring together and often disconnect family members. The gay young man, here called Emílio, has the sad smile of the all-knowing narrator. This time he is for the most part a resigned observer who stands aside while his parents are exposed ruthlessly, as they had previously been, under different names, in *A estrela do lar* and *A cerimônia do adeus.* In *Pérola,* seen, in just under five years, by more than half a million spectators, the action revolves around the mother's (mostly material) ambitions, such as the addition of a garage to the house and, especially, the swimming pool she has built despite the objections of everyone in the family, including husband Vado (Sérgio Mamberti). Much too big for the small yard, the pool comes to represent Pérola's oversized emotions and misplaced struggle for status in the provincial Bauru that Emílio longs to flee. But this last look at Rasi's mother figure is different. This time everything is tinted by death; *Pérola* is his mother's requiem (Rasi wrote the play in honor of his mother, after she died in 1993). As Macksen Luis (1995: 12) reminds us,

> *não se pode esquecer que a peça tem na sua gênese a morte. O fim desta mãe teatral, que faz o mundo a seu modo, é também o fim de um tempo (o amadurecimento do autor).... Pérola ... escolheu o seu papel na vida e o viveu até o fim. Mauro Rasi mostra na vida e no teatro o fascínio que esta escolha exerceu sobre ele.*
>
> [one cannot forget that this play has death at its core. The end of this theatrical mother, a woman who made the world the way she wanted it to be, is also the end of an era (corresponding to the playwright's maturity).... Pérola ... chose her role in life and lived it to the end. Mauro Rasi shows in life and theater alike the fascination this choice has had over him.]

Gone from Rasi's next play is the dramatic memorialism of childhood recollections seen in *A cerimônia do adeus* and *Pérola. A dama do cerrado* (prem. 1996; The Lady from Goiás) is Leda Florim (played by Susana Vieira in the Rio de Janeiro production), a former Miss Goiás State who, after years as the lover of one or another Brasília pol, falls in love with a senator. When the president taps the senator for a cabinet post, the man ditches Leda, who, in turn, seeks revenge by airing the intrigues and gossip she had learned in her twenty years' brush with power. Leda's favorite confidante is her hilariously over-the-top gay hairdresser, Fúlvio (Otávio Augusto), owner of a decadent salon in a lower-middle-class Brasília suburb. The play mixes fiction with real-life political events and documented cases of corruption and abuse of power. As a result, between cuts, perms, and color jobs, Leda and Fúlvio rake over the coals some of the biggest names in the country's political scene of the last two decades.

In *As tias de Mauro Rasi* (prem. 1996; Mauro Rasi's aunts), the focus is on his father's four sisters. For the creation of the four characters, Rasi amalgamated traits drawn from an extended family that includes the wives of his eleven uncles and four of his mother's cousins. Again, they are observed by Rasi's alter ego, Emílio, as they live their mostly pedestrian existences—peppered here and there by eccentricity and a dash of tragedy—in boring Bauru. The family-centered cycle of Rasi's dramaturgy closes with *O crime do Dr. Alvarenga* (prem. 1999; Dr. Alvarenga's crime). After the homage to his mother in *Pérola*, now Rasi wanted to honor his father, who died later that same year. In the play, Rasi added a profile of his father to a text by the same title that Rasi senior had written in the 1950s but which had not been professionally staged before. The plot focuses on a love triangle involving a Nobel Prize–winning scientist called Alvarenga (played by Paulo Autran), his wife, and a young biologist with whom he falls in love. Rasi's added text, seen as usual through the eyes of his alter ego, Emílio (Guilherme Piva), juxtaposes the real life Osvaldo Rasi with *his* alter ego, the man Rasi senior would like to have been.

Rasi's latest play, *As ladies na madrugada* (Ladies in the wee hours), takes place outside the family realm. With it he is really returning to his first dramatic attempt, which flopped in its 1974 version. Rasi had cut his teeth during the early days of *besteirol* (literally, silly stuff) in the 1970s. This irreverent, light-weight comedy style is a Brazilian-seasoned combination of improv art, stand-up comedy, and sitcoms that would serve Rasi well later on in his career (as it would Miguel Falabella, Vicente Pereira, and several other playwrights of the younger generation), but the transition to a more conventional form of theater was not at first very smooth. He persisted for several years until hitting it big with *A cerimônia do adeus* in 1987, but he never forgot the 1974 disaster and returned to it twenty-five years later. The 1999 version of *As ladies na madrugada* has been refined and music added to the intrigue-laden plot that involves eight strangely acting people on board a "fascist liner" sailing from Buenos Aires to Genoa just days before the beginning of World War II.

A Major, Constant Referent

Although I have built this chapter around plays and playwrights, the work of a key director has been a constant referent to the issues raised here. José Celso Martinez Correa (Zé Celso) bridges different periods and his presence on the Brazilian stage stretches over almost half a century. His groundbreaking interventions with the Teatro Oficina of the late 1960s and early 1970s continued into the highly controversial productions that followed Oficina's metamorphosis into Uzyna Uzona in 1981 and extended through the 1990s and into the first years of the new millennium. The paramount position he occupied in Brazilian theater through his forced exile in Portugal (1974–78) was lost however as other directors and *encenadores* (Antunes Filho, Gerald Thomas, Gabriel Villela) moved to the fore in the 1980s and 1990s. Even if his more creative years are behind him, Zé Celso continues to experiment, finding new ways to break out of old molds and with his talented young company to create theater out of discontinuity and chaos.

Although transgression in Zé Celso's work is an ampler notion (as evidenced, for example, by the contrarian, political project that was his staging of Oswald's *O rei da vela*), occasionally it takes a blatantly homosexual, or, as Zé Celso himself terms it, homoerotic form (Sá and Frias 1997: 8). In such instances, Zé Celso questions the homogenic place of Oswald de Andrade and Nelson Rodrigues in Brazilian theater while contesting the heterosexual imperative that informs their work and their representation of homosexuality (as seen in chapter 2). He has done so throughout his career, in stagings that subvert scenes (i.e., add homosexual transgressiveness when it is not explicitly in the script), as in the impalement scene at the end of *O rei da vela* in 1967 (see chapter 2, note 31) and the kiss of the dentist and the title character in Oficina's staging of Nelson's *Boca de ouro* (Golden mouth) (1961) in the 1990s, to cite only Brazilian plays; the same is true of his readings of Western classics, as in *Ham-Let* (1993) and *As bacantes* (1996; The Bacchae).

Final Thoughts

Thirty or so years after the heyday of the male-accented plays of the 1970s, it seems that at least some of them, like *O assalto*, *Greta Garbo*, and *Blue jeans* have staying power, despite the fact that, in hindsight, they seem to be much too interested in the shock value of a taboo subject. Whether the gay boom of the 1970s did in fact venture into new artistic territory and thus will become a relevant chapter in the overall history of the theater in Brazil, only time will tell. From our vantage point, though, it seems clear that the better works among them were fundamental in changing the representation of homosexual transgression on the Brazilian stage.

The more successful of these works portray characters who embody the already mentioned cultural process José Esteban Muñoz calls "disidentification." Characters like Pedro/Greta Garbo and others outside the sexual mainstream negotiate majority culture "not by aligning themselves with or against exclusionary works but rather, by transforming these works for their own cultural purpose." Transposing Muñoz's ideas and terms about racial and sexual minorities in the United States to an examination of the process of identification in the plays and characters under consideration helps to detect in the Brazilian theater of homosexual transgression intersections of identity and difference in a culture where the oppressed are left "to negotiate a phobic majoritarian public sphere that continuously elides or punishes the existence of subjects who do not conform to the phantasm of normative citizenship" (Muñoz 1999: 4).

Mainstream theater criticism has largely ignored this body of work and no scholarly article I am aware of has ever focused solely on any one of the plays I examine in this chapter. Nor is there any evidence of preoccupation with misalignments or intersections of difference in these works. There were newspaper reviews of the plays when they first opened (including Sábato Magaldi's excellent piece on *O assalto*, later published in his book *Moderna dramaturgia brasileira*) but almost as a rule these reviews skirt the homoerotic content. One scholarly article, Luis Canales's "O homossexualismo como tema no moderno teatro brasileiro," does consider several of these plays in a pioneering piece published in *Luso-Brazilian Review* in 1981, but the survey format and sketchy, thematic treatment impede any depth of analysis of *Greta Garbo* or the other plays Canales reads. As the next chapter will show, it would take a major crisis to change this state of affairs: the arrival of HIV and AIDS coupled with a more sophisticated critical lexicon and greater visibility and new political advances for women and minorities inflected the cultural discourse of transgression and altered the direction of gay-accented theater in Brazil.

chapter 4

AIDS, Subalternity, and the Stage

General Remarks

Not only a major public health problem, AIDS is a focal point for many of the social ills that plague numerous nations, including Brazil. The Brazilian artistic community has reacted to the epidemic by means of a multifaceted engagement, ranging from the relatively quiet act of writing an elegiac poem to loud participation in meetings and demonstrations. Theater, by nature a confrontational art form, is a particularly strong and potentially eloquent medium through which to question and intervene in times of crisis; in Brazil, for instance, it played a key role in the resistance during the darkest years of the dictatorship in the late 1960s and early 1970s. Thanks both to their craft's directness and to its human dimension, Brazilian theater practitioners have been able to touch their audiences in significant ways as they have engaged with the rich cultural metaphor of AIDS, linking life and death, race, class, politics, and our perceptions of Self and Other.

HIV and AIDS have brought further complexity to the notion of the subaltern, which bears directly on the theatrical representation of seropositivity in Brazil. The most pressing question is how the occurrence of HIV and AIDS in Brazil has complicated the cultural process of determining who is entitled to speak to and for whom. Also significant is whether playwrights (regardless of sexual orientation) who contribute artistic responses to HIV and AIDS as well as those who perform relevant cultural interventions take on a patina of otherness through their association with the condition. How can the AIDS subalterns deflect strategies and discourses meant to isolate them by virtue of this assigned otherness? Fernando Coronil (1994: 647–48), among others, has built his critique of Gayatri Spivak mostly around the issue of otherness, claiming that she has "in effect homogenized and pushed the subaltern out of the realm of political exchange," resolving the contradictions surrounding the issue through "the subaltern's relegation to the margins and transformation into an outsider, an Other," reconstituting the subaltern "not only as a unified subject which cannot speak, but as a mute object—positioned outside agency." Instead, Coronil views the subaltern as "an agent of identity construction that participates, under certain conditions within a field of power relations, in the organization of its multiple positionality and subjectivity," for "dominance and subalternity are not inherent, but relational characterizations. Subalternity defines not the being of a subject, but a subjected state of being" (648–49). More specifically addressing subalternity in Brazil, Phyllis Peres (1994: 114) explores "the conditions under which subaltern discourse is produced and then imperfectly apprehended" by someone who is an outsider in relation to a particular community or worldview. For, as she argues in "Subaltern Spaces in Brazil," "Brazilian historiographies (whether historical, literary, or cultural) have silenced subaltern discourses by exalting the Brazilian subalterns as exemplars of an elite concept of nation. Brazilian subalterns can, indeed, speak in traditional Brazilian historiographies, but only in the voices of the elite. The integrity of subaltern discourse . . . is appropriated by Brazilian elites as discursive fragments that can neither be produced nor apprehended on their own" (114–15).

As chapters 1 and 2 showed, this was the fate of sexual minorities in Brazilian theatrical historiography and canon formation. Chapter 3 looked at a period when the sexual subaltern could begin to speak and be understood, gains that were seriously threatened by the onset of AIDS in the early 1980s. This chapter, in turn, identifies how we might hear the theatrical expression of Brazilian subaltern discourse during the AIDS crisis. To further complicate matters, in a subaltern society even the chronological, evolutionary process of the theatrical representation of AIDS is disturbed as translations of works belonging to a later stage are imported into the peripheral culture, bypassing the important experience of the earlier stages and strengthening the hegemonic nature of the representational process.[1]

Like anyone facing a health emergency, a playwright confronting the subject of HIV and AIDS must learn to handle a range of emotions that includes anger, fear, denial, despair, stoicism, sarcasm, prejudice, and a general feeling of disbelief. As a consequence, theatrical representations of AIDS reflect diverse approaches, from escapist fantasies to nervous comedies, from the richly detailed realism of testimonials to the far-reaching ambitiousness of allegory and fable.

Not unlike their colleagues in other cultures, Brazilian playwrights and directors who represent AIDS in their works must not only grieve for friends and colleagues[2] while facing discrimination themselves, they also must contend with the usual business that attends a stage production (payroll, rental payments, profit margin, critical reception, ticket sales, et cetera). Community-based groups are not normally besieged by such commercial concerns, but their often emotional involvement with the issue may raise other problems. Quite frequently, by the time such performances open, seething rage flies off the stage, language fragments into expressions of perplexity, and the spectator can only ponder how long the cast can embody such revolt and retain their sanity. Still, some of these performances constitute a vital instance of counterdiscourse in present-day Brazil, as do other theatrical acts, such as the unfurling and display of the native version of the AIDS quilt (called "Projeto NOMES" in Brazil), with its tremendous power to affirm and celebrate at the same time that it protests, contests, and subverts official cynicism. Less conventional than straightforward stagings, performances such as the AIDS quilt ceremony, readings of nondramatic texts, and other forms of theatricalization have explored distinct modes of communication in voicing their concern and support. A good example is the January 1997 book signing in Rio de Janeiro's Estação Botafogo of Herbert de Souza (Betinho)'s new book, *A lista de Ailce* (1996, Alice's list); as a group of friends and admirers surround the very frail author, an event held at a space normally unconnected with theatrical convention turns spontaneously into a theatrical act, with each individual gesture or statement fulfilling a new role in the engagement of the unmentioned condition. Following Betinho's death in August of 1997, Elias Andreato adapted *A lista de Ailce* as a monologue, a production that premiered 23 October 1997 in São Paulo's Teatro Ruth Escobar and was directed by Andreato and starred Angelo Antônio.[3]

There has been a wide variety of AIDS plays in recent years in Brazil, from mainstream works that have been staged and published (such as Plínio

Marcos's *A mancha roxa*) and that have reached a relatively large number of people to a more ephemeral kind of theater, such as that practiced by groups whose main goal is educational, such as the Rio de Janeiro–based Oficina de Teatro Expressionista para Homens que Fazem Sexo com Homens. In both camps, the best works steer clear of the anger and shrillness that can thwart the impact of theatrical representations of AIDS.

Some of the commercially produced plays also have an educational focus. In many ways, all plays about AIDS show some degree of didacticism, regardless of authorial intent; even when a play was not meant to be a vehicle for teaching (or preaching), its depiction of living with HIV may come across as such. Perhaps the best publicized of the educationally oriented commercial plays was the Porto Alegre staging of *O homem com a flor na boca* (*L'uomo dal fiore in boce*; The man with the flower in his mouth) in 1992. Obviously a pre-AIDS piece, Pirandello's 1936 play—essentially a dialogue between a patient with oral cancer and a healthy man—is reported to have lent itself well to its contemporary producers' educational goals. In this production by Manuel Aranha (b. 1947), who also directed and performed one of the roles,[4] part of the proceeds went to community groups involved in AIDS education, and each show was followed by a discussion with the audience on several aspects of HIV and HIV infection: prevention, prejudice, changes in goals and life perspective, the meaning of death, and so on.

The appearance of AIDS in Brazil also occasioned rewritings and new productions of pre-AIDS gay texts such as Zeno Wilde and Wanderley Bragança's *Blue Jeans* (examined in chapter 3) to reflect the new realities produced by the epidemic. The fate of Wilde and Bragança's work illustrates how AIDS can be seen as a poignant measure of the gulf between the Brazil of 1980 and that of 1992. The new, musicalized version—developed and directed by Wolf Maia—drew considerable attention and large audiences lured by the presence of some big television names in the cast. However, while it engages the spectator in an urgently needed reconsideration of the world of male hustlers in Brazil, the updated action, on the other hand, fails to confront AIDS with the forcefulness required. In addition, it precludes the experience of seeing the earlier period with sad irony, leading the viewer to conjecture on what it would be like if the original text (1980) had been restaged in 1992 and if there might not have been a deeper sense of impending tragedy, as the audience would know what was about to happen not long after the turn of the decade. In short, a consideration of the fortune of *Blue Jeans* strongly suggests that speaking more adequately to a radically different gay experience in urban Brazil has proven a difficult task, one that involves more than just an update of old vocabularies, one that in fact requires the conceptualizing of entirely new processes of articulation.

Theatrical reaction to the disease in Brazil also has prompted the staging of other plays that are not about AIDS, for example, a production of Ibsen's *Espectros* [*Ghosts*] that opened in São Paulo in the mid 1980s. Staged in our time, these works cannot escape the implications of an epidemic lurking in the background, a development paralleled by the new connotations taken on by vampire stories in literature and film (as in both versions of Anne Rice's *Interview with the Vampire*). However well-intentioned, the latter-day Brazilian production of *Espectros* (directed by Camila Amado and featuring the great Lélia Abramo as Mrs. Alvig) was marred by obviously anachronistic, heavy-handed allusions to and even a direct mention of AIDS. Such unfortunate overkill does more than merely ignore the fact that syphilis is never mentioned in Ibsen's play; it actually counters the playwright's point that sexually transmitted diseases are to be understood as both real and symbolic. Still, this kind of production might be of use for those studying how a new era and a peripheral society can affect the staging of pre-AIDS works, especially the type of drama which, like Ibsen's play, is concerned with the moral and social repercussions of contagion and stigma.

Several of the AIDS texts produced commercially in Brazil have been translations of foreign plays such as William Hoffman's *As Is* (1985) (*Por que eu?;* staged in Rio de Janeiro in 1987) and Tony Kushner's *Angels in America* (1992) (the Brazilian version, *O milênio se aproxima*, staged in Rio de Janeiro in 1995, is in fact an abridgment of only the first half of Kushner's play, *Millennium Approaches*). In addition to the problem of it inhibiting the autochthonous development of a theatrical representation of AIDS, the initial prevalence of U.S. AIDS works on the Brazilian stage posed other risks. First, there seemed to be the perception that native authors might feel less inclined to offer dramatic portrayals of HIV situations, should they become convinced that U.S. playwrights were better qualified to deal with what in Brazil was thought of, initially, as an "American problem" or "an American disease." A related issue here is the risk of being exposed to one foreign perspective to the exclusion of others, leaving out, for example, to name just one important AIDS culture, German imports. However, as the number of AIDS cases in Brazil grew dramatically throughout the 1980s, the need also grew for Brazilian voices to address the problem of HIV infection, and native texts accordingly began to appear.

Leaving aside translated texts, I have identified six paradigms that I believe typify the different approaches to the representation of AIDS in Brazilian theater: the neorealist paradigm, the neoexpressionist paradigm, the collective theater paradigm, the allegorical paradigm, the evocative paradigm, and the postmodern paradigm. I begin with an examination of Plínio Marcos's *A mancha roxa* as representative of the first paradigm and proceed in a more or less sequential fashion to the analysis of the other five.

The Neorealist Paradigm: Plínio Marcos's *A mancha roxa*

The Neorealist paradigm identifies those theatrical representations of HIV and AIDS that most closely parallel the often grim realities of the condition for those who have had to confront the social and personal crisis triggered by the virus.[5] I chose to begin with Plínio Marcos (whose work has already been discussed in chapters 1 and 2) because of his strong interest in marginality and social deprivation and because *A mancha roxa* provides a gritty depiction of the predicament of living with AIDS in the underworld of a women's prison in Brazil.

Plínio Marcos remains to this date the only major Brazilian playwright to have written about AIDS. His *A mancha roxa*, published in 1988, is perhaps the best-known AIDS-related Brazilian play.[6] It has been produced three times so far, twice in São Paulo (in 1989, under the direction of the playwright's son, Leo Lama, and in 2001 at São Paulo's Vergueiro Cultural Center) and once in Rio de Janeiro in 1993, directed by Eduardo Loyola.

Sexual desire linked with danger has become a truism in the age of AIDS. In *A mancha roxa* Marcos adds to this danger by considering sexual desire behind bars, placing his characters in a world of violence, drug abuse, and homosexual rape. By never mentioning the disease by name (a choice made by its pioneering counterpart in the United States, Larry Kramer's *The Normal Heart* [1985]), Marcos's play comments above all on the debate about the need to show AIDS versus the drive to hide AIDS. The need to show AIDS stresses that the disease is something we must confront, that it is a problem for all to acknowledge and tackle; the need to hide AIDS, on the other hand, insists on respect for the suffering of patients and accepts the claim that the nature of the condition may be upsetting to some. This debate is in fact held against the background of a much larger issue, that of marginality. In Brazil, where the elites have traditionally conferred on themselves the right to designate those who are entitled to be part of the social corpus (consequently excluding all others as outcasts, and perversely confirming Edward Said's definition of culture as "a system of exclusions" [1983: 11]), the HIV-positive individual has been added to the numerous other undesirables, or "marginais"—an exclusionary act that may aggravate further the already serious process of social disintegration of the region.

Hardly known for insisting on ambiguity over moral indignation, Marcos in *A mancha roxa* again resorts to the hallmarks of his works from the 1960s and early 1970s—an abundance of profanity and low-life posturing, unrelenting aggressiveness, and threatened or actual physical violence, gloomy, filthy, confining settings such as prison cells (*Barrela*), brothels (*Navalha na carne* and *O abajur lilás*), cheap rooming houses (*Dois perdidos numa noite suja*), and trash pickers quarters (*Homens de papel*). In *A mancha roxa* the number of characters may have increased, the source of the discord is a detestable novelty, but the crudity, the coarseness, the open-wound approach are vintage Marcos.

Marcos himself has stated that *A mancha roxa* is his most violent work (Comodo 1993). In its most uncompromising moments, the play achieves a neorealist blend of verité and melodrama, a style that hews closely to the rhythms of the characters' constant haggling, mounting despair, and encroaching defeat. The action takes place in the squalid environment of a women's penitentiary. Set in a single cell where six inmates are confined,[7] the play spans a period of a few hours, alternating between the dramas of the women as they each seek respect, love, and acceptance, without having much of themselves left to invest. The women gradually discover, or are forced to admit, that they carry the virus—now that they can no longer hide from the others the very visible, revealing symptoms, the purple skin lesions or "*manchas roxas*" of the title.[8] Their drama is collective but each individual inveighs against the other, ironically denouncing her for being sick with the same disease as the attacker, and for being a carrier of the same virus the attacker has contracted and possibly transmitted.

During casting for the São Paulo staging, the production team was rudely reminded of the stigmatization associated with AIDS and incarceration in Brazil. No less than seventy-nine performers turned down invitations to audition for the play before seven actresses (Beth Daniel,

Camila Bolaffi, Cláudia Campos, Dione Leal, Elaine Gonçalves, Graça de Andrade, and Leila Pantel) finally agreed to be involved with the production, and these were amateur actresses who did not receive financial compensation for their work and probably saw their performing in a Plínio Marcos play as a career boost.

The press, too, virtually ignored the production, which prompted Marcos to return the awards that it won later that year. In doing so, Marcos was also protesting the press's silence regarding his AIDS prevention work in São Paulo's penitentiaries. In fact, *A mancha roxa* grew out of a series of visits, talks, and a video tape he did for the State of São Paulo Department of Corrections, having been chosen by the inmates themselves as the art world personality they trusted most. Marcos visited both men's and women's penitentiaries as part of his volunteer work. After several days of prostration and depression caused by what he saw in the prisons, he went into a "writing rage" that resulted in *A mancha roxa.* Although one almost expected a play about men (when the play was written, three out of four people with AIDS in Brazil were male),[9] Marcos—horrified by a number of murders of HIV-positive male inmates by prison wardens and HIV-negative inmates in the São Paulo corrections system,[10] and reportedly not seeing among the male prisoners the compassion and sense of unity displayed by the women—decided against writing about men. But there is another dimension to Marcos' choice. It is a tribute to Marcos's vision that *A mancha roxa,* the first mainstream Brazilian theater production to deal with AIDS, altogether dissociates the disease from gay men. By choosing to focus exclusively on women with AIDS, Plínio Marcos stresses the fact that the HIV virus does not discriminate and does not take into account sex, race, or station in life. At a time when denunciation of gay men as "vectors of the plague" approached hysterical dimensions, his deliberate exclusion of gay men from the play contributed to educate a large number of people about HIV risk, and in doing so it helped to cool off the social atmosphere, enabling sensible parties to steer the debate towards a more rational center.

As in *O abajur lilás,* with which it has many parallels,[11] the "tainted" bodies of the women in *A mancha roxa* are never eroticized. At first, with the exception of Isa, the inmates aren't even distinct individuals, for the five other women act as a block. In tandem, they torment Isa, the first of the inmates to show "*manchas*" on her body. One of the five, Isa's lover Linda, later breaks away from the block as she defends Isa—but she does so for selfish reasons, terrified the other women might declare her "infected."

One by one, each of the other women breaks away from the unit as her contamination becomes apparent to the others and she fights for survival amid all manner of accusation and cruelty. As desire gives way to repulsion, eroticization becomes an impossibility, and aggression quickly takes over. For a while, when it seems that all of them are ill, the sting of difference and abnormality disappears. That period is but a brief lull, though. We soon learn that of the six inmates the only one who is not infected is a reminder of suffering and sainthood and is treated with sarcasm by her cellmates, who give her the name Santa when they learn she had been incarcerated for killing her husband. In contrast to the initial five against one opposition (when only Isa was known to be sick), now it is the HIV-negative individual who is in the minority and who can no longer inveigh against the other women. Operating again as a unit, the five women decide that Santa must now be brought into the fold. They proceed to make her their equal, an initiate in the new sisterhood, by forcing her to be a communicant in Isa's body and blood.

The spread of the disease, from one inmate to all inmates and, in a long, dreamy, feverish passage (36–40), from the prison cell to the world at large, is signaled by the use of lighting (30–31, 38–40). Purple light bathes the set, slowly pervades the stage area, and gradually spreads to the audience. Otherwise, there is no authorial direction for lighting, leading one to assume that traditional stark lighting is to be used in the more realistic scenes, such as the needle sharing (17–18) and the threatened use of supposedly infected blood as a weapon (26).

The six-woman unit relates to the world beyond the prison walls through the figure of Grelão, the matron warden whose presence or voice (she is often heard from offstage) is a constant reminder of a ruthless outside force. Simultaneously outsider and insider (having once been an inmate herself), Grelão mediates through corruption, bribes, blackmail, and threats of rape, occasioning frequent bursts of rebellion as the women denounce the system that led them to crime and infection. Power becomes indissociable from prejudice as the women rage against the penal system and society's drive to hide AIDS:

> *Os próprios filhos da puta que tomam conta disso aqui, diretor, juiz, promotor, todos que socaram a gente aqui dentro, todos vão inventar uma história para esconder que estamos morrendo de roxa aqui dentro. (28)*
>
> [The sons of bitches that run this place, the director, judge, the prosecutor, everyone who dumped us in here, they are going to make up something to hide the fact that we are dying in here of the purple disease.]

Quickly however, reality settles in and they accept the uselessness of their rage. One of the inmates, identified only as the Professora, speaks for the group and then rejoins her silent companions:

> *O Estado, o Estado, o Estado é responsável por mim. . . . O Estado é culpado. O Estado é culpado. O Estado é culpado.* (Vai perdendo o ânimo.) *O Estado. O Estado . . . O Estado . . .* (Pausa. Silêncio.) (Virando-se lentamente para as outras.) *Ninguém ouviu. O Estado é surdo. Os promotores, os juízes, os políticos são todos surdos. O Governador é surdo. Todos são surdos.* (34)
>
> [The State, the State, the State is responsible for me. . . . The State is guilty. The State is guilty. The State is guilty. (*Losing heart.*) The State. The State . . . the State . . . (*Pause. Silence.*) (*Turning slowly toward the others.*) No one listened. The State is deaf. The prosecutors, the judges, the politicians, they're all deaf. The governor is deaf. Everyone is deaf.]

Theater about AIDS is raw and powerful, even when to some ears it is unpolished, or perhaps especially when it is unpolished. In *A mancha roxa* there is plenty that is unpolished, as for example, the use of refrains such as "*Pelo sangue, pela porra, pela merda*" (8, 15, 36) (through blood, cum, and shit) and a recurring song, delivered by Professora, that, while bordering on pamphleteering, serves as a reminder of the power that unleashed anger can wield. In Marcos's play there is also plenty that is unbearable about words and gestures and scenes, plenty that makes one want to turn away—and in this sense Marcos remains the "*repórter de um tempo mau*" (reporter of bad times) of the 1960s and 1970s (Schoenbach 1976). Yet something about *A mancha roxa* is steadying and almost comforting. Its challenge makes us consider once again the way Brazilian women are brutalized by society and discarded as they become old or ill or incarcerated. Neither despicable nor heroic, these women are ordinary human beings who are angry and scared as they try to survive against enormous odds, dreaming of an unlikely chance to get out (be it of prison, or of this virtual death sentence) and start over. The prison cell is, at first, a locale for small, petty fights, as individual dramas resist coalescing into a collective tragedy, only to be transformed, at play's end, into a large arena featuring one sole conflict of enormous proportions.

Still, as a portrayal of HIV infection among six women prisoners (the group includes lesbians and African Brazilians) by a white, heterosexual, HIV-negative male playwright, *A mancha roxa* refers both to the longstanding problem of the portrayal of the Other in Brazil as an exclusionary act and to the more pressing matter of agency and intervention in cultural representations of AIDS. In Marcos's theater, women are rarely represented in ways that foreground an accurate understanding of their plight in Brazil, and accusations of misogyny have always dogged his career. The sad gallery of pathetic prostitutes who inhabit so many of his works may do more to reinforce social barriers than to voice grievances or foster understanding. In *A mancha roxa* too, women are more vectors than victims, suspects who participate in their own infection. The political consequences of these representations can be disastrous for the disenfranchised, with a possible increase in prejudice against people with AIDS and reinforcement of the general belief that such dangerous beings should be isolated or incarcerated.

As Alberto Sandoval (1994) has pointed out with regard to Latinos in the United States and Puerto Rico, AIDS is as much a crisis of representation as a crisis of public health, and the crisis of representation has been vividly illustrated by drama and the theater.[12] The same claim can be made about minority groups in other areas of the continent; in Brazil, too, the crisis in representation can be seen at different levels and in different venues, including the theater. Perhaps nothing makes such a crisis in representation more patent than Plínio Marcos's status as the author of the most acclaimed AIDS play in Brazilian theater so far. Marcos's theater shows in its early stages an undeniable acquaintance with marginality and oppression, but three decades after the potent impact of his art was initially felt his dramatic works are very much a part of the canon, his early antiestablishment credentials notwithstanding. The stage is now set for new, more diverse voices to be heard in the theatrical portrayal of the AIDS experience in Brazil.

The Neoexpressionist Paradigm: Vagner de Almeida's AIDS Trilogy

What I call the Neoexpressionist paradigm in Brazilian AIDS theater is characterized by a strong reliance on images and metaphors to express internal conflict as they conjure up the HIV and AIDS experience. The plays of Vagner de Almeida and other playwrights of the 1980s and early 1990s suggest associations and connotations that might offer a glimmer of understanding to all those who have been directly or indirectly touched by the crisis. To do so, these playwrights resort to a number of the tenets of expressionist theater—referred to below—liberally interwoven with personal touches that depart from the doctrine they originally espoused.

Highly creative and energetic, Vagner de Almeida (b. 1957) wears many hats in Rio de Janeiro, from artist to teacher to counselor to cultural activist. He began his involvement with the theater as a young man, first as an actor, and later as a director and playwright in the city of Petrópolis, in the state of Rio de Janeiro. In addition to expressionist theater, Vagner was also influenced by Grotowski's poor theater, and by his reading of Artaud, Fassbinder, and Pasolini. In the early years of his career, Vagner staged a series of collages of scenes culled from classic texts (e.g., his *Retalhos* I, II, III [Rags I, II, III]), and from texts dealing with deprivation (such as *Fome, sede, privação* [Hunger, thirst, deprivation]).

Like most alert members of Rio de Janeiro's gay community in the 1980s, Vagner had observed the AIDS crisis growing all around him and was shocked by the silence in the media and by the lack of mobilization in society as a whole and in the gay community in particular. Reacting to the denial that existed about the extent and severity of the problem and dismayed by the Brazilian inertia in comparison with the mobilization in the United States, with which he was well-acquainted—Vagner began to take action. As Richard Parker puts it, Vagner de Almeida *"foi uma das primeiras pessoas a conscientizar-me a fazer alguma coisa para alertar socialmente que a AIDS no Brasil era um paiol de pólvora com um curto pavio pronto a explodir"* ("Review of 'Adeus irmão,'" 1989: 47) (was one of the first people to make me realize that something needed to be done in order to alert Brazilian society to the fact that AIDS was a powder keg ready to explode).

Vagner believed he could adopt the tenets of expressionist theater to explore a wide range of themes and emotions and escape the limitations of stark realism and the frustrations of the so-called rage and remembrance AIDS plays. Vagner also had to evade the inadequacies of both traditional theater and the authoritarian dispensing of information, the former because of "its dependency on illusion and behaviourism (that ultimately intensifies individualism)" and the latter because it "ultimately intensifies our awareness of sickness rather than health" (Richardson 1993: 297). Tinkering with expressionistic theater helped Vagner navigate these murky waters. As he puts it, "The very idea of expressionism—to take underlying internal conflicts and express them outwardly—seemed appropriate as an approach to the difficulties" that had plagued previous attempts at dramatizing AIDS. In addition to transcending the mere transmission of facts and general information about the disease, expressionist theater would allow for the desirable exploration of "emotional and psychological dimensions of conflicts and tensions raised by both homosexuality and AIDS among the broadest possible spectrum of men who have sex with men" (Almeida et al. 1996: 3). Still, he is clearly not a practitioner of theatrical expressionism in its orthodox form; he is what could be described as a neoexpressionist. In a typical Brazilian cannibalistic, *bricoleur* vein, what Vagner produces, beyond the use of some basic expressionist techniques, is a very eclectic theater that draws on traditional stagecraft and other media and offers solutions of its own.

Returning to Brazil in 1988 after a long stay in California, Vagner began to work on his AIDS trilogy, which comprises *Adeus, irmão, durma sossegado* (1989; Good-bye, brother, sleep well), one of the first Brazilian plays about AIDS to be staged (Teatro Aliança Francesa de Copacabana, Rio de Janeiro); *Estou vivo* (I'm alive), which opened in September 1992, at the Teatro Henriqueta Brieba, also in Rio de Janeiro, and was the first Brazilian play about AIDS to go on a national tour, under the auspices of SESC (Serviço Social do Comércio [National Commerce Industry's Social Services]); and *Os desgraçados* (1991; The miserable ones), which premiered at the Centro Cultural Noel Rosa at Vila Isabel and later moved to the Teatro Escola Pedro Alvares Cabral in Copacabana. Vagner directed and acted in all three productions.

The very title of *Adeus, irmão, durma sossegado* alludes to the problem of the invisibility of AIDS in Brazil. The first letters of the title form an acronym for the syndrome without actually naming it.[13] The official silence surrounding the disease throughout most of the 1980s is alluded to and denounced in several of the fifteen individual scenes or tableaux that make up the play. Whether inserted into or interspersed between scenes, editorial comments lash out against the inaction of government, the media, and society as a whole. In *Adeus, irmão*, these interventions take on additional force as the playwright steps out to deliver them. In its most direct form, authorial editorializing can offend an audience interested in forming its own opinion. But such is the urgency of AIDS that previously established certainties lose their validity. In 1989 it was necessary that Brazilian audiences be exposed to the direct comments of the playwright and that these comments be delivered while he looks them in the eye, an example being the line, "*Morrem vitimados não só pela doença mas pela solidão e esquecimento das pessoas*" (They die victims not only of the disease but also of loneliness and rejection) which follows a scene in which the parents of a hospitalized woman with AIDS abandon their daughter in her hour of need.

There are also several direct messages delivered not by the playwright but by actors playing a role. Pedro, a young man who has AIDS, wakes up in a panic in the middle of the night and has a conversation with his lover Paulo that includes the evidently editorial line, "*O povo precisa ver o aidético como gente, não como bosta*" (People need to see the person with AIDS as a human being, not shit). Most memorable, though, is a long speech by a woman in a medieval-looking habit who carries a cross and inveighs against the kind of thought that posits the illness as some kind of plague or divine retribution for behavior perceived as sinful. Why, she asks rhetorically, call this virus-caused endemic disease that can afflict anyone a "*praga pré-apocalíptica*" (pre-apocalyptic plague) or "*peste gay*" (gay plague)? The message concludes, "*AIDS não é castigo de Deus*" (AIDS is not a punishment from God).

The play makes good use of unseen characters who are denounced for uncaring or hostile behavior, such as graffiti artists who write things like "gay plague" on the walls, an insensitive reporter who interviews an incarcerated young man with AIDS, or a doctor who fails to show up for an appointment with three patients. The invisibility of these characters denotes the impunity of the perpetrators and the frequency of the pain and injury occasioned by those who evade their professional responsibilities and moral obligations. Their absence from the stage suggests society's reticence to face what is a clear threat to all.

Denunciation of individual omission and societal neglect is also expressed in *Adeus, irmão* by means of the parallelism in the first two scenes. Each scene depicts a set of parents talking about their ailing child, a son and a daughter, respectively. As each scene progresses, the parents, and we, are made aware of the two deaths. As an offstage voice coldly announces the recent obits, the parents react differently in each scene. In the first, they refuse to acknowledge even that someone is knocking at the door, which suggests their failure to acknowledge their son's existence and/or disease, or perhaps to accept his death. The parents in the second scene do acknowledge the knock at the door but, terrified of the stigma and other social consequences of infection, deny having a daughter called Maria da Silva. The anonymity of the parents and the near-anonymity and lower-class connotations of the daughter's name (da Silva being the most common last name in Brazil and one prevalent among the poorest segments of the population and Maria being the most common woman's first name) bespeak the nature of the infection as it spreads quickly among the poor and disenfranchised and in areas where ignorance and intolerance thrive. The voice insistently repeats the notification and, in a last attempt before going away, adds the name of the disease to that of the deceased: Maria da Silva da Aids. In death, Maria has lost some of her anonymity (by virtue of having acquired a longer last name) and attained an identity that is indistinguishable from the condition that led to her death. As the scene closes, the associative process is complete and the body—effaced by parental denial—disappears while identity and disease coalesce in death.

Perhaps the most effective scene is the interaction of four prostitutes (a woman and three *travestis*) as they try to read and interpret a brochure that describes in erudite language the risks of a number of sexual practices. The woman, Manon, does most of the reading because she claims to have taken acting lessons and, in any case, the men are barely literate. With a good deal of humor tempering the criticism of the detached scientific terminology the woman is reading aloud to them, one of the *travestis* provides a "translation" of the technical information into the real if vulgar language accessible to those the brochure was designed to reach.

The play's final scene shows a man (Nonô) with AIDS and his HIV-negative lover, a woman (Naná) who watches him dispose of his belongings. As he does so, he lapses into reminiscences about his past, including the moment he learned he was HIV-positive. His speech is interspersed by the comments Naná makes as she looks at an old photo album. The scene ends with Naná singing a lullaby ("*Dorme, nenê, do meu coração*" [Sleep, beloved baby]) as Nonô lies with his head on her lap and falls asleep or, perhaps, dies. At this point the other actors enter the dark stage carrying lit candles that they blow out moments later. As the lights come back a stern-faced cast walk up the aisle and we again hear the passage "Fortuna Imperatrix Mundi" from Carl Orff's *Carmina Burana*, which was heard as the play opened.

The second play in the trilogy, *Estou vivo*, revisits the material presented in *Adeus, irmão*. Most of the characters and situations and a good portion of the text from the first play are included in this second part of the trilogy. *Estou vivo*, however, is a much longer play, as the monologues and dialogues have been expanded and additional characters and situations have been created. It soon becomes evident that the changes have taken their toll. Gone are most of the bite and edginess of *Adeus, irmão.* Without the incisiveness of the first part, the new play, unnecessarily long and repetitive on occasion, seems to be ending at least twice before it finally does.

The scenes, now presented in a different sequence, are bracketed by the appearances of a somewhat pretentious character, Miss Saigon, who performs two longish, lip-synched musical pieces at the beginning and at midpoint, and who, no longer in drag, closes the play as José da Silva, a man with AIDS, and delivers the upbeat monologue that lends its title to the play. Stressing survival against all odds, José invites all to celebrate life and keep fighting for what's right. Although the optimistic message seems to belie much of what precedes it, its honesty and genuineness demand that this scene be read as an instance of agency and intervention on the part of those who, finding themselves at the eye of the storm, decide to speak their minds and fight for their lives.

Editorial comments, too, are more numerous, and lengthier in *Estou vivo.* Shrill and proselytizing, they constitute the message it is hoped the public will retain on leaving the theater. In fact, the play's longest monologue, delivered by an AIDS educator, acknowledges as much: *"Este é um espetáculo de teatro para o qual não deveríamos usar a palavra 'espetáculo' mas sim uma 'manifestação' a favor da conscientização do perigo dessa doença"* ("This is a show that should not be called a 'show' but rather a 'demonstration' that aims to raise awareness of the danger of this disease). Making a rhetorical distinction between an "ideological virus" and a "biological virus," the educator claims that the former, "the virus of prejudice and discrimination," although by far the more dangerous of the two, can be stopped by "the vaccine of solidarity." Staring at the audience, she concludes: *"Fique cada qual apresentado hoje a um grito de alerta. Nesse grito de alerta ressoa o eco de que uma pessoa com AIDS é gente como outra pessoa qualquer e digna de respeito e humanidade"* ("Each and every one of you has been exposed today to a cry that echoes the message that a person with AIDS is a human being like any other and as such, worthy of respect and humanity").

As the production went on tour, the scenes became provisional since at times it was necessary to adapt them in response to specific local exigencies; sometimes unexpected problems with members of the cast demanded changes in content or even deletions of existing scenes, and/or creation of new ones. And finally, some of the scenes were reworked so that they became open-ended, serving as points of departure for postperformance discussions with the audience; the responses, predictably, were as varied as the make-up of the audiences.

The changing face of AIDS in Brazil in the early 1990s is denoted by the inclusion in *Estou vivo* of new characters nonexistent in *Adeus, irmão*, male and female, young and old, of different sexual orientations and from all social classes. In addition, an effort is made to stress the fact that a healthy existence should not be determined solely by one's HIV status. Still, in *Estou vivo* as much as in *Adeus, irmão*, the outcasts remain at center stage and the theater an outlet for their voice.

The commitment to the dispossessed seen in the first two parts of the trilogy remains strong in Vagner's third AIDS play, *Os desgraçados*. The allusion to Victor Hugo's novel is evident in the title as well as in the focus on the disenfranchised, but unlike Hugo's *Les Miserables*, Vagner's work is not interested in plot development, presenting rather a series of situations and brief scenes.

Never mentioned, the disease hovers over the general situation being depicted—the oppressive panorama of deprivation, despair, and discrimination in contemporary Brazil. By far the angriest and most blatantly political of the three plays, *Os desgraçados* wastes no time finding ways to suggest that these social conditions are certain to spur the spread of the virus, instead striking the spectator with a seemingly endless series of hard blows, verbal and visual. So relentless is this sensorial assault that the production risks failing to obtain the empathy of an audience overexposed to so much filth and ugliness.

Of the three plays, *Os desgraçados* is also the one that makes the most use of expressionist techniques. Class conflict and social oppression are portrayed not through plot, dialogue, and character development but rather by an array of signation, including facial expression, gestures, movements (actors moving in slow motion), sets (rundown buildings, filthy streets, dark alleys), wardrobe (tattered clothing, rags), make-up (heavily smeared black make-up stressing pent-up emotion), and sounds (groans and screams, cacophonous distortion). Characters are schematically designed as nameless figures (beggars, street people, slum dwellers, rape victims, prostitutes), all of them unwitting participants in the victimization process. The scenes are short and not always causally linked while the dialogue, which more often than not lacks in interpersonal communication, varies from brief telegraphic phrases to long, rambling speeches. The latter draw from a variety of accepted symbols of unity and harmony, such as the Brazilian National Anthem and "Silent Night" (both delivered as a recitative by an irate, defiant cast) as well as several articles of the 1988 Constitution, angrily recited as foils to the abuse and abandonment of women and children and the criminal disregard for the civil rights of a large segment of the population. The violent questioning of such icons of benevolence and justice is not, however, aided by the use of excessive repetition. This is egregiously clear in a long scene (of about twenty minutes) consisting entirely of the echoing of two speeches voiced each time by a different actor and in a different tone, relaying a message that, although intended as inflammatory and solidarity-building, may lead, by lack of nuance, not to the expressionist goal of attaining spiritual regeneration but to further apathy and neglect.

The aggressiveness of the performance is both its strength and its weakness. To paraphrase what Laura Jacobs (qtd. in Kistenberg 1995: 110) says of a Karen Finley performance, confrontational complaint does not change the spectator's mind if he or she disagrees with the artist, while if the spectator agrees with the artist, then the performance becomes little more than a depressing catalog of woes. Still, Vagner's play does fulfill its function, not only as the closing part of the trilogy but, more importantly, as a powerful if perhaps too strident wake-up call for the elimination of the social conditions that enable the unhindered propagation of AIDS in Brazil.

Vagner de Almeida's trilogy emerged from a desire to touch the emotions and address the concerns both of intended target groups and, more significantly, of the public at large. As such, the three plays constitute successful "acts of intervention" (Román 1998). Empathy is reportedly the overriding sentiment experienced by audiences after seeing these plays that aim to use theater as a tool in AIDS education. As such, they provide information about AIDS, raise awareness about risk, and challenge negative attitudes toward, and promote compassion and understanding for, people with AIDS. The same is true of his work with the Oficina de Teatro Expressionista, which I consider next.

The Collective Theater Paradigm: The Oficina de Teatro Expressionista para Homens que Fazem Sexo com Homens

Understanding how Brazilian theater attempted to give agency and voice to the subaltern in a time of crisis and thus contribute to making sense of HIV and AIDS calls for an examination of forms of representation based on collective action to resist otherness. The personal struggle to fight relegation to the margins becomes the basis for the subaltern's construction of his or her experience with the condition and becoming a participatory agent of identity construction. The plays grounded in this belief form the third paradigm, which is manifest in the work of the ever-surprising Vagner de Almeida.[14]

AIDS prevention faces different challenges in subaltern societies such as Brazil. Poverty and indigence, high illiteracy rates, class discrimination, male and female prostitution, and deep-seated racism and homophobia combine to present AIDS educators with a formidable challenge. As a tool Brazilian AIDS workers have resorted to in their outreach efforts, theater has been particularly effective, thanks in no small measure to its ability to empower the voiceless and thus intervene in the naming practices and constructions of difference whereby the established structures of power formulate social determinants of meaning and subjectivity.

Although my focus here is the group Oficina de Teatro Expressionista para Homens que Fazem Sexo com Homens, other groups now active in Brazil merit as much attention and praise for their work with communities at high risk of contracting AIDS. Especially interesting is the involvement of several groups and individuals in *favelas* (shantytowns) and prisons. Most of these groups stage simple but often very effective plays that result from collective work and thus serve to illustrate the paradigm under discussion.

Of enormous importance for AIDS prevention in Brazil is the pedagogical work of theater groups such as Salvador's Tribo do Teatro, which performs in schools, orphanages, and community centers in the poor outskirts and sprawling slums of that city. Created in 1994 as part of a larger project called "Educação, um exercício de cidadania" (Education, an Exercise in Citizenship) with funding from the nongovernmental organization, CRIA (Centro de Referência Integral para Adolescentes [Center for Holistic Assistance of Adolescents]), their latest production, "Quem descobriu o amor?" (Who discovered love?) was presented during the 1996 school year. Featuring a young cast (whose members were just twelve to twenty years of age), the play is a sequence of short scenes followed by debate with an invariably enthusiastic audience. On subsequent days, student volunteers are trained to continue the educational and outreach work initiated by the play (Rossetti 1996: 5).

Under the direction of Murilo Mota, GRAPAAR (Grupo Resistência Adquirida para Prevenção de AIDS com Arte na Rocinha) [The Acquired Resistance Group for the Prevention of AIDS through Art in the Rocinha District] has focused on dramatizations of prevention strategies among teenagers living in an area with high unemployment and few opportunities for social advancement. The group has staged two collective creations so far. The first, *O alvo* (The target), moved to Teatro Dulcina in downtown Rio de Janeiro in September 1999, after numerous presentations in working-class communities all over town. Their second effort, *Bienal do Mané* (Mané's biennial), which opened in October 2000, had a cast of thirteen young actors and involved a dramatization of AIDS prevention combined with a discussion of the meaning of citizenship; this time around the group was less interested in gaining the recognition of the theater establishment in downtown Rio and focused instead on their target audiences in public schools and sympathetic churches (the work premiered at Rocinha's Methodist church).

Equally noteworthy in connection with this paradigm is the work three English directors conducted with slum dwellers and prison inmates in Brazil. Cicely Berry, a director of the Royal Shakespeare Company, was instrumental in the creation and the first years of existence of the group Nós do Morro, based in the Vidigal slum in Rio de Janeiro. Paul Heritage, of the Drama Department of the University of London, has long been associated with Brazilian theater, as a researcher and scholar and also as mentor of theater groups formed by prison inmates, mostly in the maximum security penitentiaries at Papuda in Brasília, Carandiru in São Paulo, and Lemos de Brito in Rio de Janeiro. James Thompson, cofounder, with Heritage, of TIPP (Theatre in Prison and Probation), saw their work expand quickly to prisons in Holland, Spain, Greece, and Brazil, where for the past three years he has directed prison inmates in AIDS-related plays in the São Paulo penitentiary system.

I will focus more extensively here on the Rio de Janeiro–based Oficina de Teatro Expressionista para Homens que Fazem Sexo com Homens (OTE).[15] Part of Projeto Homossexualidades[16] and sponsored by, among others, ABIA (Associação Brasileira Interdisciplinar de AIDS) and Grupo Pela Vida,[17] OTE is made up of a core group of forty-five to fifty participants who are collectively responsible for the entire production, from choosing the subject matter and writing the text to selecting and executing wardrobe, make-up, props, sound track, and other details.[18] With the work of groups like OTE and Teatro Vida, and secure from alterity, misrepresentation and the power of an authoritative playwright, the Brazilian person with AIDS has found his or her voice. The existence of such groups is crucial if the person with AIDS is to be represented as a resister and not a victim.[19] Such change stems from these groups' portrayal of the person with AIDS as a valuable member of a social unit, a community of friends, supporters, and survivors. In these works the person with AIDS is presented as a sympathetic character rather than a helpless victim and as someone whose energy and affirmation will spur the audience to work for social change in the world outside the theater. Finally, in this kind of theater, empathy is of paramount importance. For these plays to be effective, audience members must be made aware that they have much in common with these characters and that they face some of the same situations and risks.

Part support group, part educating team, OTE has adopted the crude language of the streets to speak to those most at risk in contemporary urban Brazil. Undaunted by intolerance, the group seeks to combat internalized homophobia and turn transgression around in order to expose its true meaning. Humor, nudity, and simulated sexual acts are often included in their productions, as *"esta modalidade de arte faz com que os participantes expressem suas bifacialidades sem temer a crítica alheia; trabalha-se a auto-estima, a valorização do Eu, deixa-se à parte a autopiedade e avança-se em direção à verdadeira expressão que há em cada um"* (Almeida 1994a: 9) (this type of art lets its performers express their dualities without fear of criticism; we work to improve self-esteem, leaving out self-pity and proceeding toward one's inner truth). The group works under the premise that access to information alone is insufficient to begin effecting behavior changes in human beings and that bombarding people with slogans (such as "Pratique Sexo Seguro" [Practice Safe Sex] and "Proteja Seu Pinto: Sempre Use Camisinha" [Protect Your Dick: Always Wear a Condom]) and cognitive messages is less effective than a sustained effort at improving the self-esteem and raising the awareness of risk among target populations.

Vagner de Almeida serves as ABIA prevention group discussion facilitator and OTE stage director. With a strong background in acting, directing, and playwriting (including the AIDS trilogy examined above), Vagner was the logical choice for leader of ABIA's Oficina de Teatro Expressionista when the program was launched in the early 1990s. As none of the participants had any previous stage experience, preparation was an arduous endeavor, with posture, diction, and acting lessons preceding and often replacing the dramatic exercises and previously scheduled play rehearsals. In the first twelve months, regular weekly sessions were held,

> focusing on expressionist bodywork and pantomime, dramatization of sexual negotiation and interaction, and collective discussion of issues such as sexual identity, desire, pleasure, the impact of HIV and AIDS, and the experience of stigma and discrimination in Brazilian society. Workshop activities were documented and monitored through the use of video recordings, pre- and post-workshop interviews with participants, and focus group discussions with regular participants. (Almeida et al. 1996: 3–4)

In its first year, OTE borrowed and adapted street theater tactics for their communication exercises. One such tactic was their "Intervenção Corpo a Corpo" (Body to Body Intervention) in which some of the thirty actor-educators would appear unannounced to conduct brief performances for, or simply interact with, the patrons of bars, dance clubs, parks, beaches, and saunas favored by gay and bisexual men in Rio de Janeiro and São Paulo (Terto and Godinho 1994: 14–15).

As the program entered its second year, attendance and participation in sessions kept increasing. Through the many months of debate and discussion, Almeida's dedication to the project deepened as he got to know the members better and, through them, came to a clearer understanding of the nature of their problems. Furthermore, the urgency of the project was becoming more evident, for while other project activities attracted an older and more educated, more middle-class public, the OTE sessions were more popular among younger, lower-class, more at-risk men:

> The majority of workshop participants were between the ages of 16 and 25, from lower-class neighborhoods such as *favelas* or the suburbs outside of central Rio, and, consequently, in large number black or mulatto in terms of race or ethnicity. With extremely limited educational opportunities, a large percentage of these men were either unemployed or underemployed, marginalized through racism, class discrimination, and, above all, homophobia, from the broader structures of Brazilian society and culture. (Almeida et al. 1996: 4–5)

OTE sessions provided these youths with a forum and an audience, a place where they could voice their opinions and where they could be heard with consideration and respect. It soon became obvious that before safe sex and AIDS could even be tackled, key social issues such as race and class prejudice had to be addressed. The meetings then became vehicles to combat such feelings and at the same time to heighten self-esteem and foster solidarity and an awareness of one's civil rights and freedom of expression. In the workshops and related group activities one could begin to see the formation of a true gay community, the creation of which has been impeded by the all-too-powerful repression—social, political, religious—that lies at the core of life in Brazil.

It was not until this time, well into the second year of the project, that a group of regular participants in OTE workshops began to develop the play they later named *Cabaret Prevenção*. All those who were given lines to speak were amateurs who answered casting calls to play people very much like themselves; some were given monologues, others only a few lines. Naturals all, they knew exactly what to do because of their firsthand knowledge of the issues portrayed in *Cabaret*. After one year of rehearsals, the production opened in January 1995 and ran successfully until March 1995, with a combined attendance of over 3,000 people and with an average of 83 people at each performance.[20] These were held in Teatro Alaska, chosen precisely for being a traditional gay space in Rio de Janeiro's Zona Sul, and which had long been used for drag performances and sex shows with male strippers, including a runaway hit that crossed over audience lines, *Os Leopardos*. The creative process was collective at every step of the project, with the participants themselves in charge of the text,[21] the theatrical aspects of the production (make-up, wardrobe, lighting, props, and so on) and also publicity, marketing, the creation of a poster, and the production of a video that documented all stages of the project (Almeida et al. 1996: 6). In order to emphasize the urgency of the issues the show dealt with, there were no sets, the wardrobe was made from used items and recycled materials, and only four colors were used in the staging (black, white, red, and purple).

Cabaret Prevenção, with a running time of about an hour and a half, consisted of seventeen consecutive skits on topics that had emerged in the workshops, key issues perceived by the participants themselves, such as "seduction," "machismo and homophobia," "seropositivity," and "street violence" (Almeida 1994a; 1994b; 1997). Each group member would write a scene, which was subsequently revised following a critique from the rest of the cast. Selection of the eleven topics and of the play title was done through ballots cast by the participants.[22] During the rehearsal phase, the diverse scenes were tied together through projected images (from slides), music, and dance.[23] It was also decided that authors would not perform

Ad for performance of *Cabaret Prevenção* with cast from the Oficina de Teatro Expressionista (Projeto Homossexualidades, Associação Brasileira Interdisciplinar de AIDS). Directed by Vagner de Almeida. Teatro Alaska, Rio de Janeiro, 1995. Photograph and artwork by Vagner de Almeida.

the particular skit they wrote and that there would be role rotation on a nightly basis.[24]

During the writing of the skits, the group had to face the issue of humor in AIDS-related theater. There were no models to look to in commercial Brazilian theater. Whereas the mainstream American theater can boast at least one very good AIDS-related comedy—Paul Rudnick's *Jeffrey* (1993),[25] which later became a film by the same title—its Brazilian counterpart has yet to put forth comedies about HIV infection. There may well be comedy manuscripts waiting to be staged and or published, but it seems that in Brazil, as in most places, imposing a comedic treatment on HIV infection constitutes a formidable challenge, one more likely to be taken up by groups outside the commercial theater (such as OTE and Teatro Vida). Still, it is surprising that the almost surreal indignities that can bedevil AIDS patients in Brazil have not spurred some kind of absurdist comedy or that in the subaltern context of Brazilian society an AIDS comedy is still viewed as too jarring.[26] For humor is a key element in the human psyche, exists as an important survival strategy, and plays a major role in the collective life of a nation predicated on transgression and carnivalization. Rather than deter OTE, the lack of AIDS comedy in Brazil encouraged their creation of original humor for *Cabaret Prevenção*. With the belief that the juxtaposition of pathos and comedy accurately reflects life for a number of people with AIDS in Brazil and that ultimately the humor underscores the devastation, OTE members created two original scenes, "Meu Corpo Nu" (My naked body) and "Meu Pau, Meu Cu" (My dick, my ass), the former a hilarious look at our overcritical attitude toward our bodies, the latter an ingenious defamiliarization of sexual activity by means of a lighthearted dialogue between those parts of the male anatomy. Because they were drawing mostly from their own life experiences, the scriptwriters could extend the range of representation beyond the stereotypical.

Cabaret Prevenção turned out to be an ample event, encompassing related activities such as the video production and even the party celebrating the success of the show. It became an integral part of the effort aimed at community education, mobilization, and AIDS awareness; for example, at the door playgoers were handed, in addition to the playbill, educational materials, brochures, and condoms. To a large extent, *Cabaret Prevenção* was so successful because its medium of choice, the theater (and other performance genres such as *carnaval*) have had a long history of close association with the gay subculture in Brazil (Almeida 1996: 7). As Almeida writes in his conclusion,

> By situating the question of AIDS awareness within this broader context of cultural production and cultural activism, and drawing on cultural forms which have an important place within the context of the gay subculture, the Expressionist Theatre Workshop and the production of *Cabaret Prevenção* were thus able to build upon already existing structures of meaning in order to mobilize community awareness and action in response to the HIV/AIDS epidemic. (7)

As a theater group made up of individuals who were previously deprived of political consciousness and an expressive voice to protest their oppression, OTE could do the kind of work that shows how "groups outside the social mainstream often use art to explore social power in ways that those already possessing it apparently don't need to" (Grover 1986: 29). Working from society's margins and speaking with the voice of the endangered outsider, OTE shares many of the strengths and liabilities Alexandra Juhasz (1995: 228) examines in her work on alternative video; like their television counterparts, OTE participants "may lack professional training, massive funds, full-time attention to their artwork, or often even an adequate sense of self-worth. Yet these very weaknesses are [their] strength. Speaking to specific publics about specific goals, alternative [groups] bridge the gaps between producer and spectator, viewer and viewee, addressing them not as a purchasing public but as an engaged and articulate community."

The Allegorical Paradigm: Luís Alberto de Abreu's Book of Job

The theatrical representations identified in this paradigm investigate meanings that tend to become apparent only with careful scrutiny. Spanning a wide range of emotions and ideas, these allegorical explorations of punishment, contamination, powerlessness, and, sometimes, relief through death prove gripping. The best among them may offer very little in the way of solace but on the other hand will—as does Luis Alberto de Abreu's questioning of stoicism—reward the spectator with a new understanding of great suffering and irreparable loss.

A strong, very talented voice in contemporary Brazilian drama and one at ease in mainstream as well as noncommercial theater, Luis Alberto de Abreu (b. 1947) is the author of a number of successful plays, including the award-winning *Bella, Ciao* (1982). Abreu has been involved with some of the most original groups in contemporary Brazilian theater, including

Teatro da Vertigem and Núcleo dos 10. In addition, he is a principal player in the Projeto de Comédia Popular Brasileira and a respected teacher of free workshops for aspiring playwrights offered at the Teatro de Arena in downtown São Paulo, a stage with profound resonance in the history of Brazilian theater.

The crowning moment so far in Abreu's career is undoubtedly his collaboration with director Antônio Araújo (b. 1967) and the group Teatro da Vertigem for the staging of Abreu's adaptation of *O livro de Jó*. A young, highly original ensemble based in São Paulo, Teatro da Vertigem is strong in research and experimentation. Its members have solid backgrounds in music, dance, and acting. Founded in 1991, the group dedicated its first year of existence to the study of basic principles of physics, particularly the realm of mechanics, and their application to the human body in actors' gestures and movements. Their research created a repertory for body training and consciousness and enabled the group to present a series of innovative works staged in unconventional locations, including the critically acclaimed *O paraíso perdido* [1992; Paradise Lost] which ran for eight months in the Church of Saint Iphigenia in São Paulo, and of the work at hand, *O livro de Jó* (1995), staged in a hospital, also in São Paulo (*O livro de Jó* Playbill 1995: 11).

Luís Inácio Stadelmann's Portuguese translation of the Book of Job[27] (from the Jerusalem Bible) was the text from which Abreu selected and adapted the key passages that eventually made up the playscript. Metaphors and allusions relating to previous epidemics proving unsatisfactory,[28] biblical allegory seemed the right choice for a playwright with a strong interest in myth. For Abreu, the theatrical exploration of myth involves several stages, beginning with a careful study of a myth's identity, structure, and trajectory into the borrowing culture; if the mythical figure, as in the case of Job, has a religious significance, the figure must be extracted from such a context before it can fit into the new, dramatic configuration (telephone interview). In the text he wrote for the playbill, Abreu expounds on the particular problems posed by casting myth as hero. Drawing a distinction between the "wise mythic hero" (like Elijah, Buddha, and Oedipus at Colonus) and the "blind hero" (such as Coriolanus and Oedipus at Thebes), Abreu places Job among the former, and continues:

> A hero's character determines his course. The blind hero takes his sword and follows the warrior path, until his action leads to excess, exorbitance,

> "hubris" and, therefore, the tragic end. The wise hero refuses the warrior path, thus avoiding error and misfortune but, on the other hand, missing out on crucial dramatic elements. As opposed to the blind hero's active and external journey, the wise hero follows a course of inner struggle, in which he avoids temptations, [examples being] Christ in the desert, Buddha under the tree of Life, and Job . . . refusing his wife's pleas for an all-out battle with God. (*O livro de Jó* Playbill 1995: 7)[29]

Highlighting the dramatic contours of a hero whose actions preempt conflict was therefore a major challenge, one which Abreu met by modifying the role of Job's wife, giving her considerably more visibility while at the same time reducing that of Job's three friends, Eliphaz, Bildad, and Zophar. In Abreu's text, Job's wife is far from the almost irrelevant individual seen in the biblical text, appearing instead as a resolute instigator of resistance, a de facto antagonist in fierce combat with her husband's resignation. As Abreu puts it, "Job's wife, like a blind hero, lifts up the sword that Job refuses to brandish and starts a battle as legitimate and grandiose as that of the protagonist's" (7).

Another major challenge faced by Abreu and director Antônio Araújo was that of extracting the mythical element from its religious casing. As already mentioned, Abreu considers this a crucial step in the theatrical use of myth. Here, the textual adaptation involved the editing out of theatrically inappropriate, though very beautiful, devotional language. In Abreu's explanation,

> Notwithstanding the current surge in mysticism, I consider theater to be essentially a profane activity, derived but disconnected from religious rites, the offspring of a secular and democratic Greek culture. Therefore, in the Book of Job, I was more interested in the mythic hero, in the human and dramatic story, than in the sacred one. If religious books bring us divine revelation, let theater bring us human revelation, as it always has. (7)

Other, related choices made in order to achieve that goal include omitting Job's return to prosperity and stressing his trials and tribulations as well as his unyielding resistance to rebellion even in the face of unbearable suffering.

Abreu says that in selecting biblical passages for the dramatic text he did not have to worry too much about finding passages that were relevant or appropriate as comments on AIDS, so clear are the parallels between Job's condition, the AIDS situation, and the human predicament of having to face the incurable, fate, or the end of life. The transparent similarities also made superfluous the explicit mention of AIDS in the play (telephone interview).

The verbal matrix itself was determined by the staging conceptualization provided by the director, whose close collaboration with the playwright was essential for the project. Brilliantly created and directed by Araújo, the performance took place in a derelict hospital (Hospital Umberto Primo) in São Paulo in early 1995.[30] This occasionally devastating, often brutal theatrical plunge into the heart of sorrow vehemently disproves Joel Shatzky's suggestion (1992: 134) that plays that treat AIDS symbolically are less electrifying than are realistic, direct works such as *The Normal Heart.* The audience, reaching the maximum of sixty people per show in the performance I attended (25 August 1996), was mesmerized, with some spectators sobbing and at least one person fainting—apparently a common response since the earliest performances and the reason why the production team sought special training in first aid (Cláudio 1995: 84–85). Following the cast almost procession-style through the darkened, mostly empty spaces of the enormous building, through reception areas, wards, operating rooms, hallways and stairways, the audience is bonded in empathy and awe. The atmosphere is aided by the striking use of indirect lighting, with the spot located at the end of a long corridor, for example, or behind glass windows, or barely visible through a half-open door. Subtle changes in lighting source and the occasional use of filters contribute to the creation of an atmosphere of dream turned nightmare.

As in *A mancha roxa, Os desgraçados* and other AIDS plays, the disease is never mentioned explicitly in *O livro de Jó.*[31] By revisiting Job's plight at some undefined time in the past, Abreu's work evades the issue of naming the disease and thus evades the fury of critics like James W. Jones (1993: 228–29) who maintains that "not naming AIDS becomes merely another capitulation to the signification a homophobic culture has already ascribed to AIDS," an action he believes will only reinforce the equation "Homosexuality = AIDS = Death" and "push the disease to the edge of fiction." The validity of Jones's point is limited at best to works portraying the experience of gay males living in the present or recent past, and even so a case can be made for the rich signation and esthetic value of this language of indirection. In the Brazilian theater, the forcefulness of suggestion and allegory has been solidly affirmed by Abreu's deeply moving rendition of *O livro de Jó.*

The unnamed condition, however, pervades the staging, with the piece performed in a hospital and the inescapable presence of blood.[32] In his reflections on the performance, Araújo explains his choice of place for the staging of *O livro de Jó*: "A hospital [is] the place 'par excellence' of pathos, of suffering, of the imminence of death. It is a kind of taboo-place, where we confine death, and [where we are] confront[ed] with death. Whence the fear and unease associated with it (*O livro do Jó* Playbill 1995: 8). For him, the choice of location is determined by the issues to which he is giving theatrical form, hence his controversial decision to present his theatrical exploration of *Paradise Lost* in a Catholic church. Araújo explains further in the playbill,

> When we take an audience to a place which has a certain emotional register and a special significance, we want this place to modify, interfere with, and contribute to the audience's understanding of the play. We could say that our choice of non-conventional locations has to do with an intervention in the audience's perceptions and not with architectural research or "space aesthetics." This intervention reaches beyond the audience, becoming an intervention which is social, an interference in institutions. (8)

Reflecting on the decisions to juxtapose the current epidemic with the story of Job and to stage the play in a hospital, Araújo touches on several issues shared by different societies worldwide: "We daily confront this imminence of contagion, which has so deeply changed the way we express our sexuality. No one is immune to it, and our imagination is haunted by the agony of terminal patients" (8). Perhaps nothing in this performance leaves a longer lasting impression on the spectator than the pervasiveness of blood.[33] Thanks to its omnipresence in the play, AIDS is not a "hidden meaning" but rather an "absent presence" throughout the show (Román and Sandoval 1995: 564). For most humans, the sight of blood is a tantalizing and, at the same time, frightening experience, a simultaneous reminder of the essence of life and the certainty of death. In the time of AIDS, blood has taken on the additional meanings of risk, danger, and even terror. When our way of life is under severe threat, when the world around us experiences a grave crisis, as in times of war and plague, art tends to revert to archetypal images such as fire and blood. The tension of opposites associated with blood—the tension between living and dying—no longer maintains its former equilibrium. The new context created by AIDS has forever changed the way people react to blood.

By giving blood such an intense presence in the staging, Araújo seeks to decouple the fear of contagion from the fear of individuals. In a tour-de-force as Job, Matheus Nachtergaele[34] is naked for most of the seventy-minute performance soaked in a bloodlike liquid (far more convincing than traditional stage blood). Because of their close proximity to the actors, including the blood-dripping Nachtergaele (who at one point plunges into a tank full of the bloodlike substance, a mixture that includes liquid Vaseline, surgical detergent and color additives), the audience is challenged to rethink their fear of contagion. Confronted with the ugliness of Job's condition, the spectator is reminded of the thread that connects him to those who suffer.

Staged in the shadow of a fatal disease, one loaded with social and political nuances, the story of Job poses new questions about such time-tested concepts as allegory and catharsis. To quote Douglas Crimp's by now classic statement (1988: 3), "AIDS does not exist apart from the practices that conceptualize it, represent it, respond to it. We know AIDS only in and through these practices"; allegorizing AIDS poses some problems,

Matheus Nachtergaele as Jó is immersed in blood in Luis Alberto de Abreu's re-telling of *O livro de Jó*. Directed by Antônio Araújo. Teatro da Vertigem. Hospital Umberto Primo, São Paulo, 1995. Photograph by João Caldas. Arquivo Multimeios/Divisão de Pesquisas. Centro Cultural São Paulo.

the most pressing of which is that of defining AIDS as something "radically *other* in crucial ways: a disease of *others*, and a disease that is *something other*, that must be understood by means of figures, extended tropes, free-playing semiosis—something to be looked at, examined from a distance, a *spectacle* of representation" (Morrison 1992: 171). Although, as theater, it cannot evade its essential spectacle-ness, *O livro de Jó* helps to mitigate the marginalization of AIDS by reducing to a minimum the distance between spectator and actor/character, between "us" and "them," and in so doing, invests the spectator with clear responsibilities in the receptive and interpretative processes. For, as David Román and Alberto Sandoval (1995: 562) put it,

> The allegory of AIDS functions in relationship to the politics of representation and reception in the contemporary theater. The spectator's allegorical interpretation is not limited to personal awareness of the allegory or to speculation about the authors' intentions. In the process of encoding and decoding the allegory of AIDS, the spectator intervenes in the cultural imaginary and its discursive representation of AIDS.

The issues are no less engaging when one turns to the nature of catharsis. In the swirling vortex of emotion that is *O livro de Jó*, what does catharsis consist of? Because Job loses virtually everything, he is assured of the audience's empathy, the experience of loss effecting perhaps the strongest form of empathy human beings can feel. Because he is afflicted with a horrible, contagious disease that is going to deprive him of his life, we cannot help but empathize with him, as we know that death awaits us all. But we do not want to be like him nor do we want to suffer like him. In fact, most of us know we will not suffer as much as Job or die in the same manner he will. Still, we empathize with him because we like to believe our suffering is as intense as anyone else's. What is more, our knowledge of the biblical story tells us that only conformity and unwillingness to question God's designs will save Job, and thus his struggle is in vain, destined to fail to overcome his troubles, and it may even be related to the seriousness of his condition. Finally, because Abreu and Araújo's reading of the story of Job virtually dismisses the role of the devil (it was he, after all, who dared God to test Job), it both negates any association of demonic forces with the disease and thereby eliminates a key cause or origin for the agony. Can catharsis obtain in such an extreme case of suffering, when there is no sign of relief, no hope for a reversal in fortune? Can we leave the theater cleansed of emotion when there has been no relief from suffering or even a clear cause for it? Is this really the essence of tragedy, when a good person who, through no moral choice of his own, faces a stern design he cannot change or understand and is caught in a sequence of events that will only stop with death? Such then is the power of AIDS—with its absurdity and its polarization, its stigmatization and its effacement—that it succeeds even in displacing long-established theatrical assumptions and adding new facets to, if not rendering totally moot, the most difficult of theological problems—why God allows a good person to suffer.

Abreu writes forceful plays and his characters shine with an incandescence rare in contemporary Brazilian theater. In *O livro de Jó* he tackles some very big ideas, which can be read in political, existential, spiritual, and other ways. AIDS is not too far from the thoughts of those who watch this gripping allegory about society's brutal contempt for difference. Abreu's recoding of the story of Job in light of this semiotically complex epidemic has been greatly aided by Antônio Araújo's superb stage direction, winning as a result the acclaim of critics and audiences alike. Their production of *O livro de Jó*, to borrow from John Lahr's review (qtd. in Baker 1994: 215) of the Los Angeles staging of *Angels in America*, is a victory "for theater, for the transforming power of the imagination to turn devastation into beauty."

The Evocative Paradigm: Gabriel Villela's staging of Alcides Nogueira's *Ventania*

How people organize their inner experiences regarding HIV and AIDS has also been given theatrical representation in Brazil through what I call the evocative paradigm. Plays in this category are laden with mental depictions and lyrical recollections of other places and times. Particular qualities are evoked as a character or group of characters longs for a sense of belonging, of being loved. Though seldom achieved, personal and/or spiritual growth becomes an impetus to make peace with a time of lost innocence and fewer certainties.

Alcides Nogueira's 1996 play, *Ventania*, is an homage to playwright Zé Vicente, who in the early 1980s withdrew from the theater scene at the peak of his career, following a renewed religiosity and persistent problems with the censorship of the military regime. As chapter 3 shows, before going into seclusion, Zé Vicente wrote plays that left an indelible mark on an entire generation, foremost among them *Hoje é dia de rock* (1971), a poignant look at a young poet's coming of age in small-town Brazil. Seen by many as nothing but paeans to a largely imported culture of rock, drugs, and free sex, most of Vicente's plays are in fact lyrical evocations of an Edenic time and place about to disappear.

The loss of innocence that is thematically central to Vicente's theater served therefore as a starting point for Nogueira's exploration of sex and risk in the 1990s. In revisiting the 1960s and 1970s through the lens of the mid 1990s, Nogueira attempted to evoke a strong, magical sense of liberation unknown to the generation that grew up with the specter of AIDS. Written at a time of extreme political repression in Brazil, Vicente's plays provided Nogueira with a kind of parallel on which to build his reaction to the present crisis.

Gabriel Villela's staging of *Ventania*, for which he was awarded the 1996 Mambembe Prize for Best Director, echoes Vicente's small-town atmospheres (Ventania, or high wind, is the nickname for Vicente's hometown, tiny Alpinópolis, in the state of Minas Gerais). Lyrical and dreamlike at times, crude and violent at others, Villela's staging is deeply influenced by the traditional *mineiro* culture in which both he and Vicente grew up, a patriarchal society pervaded by conservative Catholicism, bourgeois morality, and sexual repression. Villela's direction of *Ventania* also shows the stylistic influence of Grupo Galpão, with which he worked for several years before undertaking new projects and an independent directing career.

The characters show a blend of naiveté, conformity, and the desire to escape boring, oppressive Ventania. The protagonists—two brothers, Zé and Vicente (echoing Victor and Hugo, in Vicente's gritty two-character play, *O assalto*, studied in chapter 3)—differ in attitude and ambitions. Zé, played by Davi Taiu, is a "child of the Sun" and searches for transcendence through mysticism while Vicente, played by Eriberto Leão, is a "child of the Night" who undergoes a tortured inner quest fueled by drugs. Their contrast is one of several dichotomies in a play characterized by the convergence of sacred and profane elements (signified visually in the set, a church bazaar or kermis where a number of transgressive acts occur). Vicente, in spite of frequent conflicts with Zé, cannot live without his brother, a reflection of the playwright's alleged inability to reconcile compelling forces pulling him in different directions—reality and imagination, urban living and rural upbringing, among others. The brothers' difficulties and their family's travails are narrated by a satyr named Deusa de Chifon (played with gusto and intense sensuality by Rogério Romera), who is also endowed with the power to create a "ventania" (high wind) symbolic of change and disruption. Zé and Vicente's sister Luzia (played by Sílvia Buarque), blind and craving love and sex, is seduced by the satyr. After the graphic seduction scene she rejects her previous well-behaved, pious demeanor and becomes a child of the Night. Shedding her modest garments, Luzia adopts a hippie wardrobe (most of the costumes for the play were purchased in London's Carnaby Street shops specializing in authentic clothes from the 1960s) and appears nude for much of the performance, as do other members of the cast.

Luzia is an amalgamation of two characters in *Hoje é dia de rock*, blind Rosário and Isabel, whose life is driven by fantasy and an all-consuming aspiration to be a modern girl, a participant in an era alien to her community and culture. To the distrust with which Vicente approaches modernity Nogueira has added a layer of sarcasm tempered with a campy sensitivity. As in Zé Vicente's plays, the soundtrack and live singing are crucial in establishing a firm sense of time and place in *Ventania*. The inspired choice of music (American rock, together with Brazilian waltzes, folk songs, and sentimental ballads) anchors the mixing of myths and icons of the 1960s and 1970s (Elvis Presley and Jim Morrison) with those of the 1990s, but more than a dash of sarcasm is behind the choice of icon used to represent present day music (George Michael, played by Alexandre Schumacher with the right amount of tongue in cheek).[35]

In Luzia's character several traits converge to contribute to the play's denunciation of Catholicism: her being named after the patron saint of vision is one of many ironies in the play, while the comments of family members point to prejudices and hypocrisy regarding blind people and sexuality. The treatment of Catholicism is most ferocious, however, in the character of the grandmother, who moans and cries for much of the play as her dead daughter (played by Malu Valle), the mother of Zé, Vicente, and Luzia, exposes the old woman's wickedness. Played in drag by Lourival Prudêncio in a hilarious performance, the falsely pious grandmother reveals the excesses and absurdities of dogmatic, ossified religion.

As in *O livro de Jó*, the abundant use of blood on stage assures an "absent presence" rather than a "hidden meaning" for AIDS in *Ventania*; highlighting the strong AIDS subtext, the presence of blood is echoed in the intense use of the color red in the sets and wardrobe. As the conveyor of risk and death, the satyr either occasions the appearance of blood or salutes its occurrence. He is crucial in Villela's deconstruction of the role of blood as the foundation upon which traditional Catholicism creates its iconography and ritualization. As Villela explains, AIDS marks a cultural watershed worldwide—the momentous change in the meaning of blood, from a symbol of redemption to a vehicle for condemnation. Hence, within the dynamics of the play, the considerable use of blood comes to signify that communion in blood is no longer a path to grace and that the sharing of blood leads to damnation rather than salvation. According to Villela, it is the exposure to blood, and not the nudity, sex, and drugs, that leads some spectators to walk out in the middle of the performance. Unable to bear the new "truth," they reject the spectacle in what Villela describes as an "act of cowardice" ("Villela é aplaudido" 1997). Realization of the fact that they are not immune to the new state of affairs is too much for them to handle and so they flee. Thus, in decoding the allegory of AIDS in *Ventania*, and most likely in general, these spectators evade a fundamental responsibility and choose the smugness of a system of exclusion over the responsibilities of empathy and intervention.

The Postmodern Paradigm: The Theater of Caio Fernando Abreu

The last of the paradigms I have identified in the theatrical representation of HIV and AIDS in Brazil is connected with a postmodern sensibility of ambiguity, instability, and rupture. This kind of theater is not interested in minimizing trauma or presenting definitive answers. It does not provide solace nor does it seek catharsis. It focuses instead on urban young men living with dissidence and all manner of uncertainty and disjunction. For these individuals, as represented here in the works of Caio Fernando Abreu, performance pervades identity, and affirmation is to be found in fleeting liaisons. In a paradoxical way, as the following paragraphs attempt to show, the defiant transgressiveness exhibited by Dana Avalon and other Caio characters illustrates the Jamesonian interest in finding a strategy for political expression in the postmodern at the same time that these characters' dispersal of the subject, meaning, and discursive language would hardly seem to provide any grounding for an engaged art or for resistant, critical operations.

As chapter 3 has suggested, among the compelling evidence of a nascent homosexual-themed theater in Brazil are of course, the visibility and contributions of a number of openly gay actors, directors, and playwrights. Among playwrights, the work of Caio Fernando Abreu stands out, its relevance continuing to increase after his death. In the year following his demise, no less than three of his plays were staged in Rio de Janeiro alone.

The first anniversary of his untimely death (of AIDS-related causes) was commemorated with the long-awaited publication of his complete theater (Abreu 1997) and a mixed media performance that included dramatized readings of his texts and live performances of some of his musical favorites.[36]

Following the confirmation of his AIDS diagnosis in August of 1994, Caio moved back to Porto Alegre to be close to his family and numerous friends. There he set out to organize his files and his literary estate, finishing some manuscripts while revising and, in some cases, rewriting a number of previously published works. He also continued to contribute weekly "*crônicas*"[37] to prominent dailies such as *O Estado de São Paulo.* In a number of these pieces, Caio turns a staple of Luso-Brazilian letters into a vehicle for the dramatization of his condition. His experiences and feelings as a person with AIDS are presented in a variety of moods ranging from candor and resignation to anger and sarcasm. In "Mock Heroics and Personal Markings," a guest column written for *PMLA*, Sylvia Molloy (1996: 1073) writes about how the intrusion of the first person into personal scholarship "makes a scene of its own." Molloy considers using terms like "effect" or "pose" but deems them loaded with negative connotations of dishonesty and fraud and finally opts to speak of this intrusion of the personal as a calculated act—as, indeed, a performance. Although outside the sphere of "personal" scholarship with which Molloy concerns herself, the "*crônica,*" with its first person perspective (and, sometimes, bias) likewise finds itself the locus of intrusions that "make a scene of [their] own." Even within this supposed realm of the entirely subjective that is a "*crônica*" there is a dramatization, a kind of imagined staging, a shaping of everyday life into theatrical patterns.[38] Caio excels in embracing the role of dramatist while adhering all along to the conventions of the "*crônica.*" In addition, there is the underlying assumption that his readership believes that the personal writings of a dying person are genuine and sincere. Known primarily as a gifted writer of cutting-edge narratives[39] and a pioneer in the literary depiction of AIDS in Brazil,[40] Caio nonetheless had a life-long interest in the theater and left several complete plays and a few incomplete dramatic texts; at one point early in his career he even tried his hand at acting. In addition, his narratives often have a dramatic quality about them, which enables an easy transition to the stage.

The titles listed below are his dramatic texts included in *Teatro completo.* "Pode ser que seja só o carteiro lá fora" (Maybe it's only the postman out there) was the first of Caio's plays; written in 1976, it won an award from the Serviço Nacional do Teatro (National Theater Institute) but was banned by the government censors and could not be staged until 1983, in a production directed by Chico Medeiros. "A Comunidade do Arco-Iris" (The rainbow community) was his only children's play. "Zona contaminada" (Contaminated zone), his penultimate play, offers a dark vision of nuclear catastrophe. "Cenas avulsas" (Assorted scenes) is a compilation of five short scenes, brief dialogs, and drama exercises that Caio called "Diálogos." "Sarau das 9 às 11" (The 9 to 11 P.M. soirée) and "A maldição do Vale Negro" (The curse of the black valley) were both coauthored with his close friend, the theater director and drama professor Luiz Arthur Nunes; the former title is a series of independent skits and the latter a parody of nineteenth-century melodrama, for which Caio and Luiz Arthur won a Molière Award in 1988.[41] "Reunião de família" (Family reunion) is Caio's stage adaptation of Lya Luft's novel of the same title. Finally, "O homem e a mancha" (The man and the skin lesion) is the only one of the three texts by Caio produced in Rio's 1996–97 season that is included in his complete plays and the only one that had never been staged before.[42]

The first production of *O homem e a mancha*, the last of Caio's texts written for the theater, opened in January 1997 at Casa da Gávea in Rio de Janeiro, starring Marcos Breda and directed by Luiz Arthur Nunes. It had had a brief run in November 1996 at Porto Alegre's Teatro São Pedro, and Caio himself had done three readings of his text in 1994, one private (at the residence of actor Carlos Moreno, who had commissioned the work) and the other two for the public, also in Porto Alegre (Nunes 1997: 8–9).

The title echoes that of the Brazilian version of the Dale Wasserman-Mitch Leigh-Joe Darion musical, *Man of La Mancha, O homem de La Mancha.*[43] More importantly, it toys with the term, *"mancha."* As in Plínio Marcos's play examined above, several levels of signification (stain, taint, skin lesion, etc; see note 8, this chapter) exist and interact in the title, as does (when capitalized) the direct reference to the area of Spain where Don Quijote lived. Matching the polyvalence of the second noun (*"mancha"*) in the phrase are the various manifestations—seen as characters in the play—of the first term, *"homem."* Equally revealing is the choice of preposition linking the two halves; as opposed to *"da"* or *"com,"*[44] *"e"* points to this man (or man in general) and his being vis-à-vis this, or any, *"mancha"*: his reaction to it, his attitude toward it, his existence in light of it.

Disparate in appearance only, the five characters are in fact connected insofar as all five are lost, confused, and have succumbed to an illusion—an actor who has lost his ability to perform and is now apparently losing his mind as well; a lonely, retired petty official who plans to withdraw from the world, and almost succeeds; a man tormented by the strange skin lesions he may or may not have; and two versions, one younger and the other moribund, of the Knight of the Sad Countenance.

A very gifted actor, Breda moves comfortably across mood ranges and displays an exquisite sense of timing.[45] He also brings a masterly comic flair to the performance, playing some scenes (particularly those involving the younger Quijote) with comic zeal and others (when the focus is on the retiree, for instance) with an edge that recalls the neurotic comedy of Woody Allen. Switching, sometimes abruptly, from one persona to another, and breaking into diverse characters with peculiar accents and quirks adds to the already formidable challenges of the long monologue. Echoing Caio's own description of the creation of the five embodiments (Abreu 1996b: 4), Breda refers to his splitting into the different personae as a performative correlate of Russian dolls, culminating with a sort of joint appearance of the five toward the end of the play (personal interview).

The multiple manifestations would seem to suggest not a splintered personality but rather what Alberto Sandoval, writing about a different context, calls "identity formations of subjectivities-in-process." As Sandoval puts it, this process is made possible by AIDS, which functions as "the factor that pushes individuals to forge hybrid identities which are multiple, porous, and heterogeneous" (1994: 63–64). Still, the inability shared by the five to escape delusional processes prevents them from finding contentment, and when they do supplant their obsessions and reach a state of serenity, death emerges to snatch old Quijote, thus ending the play. Writing *O homem e a mancha* as his last dramatic text, Caio reflects on defining traits of his personality (such as the incapacity to deal with a pedestrian routine) and, given his frequent association with the Quijote figure, adds a thinly veiled reference to his own death. Quijote, who dreamed of fashioning the world around his illusion and only found rest in death, seems to be directing his likeness—Caio—toward acceptance and peace.

Subtitled "Livre releitura do *Dom Quixote*, de Miguel de Cervantes" (A loose interpretation of Miguel de Cervantes's *Don Quijote*), the play is dedicated to the memory of Clarice Lispector, the author who exerted a profound influence on Caio's early writing and who first established the link between Caio and the Quijote figure.[46] Although Don Quijote is the organizing figure in the play, the center of reference is the "*mancha*" and its implications—hence the importance of the character who is tormented by it. His dread of the "*mancha*" paralyzes him and in fact does him more harm than any actual disease; as a consequence of his fear he is isolated, as are the other personae, loneliness being a central theme in Caio's writings. Breda confesses that his construction of this one role was particularly difficult and emotionally draining, since he utilized his recollections of his friend Caio's physical deterioration and mood swings (personal interview).

Despite the clear allusions and even direct references to AIDS (to give but one example, the man's panic when he realizes his "*mancha*" might be purple [Abreu 1997: 103]), "*mancha*" is not, as Luiz Arthur Nunes stresses, a univocal sign; much broader and abstract, its meaning might encompass guilt, fate, the human condition. Trying desperately to look destiny in the eye, the man knows he must confront his demons just as Don Quijote faced his enemies, real and imagined. Not until he comes to terms with the "*mancha*" and makes peace with death will he be free (personal interview).

Still, even the most somber scenes are tempered with comedy; Caio's caustic humor always manages to intrude during the gloomiest moments of his theater and fiction. Remarking on the audience response to *O homem e a mancha* during the two public readings, the playwright shed light on his approach to the delicate balance of pathos and humor. Having his Quijote allude to film makers Pedro Almodóvar and Bigas Luna and singers Sarita Montiel and Marisol places emphasis on a campy sensitivity and creates a universe that, while still terrible, is fun, derivative, ironic, and very much of our time (Abreu 1996b: 4).

Despite Quijote's death, the play ends on a happy note, as the actor awakens from decline and gloom and looks forward to dedicating his regained vitality to new projects. The symmetry in the unfolding and subsequent "refolding" of the characters points to Caio's beliefs in cycles and esoteric philosophy, and the optimistic conclusion is related to his belief that the fifteen-year period begun in 1981 was drawing to a close (M. Breda, interview). For many, this was a calamitous time that included reactionary politics, capitalism's defeat of socialism, the intense backlash against women and racial and sexual minorities, and, above all, the onset of AIDS. In astrological patterns, the cycle corresponded to Pluto's transit in Scorpio (Pluto, an archetype of destruction, rules death and the most grievous situations); it ended as Sagitarius took over in 1996, the year that saw the introduction of protease inhibitors and other effective AIDS drugs responsible for a renewed hope for a cure. In considering the conclusion to *O homem e a mancha*, one must be aware of Caio's belief that he might live to see a cure for AIDS, if only he could stay well a little longer. And, in a broader sense, regardless of one's attitude to astrology and esotericism, it is important to take such beliefs into account because that was the perspective from which Caio saw the world, life, and his illness.

Dama da noite has been researched, directed, and performed so intensely by Gilberto Gawronski that contemporary Brazilian theater connoisseurs are hard put to dissociate the individual from the play. An actor, director, and theater professor at Centro das Artes de Laranjeiras in Rio de Janeiro, Gawronski has vast stage experience, which, coupled with his close friendship with Caio, has served him well in his performances of the late dramatist's plays.

In addition to his work with *Dama da noite*, Gawronski directed three other plays by Caio, *Uma história de borboletas* (A butterfly story) in 1990, *Zona contaminada* in 1992 and again in 1998, and *Do outro lado da tarde* (The other side of the afternoon) in 1998–99. *Uma história de borboletas* is the stage adaptation of a text by the same title published originally in Caio's 1977 short story collection, *Pedras de Calcutá* (Stones of Calcutta); this story of a man who witnesses the mental deterioration of a friend was performed by Ricardo Blat, who worked again with Gawronski in his award-winning performance in Koltès's *A solidão nos campos de algodão* in 1996. *Zona contaminada*, written by Caio as a play, premiered in an alternative space, the punk club Crepúsculo de Cubatão in Rio de Janeiro in 1992; the 1998 performance, also directed by Gawronski, was part of the Leituras de Teatro series at the *Folha de São Paulo* lecture hall and featured Elias Andreato, Cassio Scapin, Dionísio Neto, Grace Giannoukas, and Gawronski. The focus here is on two sisters (performed by Scarlet Moon and Ana Maria Magalhães in 1992) who survive a nuclear holocaust and are pursued by a central power represented by a voice offstage (the voice of Fausto Fawcett in the 1992 production). The mysterious force is interested in the women because they are the last two beings on the planet who can conceive embryos uncontaminated by an epidemic never directly identified but assumed to be AIDS. *Do outro lado da tarde*, premiered in October 1998 at the Casa da Gávea and then moved to Casa Laura Alvim, both in Rio de Janeiro, is an adaptation of two short stories, "Para uma avenca partindo" (For a departing fern) and "Do outro lado da tarde," both published in Caio's collection of short fiction *O ovo apunhalado* (1975; The stabbed egg). The adaptation was done by Susana Pires and Maria Maya, the two actresses in this two-character play in which the accounts given by a man (Maria) and a woman (Susana) in alternating monologues suggest a long-distance attempt at a relationship in contemporary Brazil.

Dama da noite has had seven different stagings, all by Gawronski, since its premiere in 1988.[47] Because the nature of the performance demands an alternative space, all productions have stayed away from conventional, commercial theaters. The play was first produced in 1988, in Rio de Janeiro's Crepúsculo de Cubatão and later the same year in São Paulo's Espaço Off. In 1989 it was performed in Porto Alegre's Ponto de Elis and in English at London's Apollo Club. Then it was back to Rio de Janeiro, in 1992 (at Torre de Babel) and 1997 (at the performance space in the basement of Casa Laura Alvim). Gawronski also directed and performed in a French-language version in Lyon in 1996 and presented the English version, titled *Night Flower*, at the Mabou Mines theater in New York in November 1998. Finally, a film version of *Dama da noite*, directed by Mário Diamante and starring Gawronski as Dana, premiered at the 1999 Toronto Film Festival and opened in Brazil in early 2000.

According to Gawronski, the first versions were short and deliberately provoking, as they aimed to emphasize flirting with danger and prohibition (the military regime that ended in 1985 was still vivid in people's minds and the severity of AIDS was by then clear to most in the audience). The later stagings, however, accept and sport humor, albeit of a steely nature, reflecting a change in attitude toward the epidemic, from one of fear and almost panic to a blasé and even risk-prone demeanor.

Gawronski's *tour de force* in the title role entails a good deal of physical discomfort since for the duration of the one-hour performance he must wear stiletto shoes (14-centimeter heels), a heavy black leather jacket, impossibly long eyelashes, and a red wig all but sewn onto his nearly shaved head, while delivering a nonstop monologue and moving about the entire space, sometimes running or climbing on tables, chairs, and stools. He is often busy handling a moveable wheel-like structure while attempting various grueling contortions, possibly meant to recall the moves one has to perform in order to satisfy the demands of the "roda-gigante" (Ferris wheel), the central image in Caio's text.[48]

The monologue is tinged with gender ambiguity since, "as a performative act, [it] relativizes gender categories and points to their constructedness" (Arenas 1999: 16). As deliverer of the monologue, Dana Avalon, the Dama da Noite of the play's title, is assumed to be in total control of the situation and is never challenged by the addressee, her silent interlocutor, an anonymous young man she calls "boy." Still, her delivery begs for his participation, as her existence seems to be validated by the attention he begrudgingly pays her. The youth stands for those whom society allows to ride the Ferris wheel of life, people who hold jobs, have ambitions, and take no risks, for they are terrified of contamination. As Dana sees it, these people seem to have knowledge of a password that allows them access to the wheel and, as a consequence, social acceptance, while she and many others are never given such coded approval and thus live on the margins. The monologue is in essence a statement of Dana's mixed feelings toward the youth (and those he represents) as she expresses her disdain for them at the same time she attempts to wrest some measure of affection from him. She is, as Fernando Arenas (1999: 16–17) has written, "a passionate affirmation of individual values that stand in opposition to hegemonic cultural structures;" however, as a rebel excluded from the wheel, Dana "the subject at the margins," exists "in a fragile location, at the mercy of political, economical, juridical, and epidemiological forces over which s/he has little or no control."

Dana Avalon is a superb embodiment of transgression and subversion, a symbol for the "pós-tudo" (post-everything)[49] days of the late 1980s and 1990s when a perplexed nation found itself free of military rule but haunted by uncertainties and threatened by both a severe economic crisis and a killer epidemic that did not discriminate among its victims, shattering the sexual liberation and social and political gains (modest as they mostly were) achieved by gays in late 1970s Brazil.[50] In the Kristevian sense, Dana is the abject. As such, she must look freakish, alienated, while her behavior must strike most people as aggressive—that's why she touches spectators, pets them, runs her fingers through their hair, and sits on their laps, seductive at times, reproachful at others.

A hybrid, Dana Avalon is a composite of different sexual orientations, a synthesis of genders, possibly a prostitute, and as such could not be performed as just another drag queen. While the latter would not go beyond gender inversion, Dana's impact comes from her actually displacing, instead of only inverting, the gender binary (Dollimore 1991: 312). The actor must thus incorporate male and female behavior, a man acting like a woman who is trying to seduce a man but never attempting to conceal anatomical markers of maleness (deep voice, chest hair, pelvic bulge, etc). This is a tall order for any actor, but Gawronski has mastered the role after many years of familiarity with the play. He is also inspired

Ad for staging of Caio Fernando Abreu's *Dama da noite*, with Gilberto Gawronski as Dana Avalon. Directed by Gilberto Gawronski and Helio Dias. Casa de Cultura Laura Alvim, Rio de Janeiro, 1996. Photographs and artwork by Márcia Ramalho and TCL.

by what he learned from the author with regard to sexuality. Caio believed human beings were multisexual and as such could be or perform whatever facet they chose of their many sexualities; as a result of this thinking Caio rejected the term "homosexual" and with it the idea of a monolithic gay identity. He was particularly incensed by labels such as "gay writer" and "gay literature."

Gawronski suggests that the "queen of the night" is the naked honesty that propels one to go "cruising" in search of the Other, in whatever form (money, leather, brains, pectorals, etc.) it has been idealized in one's mind. This pressing need leads a person to act and dress the way s/he imagines the Other would wish. It also entails considerable risks and the tacit acceptance of such risks—a reflection of Caio's firm rejection of complacency and of his belief that a life without dangers is not worth living. Hence the idea of the celebration of life, a veritable *carpe diem* message, that one senses in Gawronski's interpretation of Dana. For the character must personify the attraction people feel for what she stands for, a potent mixture of fascination and fear. She must whet in people the need to engage in joyous, guilt-free sex while never betraying the fact that her desire for the Other ends the moment she attains her goal.

A more direct and probably simplistic approach to the play would be to see this "queen of the night" not as the lure of risk but as AIDS itself. Explicit mention of the disease was omitted in the earlier stagings of the play because the playwright feared audiences were not ready for the shock. Later, realizing the error in his previous assumption, Caio himself instructed Gilberto to perform the text in its integrity ("Ilusões e sonhos" 1996: 2), but did not allow any other changes, accepting with pride the possible flaws in a work which, as he recalled it, was composed in approximately twelve hours in a feverish state.[51] References to AIDS in *Dama* are direct and unsparing; as she berates the "boy's" cautiousness, Dana lists symptoms, "Caganeira, tosse seca, gânglios generalizados" (Abreu 1988: 94) ("The shits, a dry cough, swellings all over" [Abreu 1990: 84]) that, she assures the young man, eventually will drive him to Emílio Ribas Hospital (alluded to visually in *O livro de Jó*; see note 32, this chapter). Later she identifies herself unequivocally as "*a dama maldita que, sem nenhuma piedade, vai te poluir com todos os líquidos, contaminar teu sangue com todos os vírus. Cuidado comigo: eu sou a dama que mata,* boy" (Abreu 1988: 95) ("the cursed queen who is going to have no mercy and pollute you and infect your blood with every kind of virus. Beware of me—I'm the deadly queen" [Abreu 1990: 84]).

The shift in Dana's identity was accompanied in later versions by a parallel alteration in her presentation, in which the feminine demeanor and attire were dropped and a style combining both genders was adopted instead, thus enhancing the gender ambiguity. As a consequence Dana changed from a lonely woman roaming the city at night in search of company to an aggressive being who rants and raves at people for their blindness and malice. Fully aware of his/her condition as hybrid and simulacrum, Dana Avalon is almost proud of being the child of a harsh, polluted, and violent era. The "dama da noite" is above all, as Arenas has written, "the product of an era besieged by panic over the body, fear of sex and AIDS" (Arenas 1999: 16). In her crude realism, Caio's queen of the night is in the end the negation of the illusion both of those who believe in finding Prince Charming as well as of those who are convinced of their emotional self-sufficiency.

Like *Dama da noite*, *Pela noite* was written as a fictional narrative, having appeared first in *Triângulo das águas* (1983; Water triangle) and later in *Estranhos estrangeiros* (1996; Strange foreigners); unlike *Dama*, however, *Pela noite* has two protagonists, a fully developed plot, and is long enough to qualify as a novella. The stage adaptation was done by Renato Farias, who also directed and acted in the production that opened at Casa da Gávea in Rio de Janeiro in August 1996.[52] It had had a pair of brief runs two years earlier, first in Rio (May 1994) and later in Porto Alegre (September 1994) as part of that city's annual theater festival Porto Alegre em Cena. Caio was feeling well enough to attend the latter production (the only time he saw the play) and was reportedly satisfied with the way his work played out on stage (Ferreira 1996: 4).

The characters are two gay men roaming the São Paulo night in search of company and sex. The game of artifice in which the two are willing participants begins with their agreeing to call themselves Pérsio and Santiago, characters in *Los premios*, a Julio Cortázar novel favored by the former. Santiago (played by Marcelo Assumpção) is a strutting, urbane middle-aged man who thinks he's got life figured out and believes in the feasibility of a stable relationship between two men; Pérsio (played by Renato Farias), on the other hand, a theater critic who wields his scathing sense of humor as a weapon, mocks marital stability, and is able to spot an Achilles' heel in an instant. Two other roles, both minor, are those of a drag queen and a male prostitute, both played by the same actor (Miguel Bellini in the Rio production).

As suggested in the text's subtitle, "Ao som de *Years of Solitude*, de Astor Piazzolla e Gerry Mulligan" (To the Tune of *Years of Solitude*, by Astor Piazzolla and Gerry Mulligan),[53] loneliness, a key figure in Caio's texts, is again central in this story of two men whose paths cross again after many years of estrangement. Farias sensed the dramatic potential in the interaction between the two men as they try to disguise their loneliness and fear of rejection. Juxtaposing the past recollections and present needs of the two men and focusing on their tentative gestures and hesitant overtures, the action softens the mutual resentment and the harshness of the "cruising scene" with a poetic treatment of the late night crowd.

In a personal letter to Renato Farias, Caio asserts his fondness for *Pela noite*, "*uma história sobre dois homossexuais que tentam encontrar a si mesmos e um ao outro, . . . o registro de emoções de dois seres humanos procurando basicamente por valores como ética e dignidade humana*" (letter to Renato Farias, September 1995, reprinted in part in the playbill) (a story of two homosexuals who try to find themselves and one another, . . . a chronicle of the emotions of two human beings in search essentially of values like ethics and human dignity). However, *Pela noite*, novella and play alike, is marred by the obvious Manicheism in the presentation of the men's views on relationships and on life in general. Santiago's seriousness and Pérsio's frivolousness are never sufficiently tempered with other traits of their personalities, a problem aggravated by the circular nature of the action. Ending as it began amid emptiness and solitude, the play emphasizes each man's lack of perspectives; neither has experienced any inner changes, nor can there be any hope either for their own relationship or for any other that they might wish to establish with others, so woefully unprepared are they to commit themselves fully to a life devoid of game playing and deceit.

The allusions to AIDS in *Pela noite* point to Pérsio's and Santiago's struggles as they deal with the crisis in their lives and try to come to terms with the "*grande peste*" (great plague) (Abreu 1996a: 121) that is constantly in the wings—a grim menace hovering above these men's every gesture. Their clipped references to AIDS suggest the inner conflicts. They are fearful of being contaminated but also experience strong resentment at being accused of being vectors of destruction (66) and feel a deep guilt for remaining HIV negative. Santiago, especially, is still grieving four years after his lover Beto's death; unable to fully accept the implications of being a survivor, he has yet to experience the healing phase of bereavement.

If the novella *Pela noite* perhaps lacked the malleability necessary for its transformation into shapely drama and if excessive Manicheism detracts from the work's impact, at least the play succeeds in illuminating the emotional devastation that the specter of AIDS has brought into these lives, and it is ultimately saved by Caio's exuberant dialogues, elastic gift for metaphor, and imaginative sleights-of-hand.

Being less committed to the theater than to the forms (short story and novel) that constitute most of his creative output, Caio Fernando Abreu was therefore freer to give vent to his impatience with drama convention and thus engage in theatrical experimentation. Ever aware of the need to demystify and de-demonize AIDS, Caio believed the disease to be but one of many mosaics of contemporary madness and HIV but one form of human contamination. In addition, he was convinced that the earth is Gaia, a living organism, and human beings its predators. As a consequence, the planet, like its inhabitants, is debilitated, immunologically affected, with the two sides mutually dependent, a point he made in his play, *Zona contaminada*, and, less bluntly, in other works. *O homem e a mancha*, *Pela noite*, and *Dama da noite* are not concerned with documenting the violence or discrimination experienced by people with AIDS or even with the suffering and disruption an AIDS diagnosis brings to a person's life; instead, what these plays reflect is a very general condition or atmosphere prevalent in contemporary society. In this state of affairs, risk outlasts fear, and danger supplants restraint. The stage works he would offer as representations of such a situation could not be but unabashedly ironic and imperfectly derivative simulacra of things they will never resemble: short stories made to conform to the theater—a pathetically anachronistic, mildly deranged man who believed he was the salvation of a defunct genre; a blunt cross-dresser who makes no claim to femininity; and two men pretending they can dodge calamity a while longer.

Closing Remarks

The plays examined in this chapter range from allegorizations to realistic portrayals of AIDS, from commercial productions to community efforts. Still, such is the nature of this disease and the reach of its implications that representations of it tend to defy absolutes. Thus, allegorical treatments will include realist touches, while even the most realist of these plays avoids extreme dramatizations of the experiences of people with

AIDS (like showing in stark realistic detail the final ugliness of a character's death), since such extremism "has the effect of distancing viewers so they cannot discern any common points between the presentation of a dire situation and their own experience" (Berthelot 1993: 306).

In addition, while plays about loss and lament are still being written, they are becoming less frequent; meanwhile, one can note an increase in the number of works that in effect take control of the situation and give positive meaning to AIDS through counterdiscourse. Plays are of course particularly effective in this regard because they are collective at many levels—in production, acting and reception by an audience. In the process, catharsis, empathy and other key dramatic elements are rethought, as the representation of AIDS creates new angles for and poses new challenges to the theatrical event.

Again, because of the nature of the disease and its multilayered connection with subalternity, AIDS theater is inevitably political, even when it ostensibly avoids politics. Never easy to achieve, the balance between art and politics is particularly elusive here, given the immediacy of the crisis.[54] The matter can be complicated further when commercial considerations are added to the picture. Still, at least two of these works, *A mancha roxa* and *Ventania*, achieve that balance. Plays that do so, as Cindy Kistenberg (1995: 49–50) puts it, "make it" in mainstream theaters because they "conform to certain audience expectations without compromising their political agenda." Other works, however, such as Vagner de Almeida's plays, Caio Fernando's *Dama da noite*, and Luis Alberto de Abreu's *O livro de Jó*, bypass the mainstream theaters because these are not venues that foster the kind of debate that in their authors' opinions can lead to social change.

Marcos's play about six women inmates of diverse cultural and ethnic backgrounds gives us some answers and allows us to glimpse some truths behind the denial of AIDS in Brazil; nevertheless, it is unable to depart from the stereotypes surrounding women and AIDS or, in a more general sense, the encompassing oppression in Brazil. Since Marcos's play first appeared, others have taken the disease and those it affects in Brazil as their subject matter. Different approaches have been taken, some of which seem more suitable to represent the experience of difference in a time of crisis.

One such approach is that favored by Vagner de Almeida. His plays give dramatic voice to the compelling social problems that have arisen with the spread of the HIV virus in Brazil. His contributions, both in the AIDS trilogy as well as in his work with the Oficina de Teatro Expressionista para Homens que Fazem Sexo com Homens, illustrate how well the theater attains an educational objective in the fight against AIDS without in the process losing its intellectual purposefulness or artistic integrity.

With a raised consciousness and rejecting models of education that do not take into account cultural specificity, the ensemble of the Oficina de Teatro Expressionista has acquired a new voice and a means to represent and confront oppression. In *Cabaret Prevenção*, sincere spontaneity and the reduced distance between real life and represented experience bespeak a pedagogical focus. Ephemeral as they may be, this and other related efforts question Susan Sontag's claim in *AIDS and its Metaphors* that one cannot give positive meaning to AIDS. For, with its insistence that laughter must be a part of the overall representation, OTE subverts prevailing notions about AIDS theater as a somber expression of rage and remembrance and, through its refusal to muffle humor in the theatrical event, humanizes the picture of the epidemic in Brazil.

Luis Alberto de Abreu's *O livro de Jó* is an allegorization of the ways disease and suffering have been constructed and an exposition of how they are conflated in complex metaphorical ways, processes bolstered by the strikingly compressed images conceived by stage director Antônio Araújo. In the end, however, metaphysical inquiries give way to those considerations related to the survival of an individual and a group. Taken by unrelenting grief, Job rants and rebels. His inability to accept his adversity resists the greater implications of guilt and isolation associated with difference and AIDS in late-twentieth-century Brazil.

By combining his theatrical experimentation with his interest in the representation of AIDS in plays such as *O homem e a mancha*, and by composing narratives that lend themselves to rich explorations in stage versions directed by such talents as Gilberto Gawronski in *Dama da noite* and Renato Farias in *Pela noite*, Caio Fernando Abreu has made a substantial contribution to contemporary Brazilian theater. A writer with a lifelong interest in the idea of contamination, Caio examined the issue of AIDS in a more direct fashion only in the late 1980s and first half of the 1990s. By then, Caio, the educated individual and tireless world traveler, could approach the epidemic without the awe or gloom of the first treatments it elicited and thus was able to produce innovative drama informed by mordant irony and satire.

Created in response to conditions vastly different from those existing in societies fortunate enough to witness the auspicious scientific advances seen in the late 1990s, the plays examined above are remarkable artistic responses to the grave social and political concerns of a less economically privileged part of the world. In addition to their intrinsic aesthetic dimension, they are worthy of attention for having attempted to let the subaltern speak, thus raising deeply disturbing questions that otherwise might have been left unvoiced. For, if art is in many ways a result of our attempts to find a way to live with dying, and if for the true theater artist his or her craft is a matter of life and death, the AIDS crisis functions as an encapsulation, a concentration, an exacerbation of that urgent need to comprehend death and mortality. That these works rank among the most provocative in recent seasons is testament to the talent and resilience of Brazil's committed theater in times of crisis.

Afterword

As this study of homosexualities in Brazilian theater began to take shape, some obstacles seemed more daunting than others. The cautious nature of the theatrical representation of homoeroticism and homosexual transgression in Brazil has presented a particular challenge. In attempting to locate such tentativeness under the diverse guises it has assumed, I had to challenge the received wisdom of Brazil's theatrical history, defying some of the major canonical icons, playwrights, and critics alike. As I dug deeper, I was repeatedly surprised at how firm their grip was on the artistic establishment during the key modernist period. And as I considered (mostly in chapter 2) how the introduction of modernism in Brazilian theater was related to the exclusions it entailed (mainly of the works of João do Rio and the transgressive nature of so much of the *teatro de revista* tradition), I became increasingly aware of the connection between the dawn of modernity in a peripheral society and what is rejected and reduced to noncanonical status. Such intersections uncover the range and pull of the repressed side, a vitality that held a special, forceful fascination for the playwrights (foremost among them Oswald de Andrade and Nelson Rodrigues) Brazilian modernism chose to induct into its ranks.

Within the Brazilian theatrical tradition, Nelson Rodrigues occupies a commanding role as innovator. As a playwright, novelist, and *cronista*, Nelson always operated as an instigator of transgression. But his works, including his plays, impart the often disconcerting suggestion that transgression, however enticing, is always a glaring aberration and that transgressors, however prevalent, are ultimately sick. Chapter 2 thus considers how it was that the man who was hailed the greatest Brazilian theater author of the twentieth century and perhaps of all times was not quite above portraying homosexuality as an odious deviance. Nor did his scorn for difference seem to bother those who worked in the early 1980s to rescue Nelson's career following his demise and that of the military regime he had supported. Sábato Magaldi (1990: 36),[1] the revered critic and editor of Nelson's complete works as well as the architect of his rehabilitation, speaks of Serginho's coming out in *Toda nudez será castigada* as a wallowing in *"a perversão do prazer masoquista"* (the perversion of masochistic pleasure).

Oswald de Andrade, a playful parodist, against-the-grain social critic, mocker of the knowing and the smug, author of mordant drama, unraveler of deep-woven cultural patterns such as *antropofagia*, and deft expert on Brazilian culture, could still deny homosexual men and women a relevant presence on the Brazilian stage. But like Nelson, the *paulista* playwright was for all his exclusionary practices still enticed by the transgressive pull of what he rejected. I have given considerable attention to the theater of these two modernist authors, as well as to that of their neorealist successor, Plínio Marcos, because together they form a vast body of iconoclastic works whose feverish search for artistic truth exploded Brazilian bourgeois conventions. Together the works of these three playwrights provide a privileged look into two related issues. The first is encapsulated in what Paul Julian Smith (1992: 219) terms "the process of disavowal by which a dominant culture expels those 'deviants' whose existence it seeks to deny." The second is the increasingly strong belief among minorities that speaking for others, as the heterosexual Nelson, Oswald, and Plínio Marcos did for homosexual men and women, is "arrogant, vain, unethical, and politically illegitimate" (Alcoff 1991–92: 6). Still, despite the clearly exclusionary treatment of difference in their plays, the theater of Oswald, Nelson, and Plínio Marcos offers some strong explorations of homoeroticism and homosexual experience in Brazil, for example through the character Arandir, whose life is changed in the wake of the pivotal kiss in *Beijo no asfalto* and the charged interactions between Veludo and Vado in *Navalha na carne.*

Aside from these mostly distorted, reluctant representations, Brazil's modernist and neorealist theater had little to say about same-sex relationships. With Lúcio Cardoso and others unwilling or unable to offer a response to these warped portrayals in a corpus that could have constituted the first sensitive representation of the homosexual experience on modernist stages, a gay-accented theater had to wait several decades until tentativeness began to give way to a more direct, though not always more effective, approach.

I was also struck at how precisely Amy Kaminsky's notion of "absent presence," which I use in chapters one and two, seemed to fit Brazilian modernist theater's perspective on homosexuality and homosexuals. The situation of homosexual exclusion, while considerably changed for males since the 1970s, still obtains in the case of lesbians, who continue to be nearly invisible on the stage eight decades after the onset of modernism in Brazil; and in those rare situations where lesbian existence has not been effaced, theirs is an other-authored, still deeply tentative, seriously misguided representation.

If this project has led me to challenge some of the sacred monsters of twentieth-century Brazilian theater, it has also placed me in a position to consider at length critically ignored plays such as those studied in chapter 3. If in doing so I gave some of these noncanonical works more than what some readers might consider their due, I am satisfied that I am providing those dramas the first extended critical treatment they have received. Even the artistic lesser of these plays are of importance to us because they contributed to homoeroticism and gay sexuality being accepted as a matter of course rather than as a novelty or an anomaly. But above all, these are important works because they mark a shift in Brazilian theater from an era when homosexuality stood for something else (capitalism's failures, in Oswald's Marxist readings; the hypocrisy and repression at the core of Brazil's middle class in Nelson's dramas; the social breakdown of a nation unwilling to look at its marginalized masses in Plínio Marcos's plays) to a time when theater could less reluctantly portray homosexual characters as themselves—a time, in short, when homosexuals began to have agency. The context for this shift and the ancestry of the post-1970 gay-themed theater in Brazil is detailed in the first two chapters. The plays examined in chapter 3 burst onto the Brazilian stage in the 1970s, an explosion of graphic language, male nudity, and explicit portrayals of promiscuity, male prostitution, and drug use guaranteed to offend as many people as it enthralled. Together, these plays set out to take Brazilian theater where it had not gone before, legitimizing homosexual characters and chronicling the lives and loves of a number of gay men who were neither total derelicts nor admirable role models.

The best known work studied in chapter 3, Chico Buarque's *Opera do malandro,* has received critical attention from other perspectives, which for the most part compared it to the plays by John Gay, Bertolt Brecht, and Kurt Weill on which it is based and considered it as a work of character peppered throughout with zest and humanity. To the best of my knowledge, however, this is the first reading the work has been given from a homosexual point of view. Like Veludo before him, Geni is often mentioned in critical treatments of Chico's play but has never before been the focus of a sustained analysis that questions "the 'in-betweenness' ... [in] the being of gendered identity" (Butler 1999: xi) or that looks at Geni, "Greta Garbo" and others as demonstrating the performative aspects of gendered roles by parodying them. Such a mode of inquiry is in fact critical as Veludo and Geni, along with Pedro/"Greta Garbo," Gracinha Tropical, and the four *tias* in Aguinaldo Silva's play, are vivid reminders of the breakdown of gender binaries and of how "homosexual communities amassing in the hidden enclaves in the urban landscape are notoriously fluid in sexual expression and manifest any number of affiliations across multiple categories of difference and oppression" (Boone 1998: 29). In their focusing on these communities, the gay-accented plays of the 1970s were able to overcome the tentativeness of previous representations of homosexual transgression in Brazil because they could now explore intersections of difference and challenge the hegemonic representations preceding them, representations that distorted same-sex desire and exoticized the male homosexual subject.

The vastly different scene following the appearance of AIDS in Brazil in the early 1980s prompted the writing and staging of a number of works authored by people who were directly or indirectly affected by the condition. The changed situation, new challenges, and the sheer number of plays compelled me to examine them in a separate chapter. These works, noncanonical all, are in fact very good examples of a committed theater as they intervene discursively in the dominant construction of HIV and AIDS and thus become important tools in promoting social change in Brazil. In addition, just as initially HIV and AIDS represented a setback and occasioned a strong backlash against same-sex love (as discussed in chapter 1), it also gave homosexuality a lot more visibility and opened many doors. One of the most relevant consequences such visibility brought to this project was that the representation of transgression on the Brazilian stage became less tentative as society grew accustomed to a more open and more serious discussion of homosexuality and the nature of transgression in general. Still, as the elevated murder rates of transgendered people suggest, Brazil's sexual others continue to be seen as a threat to the advancement of the ruling class's political and cultural project. Not all of the plays studied in chapter 4, though, are clearly engaged in the individual and collective struggle for survival that came to define life for gay men in Brazil and in many other countries during much of the 1980s and 1990s. In fact, these works eschew the easy path of victim lamentation, displaying instead a healthy diversity of approaches, as seen in the different paradigms presented in my last chapter.

As the AIDS landscape has changed significantly since the dark years of the early 1980s and the condition of homosexuality has grown more clearly apart from the epidemic, it also has become more evident that a gay-accented theater, for instance that of Mauro Rasi in the 1980s and 1990s, did not ever become quite synonymous with a theater of AIDS in Brazil. It is now becoming increasingly clear that the trend to represent HIV and AIDS in commercial theater has run its course in Brazil. But amateur groups and those involved in community work with the underprivileged use theater as a vehicle for education and protest. Two recent examples, both from the first half of 2001 are "Acorda, o sonho acabou" (Wake up, the dream is over), a theatrical discussion of disadvantaged women and AIDS, presented by Panela de Opressão, a community group based in the district of Jacarepaguá, Rio de Janeiro, and "Fruto proibido" (Forbidden fruit), put on by another Rio de Janeiro working-class community group (Artemanha), which revisited the struggles by an HIV-positive gay man. Both groups carry on the work done of the Oficina de Teatro Expressionista para Homens que Fazem Sexo com Homens and other groups that use theater as a tool for combating the spread of HIV and AIDS among underprivileged men and women (see chapter 4). The work of these noncommercial theater groups thus reminds us of the theater's impact as plays and related community work help to shape community values and goals, reinforce crucial identity politics, and alter the direction of an epidemic.

With the benefit of these five years since I began this project, it seems safe to state that for a number of Brazilian playwrights and theater people in general, the arrival of HIV and AIDS brought about three critical needs: to make sense of disease and perhaps to make sense of death; to confront difference, marginality, and transgression; and to escape a kind of theater that had been circumscribed by what Ed Cohen calls the "closet of representation" (see chapter 2). At this stage, however, it is not clear whether Brazil is moving toward a conflation of cultural and sexual identities, nor is it evident that Brazilian theater and culture in general will have to contend with the peril Sarah Schulman has identified in her 1998 book, *Stagestruck*, about representations of gays and lesbians in the United States, namely, that such representations have undermined and perhaps even erased the experiences of those who continue to suffer from discrimination or disease.

While in North America at the turn of the millennium a cure for AIDS was being discussed or even assumed (Sullivan 1996), in less developed parts of the world such optimism and euphoria are still hardly justified. In these regions AIDS is very much an epidemic (or at least it is epidemic among the neediest) and the expensive drug "cocktails" responsible for some astonishing reductions in the level of HIV in the blood are beyond the means of most patients. As a consequence, in Africa alone the epidemic has killed more people than the black death of the Middle Ages and the influenza pandemic of 1918–19; life expectancy in the worst-hit countries of that continent is expected to fall to around age 30 by 2010. As the euphoria that accompanied the introduction of the protease inhibitors subsides, experience has shown that HIV not only survives the new treatments but can grow more resistant to them; the drugs, in turn, are proving far more toxic than anyone had anticipated. The advent of these and other drugs has created new instances of Otherness, further divisions of rich and poor, healthy and ill, separating not only nation from nation, but also isolating and excluding groups and communities within a nation. More and more, then, AIDS has become a disease of the poor, dark-skinned, and illiterate—precisely those who are more difficult to be reached by preventative programs. The disease having lost its sense of urgency for the upper classes, the media has all but lost interest in reporting about it.

In the United States, the turnaround has benefited primarily white people, with minorities lagging behind, while new infection among gay young men has been on the rise; in addition, AIDS-related deaths among women are not declining as sharply as those among white men, while most women with AIDS belong to minority groups (Stolberg 1997: 1, 4). In the case of Brazil the gender, racial, and social gaps, already noticeable, are expected to widen even further (Parker and Galvão 1996: 10–11) although government officials have made a serious effort to make the needed drugs widely available to the poor and indigent.[2] Because a final agreement with multinational pharmaceutical companies is still pending, free AIDS medication distribution may well still fall victim to WTO litigation and international court rulings, not to mention other factors such as deep budget cuts and new economic austerity plans.

Adhering to no single school of thought or theory, I believe I have adopted an ample enough view (see Butler's "intellectual promiscuity of the text" [1999: x]) in order to provide a fair account of the wide diversity of drama considered in this project. There is no single homosexual experience in Brazil, and this is reflected in these plays. As we know, sexuality, as well as race, class, age, religion, and other factors interact with gender to tease meaning out of a diverse life experience. The body of dramatic texts studied here has considerable variety and their authors have individual visions and voices. Despite their vast differences, together they moved away—if ever so slowly—from the highly tentative representations of homosexual transgression prevalent through most of the twentieth century, thus pushing back boundaries and opening up for discussion a number of issues, contributing eventually to an acceptance of the fact that a gay-themed play can have the universality of drama by and about heterosexuals. And finally, the best among them reflect a commitment to the possibilities of the theater as a vibrant medium for exploring how same-sex desire fits into a myriad of issues and discussing the vastly diverse meanings of the homosexual experience in Brazil. It is my hope that the readings I have performed in the previous chapters will contribute to a shifting away from a mere listing of plays with homosexual characters and situations to the more fundamental question of what a same-sex-accented theater means in Brazil.

A reward of this project has been the interest it has generated among colleagues and students. As my manuscript goes to press, a doctoral dissertation on performative aspects of the representation of homosexuality in the theater of Brazil is beginning to take shape at the Department of Theater, Dance and Performance Studies at the University of California, Berkeley. I was honored by the invitation to codirect that thesis (as an outside faculty member) just as I am heartened by the growing number of papers on the subject being given and published in conferences and journals in Brazil and other countries. While clearly not a direct consequence of my project, these works share with mine a strong interest and profound belief in the theater as a privileged locus for explorations of agency and sexual identity in Brazil.

Notes

Chapter 1. Transgression, Homosexuality, and the Theater in Brazil

1. Cf. the work done by superstar Ronaldinho (Ronaldo Luiz Nazário de Lima) as a special representative for the World AIDS Campaign "Young People: Focus for Change." The campaign aims to raise awareness about the effect of AIDS on young people, and how they can become active participants in the response to the epidemic.

2. For evidence that soccer is hardly immune to transgression, see Luiz Henrique de Toledo, "Transgressão e violência entre torcedores de futebol," *Revista USP* 22 (June–August 1994): 93–101.

3. In a twist to the intensely publicized salvos in the debate between macho soccer players and gay leaders, more media-savvy soccer stars have begun to appear in the nude in gay magazines, for example, Vampeta and Dinei in *G Magazine* 16 (January 1999) and 17 (February 1999), respectively. This trend is in fact just another facet of the elaborate ritual of rejection and seduction that characterizes the interest in contrary registers discussed by Peter Stallybrass and Allon White (1986) in *The Politics and Poetics of Transgression* (see below).

In sports such as volleyball, where machismo is less rife, it is easier for a well-known athlete like Lilico to come out. Still, lingering doubts surround his exclusion from the national team following his coming-out interview ("Sou gay e jogo como um homem," *Veja*, 31 March 1999: 70–72).

4. Sarcastically dubbed "Copacabana Coppertone Beach" (*The Brasilians*, March 1999: 7E), the first women's soccer competition in Brazil was held in 1981. It was not until women's soccer became an Olympic event in 1988 and a women's World Cup was initiated in 1991 that Brazil began to pay more serious attention to that modality of the sport. After the initial scramble to put together a national women's

soccer team, there has been an effort to foster the practice of soccer among young women. Mild as they initially were, those efforts have begun to pay off: Brazil had respectable showings in the 1991, 1995, and 1999 Women's World Cups as well as in the 1996 Olympics, where they advanced to the semifinals, losing to China in a tight game. The emphasis, however, is on international tournaments, with local and regional competitions remaining largely ignored by the public and the media, and very visible political figures such as Eurico Miranda, a congressman from the state of Rio de Janeiro and a director of the Vasco da Gama soccer club, boldly stating opposition to the participation of women (and homosexuals) in soccer (*Veja*, 25 November 1998: 42). A more recent example of intolerance of homosexuals playing soccer is the flap over national team coach Luiz Felipe Scolari's homophobic comments to the Mexican newspaper *Crónica Hoy*, as reported in *Correio do Povo* (Porto Alegre), 25 July 2001.

For a nation so fascinated with soccer, the silent treatment the Brazilian media has accorded the women's national soccer team is baffling. Reporting from Rio de Janeiro on the day of Brazil's semifinals game with the United States for the 1999 World Cup (the United States won, 2–0), *New York Times* correspondent Larry Rohter (4 July 1999, sports section) submitted this account: "Soccer may be the king of sports here, but only the men's version of the game seems to wear the crown. Not one of this year's matches of the Brazilian national women's team has been televised live, sponsors have shied away from any association with the team, and hard-core fans who can recite the entire roster of the 1950 men's World Cup squad are hard-pressed to name even one of the current World Cup women."

5. See, for example, "Moustache x Panterinhas," *Veja*, 31 March 1999: 72.

6. Many metaphors and similes used in soccer are borrowed from warfare and military operations. Other images draw on eating and sex.

7. Two openly gay soccer referees, Valter Senra and Jorge Emiliano dos Santos, became very visible in the 1980s but could only be dealt with as "women" or womanized (i.e., weakened), as the nicknames by which they were known in the soccer world—Bianca and Margarida, respectively—attest. Jorge Emiliano died of AIDS in January, 1995. See *Sui Generis* 35 (1998): 33; and for Emiliano's obituary, *Veja*, 1 February 1995: 98.

For an intelligent discussion of the association between soccer and homosexuality, see Bech (1997: 49).

8. Their accuracy notwithstanding, it is unfortunate that Angelia Wilson's and Elizabeth Wilson's interpretations seem to exclude a key component in Bataille's theory—the ludic element that transgression contributes to a political critique, an element of fundamental importance for any parodic or subversive approach to the practices or processes contested by an individual or group.

9. Consider the abundance of derogatory Brazilian terms for men and women

who have crossed sexual boundaries—naming practices that resonate pathologically and create a disempowered Other. See, for example, Parker (1991: 43–54).

10. Because the two situations intersect in curious ways, it bears mentioning some of the lore attending the selection of the nation's patron saint. The previously unknown image was found in the fishing nets of some fishermen one day in 1717. The possibility that the image was crafted by one of the men or that it was dropped from a foreign ship sailing the coast or rivers of São Paulo was never seriously explored, nor were the circumstances of the actual finding ever described in any detail (it is known that the initial finding was the beheaded body, with the head being discovered later). The image's mysterious origin appealed to the credulous, as did the miracles allegedly linked to it, and its dark brown color (from the river mud and the smoke of candles and gas lamps) led many to see the image as that of a black saint who would intercede for abolition. A first shrine was built in 1732, and in 1888 a church was erected in the little village where the image was found; in 1980 Pope John Paul II inaugurated the Basilica of Aparecida in the same location, which now receives about six million pilgrims a year.

It was not until the 1930s that the saint's perceived "Brazilianness" began to be stressed, mostly by the nationalist regime of Getúlio Vargas. The then recent granting by the Vatican of patron sainthood to Our Lady of Aparecida was in perfect tune with Vargas's stress on autochthonous symbols and his open courting of the most visible among the nationalist icons of Brazilian modernism (figures like Heitor Villa-Lobos, Mário de Andrade, and Carlos Drummond de Andrade were employed by or cooperated with the Vargas regime).

Something previously unknown or "appearing" from the outside but seemingly ("appearing" to be) saintly was thus given a "native" name whereas something coming from abroad (as the HIV virus was almost certainly imported into Brazil) but associated with transgression maintained its foreign name. Other diseases discovered or first studied abroad are promptly given Portuguese names, for example "Paralisia Infantil" [Poliomyelitis] and "Mal de Parkinson" [Parkinson's Disease], conditions not perceived as evil because they are not associated with transgression. A useful comparison here is another sexually transmitted disease, syphilis, which in Brazil, as in much of the West, was for centuries a source of considerable stigma; yet, since it was never directly associated with homosexual transgression its patients were not, in contrast to people with AIDS, perceived as evil; on syphilis in colonial Brazil see Gilberto Freyre, *The Masters and the Slaves: A Study in the Development of Brazilian Civilization*, trans. Samuel Putnam, 2nd ed. (New York: Knopf, 1956): passim; on the relationship between syphilis and AIDS, see Sander Gilman, *Disease and Representation: Images of Illness from Madness to AIDS* (Ithaca, N.Y.: Cornell University Press, 1988).

11. Consider the visibility and adulation of young actresses and singers whose main source of talent seems to be located in their *derrières.* At the top of a long

list of names are the singers Carla Perez and Sheila and Scheila (of the band, É o Tchan) and the actresses, Gretchen and Tiazinha. In the popular TV show she used to host, Tiazinha ("Auntie") crafted a stage persona with more than a few touches of S & M.

12. That this is not an oppositional model is borne out by the fact that when two men or two women are involved, roles become more fluid in the privacy of one's bedroom, in contrast to the more rigid public stances of *atividade* and *passividade*. Transgression is further compounded in the behavior of Brazilian men who have sex with *travestis* (male prostitutes in drag). Police reports and interviews with *travestis* often allude to the fact that a large number of clients, their *ativo* outlook notwithstanding, request to be anally penetrated. See Green (1999: 254) and Kulick (1998: 158–61).

13. A psychoanalytic reading, such as Hocquenhem's (1993), emphasizes anal sex as a strategy for resisting the tyranny of reproduction and (with Hocquenhem now drawing on Ferenczi) for reversing the repression of anal eroticism brought about by the focus on cleanliness which has been so prominent in the past few centuries, anal cleanliness being associated with the formation of responsibility in the child. Homosexual desire, Hocquenhem (1993: 98) sums up, "challenges anality-sublimation because it restores the desiring use of the anus."

14. Underpinning the inquisitors' preoccupations was a concern for investing their endeavor with a semblance of legality. Remarking on this key element in the workings of the Inquisition, the Argentine novelist Marcos Aguinis (author of the acclaimed novel *La gesta del marrano*, which focuses on the Holy Office) draws parallels between the torture practices of the Inquisition and Latin American dictatorships of the recent past. Commenting on the requisite attendance of doctors at torture sessions (who advised on when to stop) and of legal scribes (who wrote down every statement made by the victim under torture, including their screams), Aguinis (1997: 6) stresses the links between the false legality and the theatricality of the entire apparatus: "Era um teatro que falsificava a lei, que fazia crer que existia a lei neste cenário de mentiras" [It was a theater that falsified the law, that led one to believe the rule of law was in effect on this stage of lies]. The trials were intricately choreographed events, as were the infamous autos da fé carried out in public spaces in Portugal (but not in Brazil). On staging and performative elements in torture, see Scarry (1985: 18, 27–28).

15. Proponents of *higienismo* championed the cause of personal hygiene and advocated the installation of sewer lines and running water. The road to a developed, "civilized" nation, they argued, must include fighting disease, malnutrition, and ignorance about health care and proper eating habits. The efforts increased in the first two decades of the twentieth century, including the full-scale attack on yellow fever (an effort largely directed at improving the nation's image in Europe and attracting more immigrants). All along, behind the talk about *higienismo* was of course the racial debate. As Skidmore writes, "Advocates of public health

measures and education were arguing that disease and illiteracy, not racial origin or inherent character . . . were the explanation" (1993: 182)

16. Relevant examples include the widely popular characters of Cintura Fina (played by Matheus Nachtergaele) in the 1998 miniseries *Hilda Furacão*, an adaptation of Roberto Drummond's novel of the same title, and Uálber (played by Diogo Villela) in the *telenovela Suave veneno* (1999) by Aguinaldo Silva, one of the playwrights studied in chapter 3. Other *telenovelas* from the 1990s also addressed male prostitution (*De corpo e alma*, 1992) and included transgendered characters (*Renascer*, 1993, and *Explode coração*, 1995). However, power and popular culture often clash in the arena of television. Searching for explanations for the low ratings for Sílvio de Abreu's *Torre de Babel* (1998; Tower of Babel), Globo network directors and the soap opera's author identified a lesbian couple, Leila and Raphaela (played by Silvia Pfeifer and Christiane Torloni, respectively) as the culprits and proceeded to eliminate them in a shopping mall explosion. While Leila and Rafaela were summarily rubbed out, gay male couples have appeared in other *telenovelas*, some even more prominently and without such harsh retribution. One notable example is the interracial gay couple Jefferson (Lui Mendes) and Sandrinho (André Gonçalves), in another Sílvio de Abreu *telenovela*, *A próxima vítima* (1995; The next victim), which was coauthored by the noted playwright Maria Adelaide Amaral.

These couples had important precursors in the 1970s and 1980s. The first homosexual character in a Brazilian soap opera was the wealthy Conrad Mahler in *O rebu* (1974; The commotion) played by Zbigniew Ziembinkski (1908–1978), the Polish-born actor and director who revolutionized Brazilian theater with his staging of Nelson Rodrigues's *Vestido de noiva* (The wedding dress) in 1943. Mahler was followed by Everaldo (Renato Pedrosa) in *Dancing Days* (1978), Claudio (Cecil Thiré) in *Roda de fogo* (1986; Wheel of fire), José Maria (Marcelo Picchi) and José Luís (Miguel Falabella) in *Mico preto* (1990; Black marmoset), and, notably, the first lesbian couple in a *telenovela*, Cecília (Lala Deheinzelin) and Lais (Cristina Prochaska) in *Vale tudo* (1988; Anything goes), which is seen as the pioneer in the portrayal of gays and lesbian as serious, respectable characters in Brazilian television. (*Veja*, 3 March 1999: 120–21).

A ten-year staple of Globo Television, widely popular in Brazil and exported to several other countries, *Você decide* asks the viewing public to call different phone lines to register their vote as to the outcome of the program. With each episode dedicated to a different topic, the program dramatizes issues that are of considerable interest to contemporary Brazil. *Você decide* has on occasion dealt with homosexuality; in the episode aired on 27 November 1997, the public voted to maintain the lesbian romance of two teenagers, and in the program of 13 August 1998, the spectators opted by a wide margin to allow a gay male couple to keep the baby they were seeking to adopt. On 17 May 1997, however, the decision was to separate another gay male couple and send one of them, Juan Pablo, back to Spain, thus rejecting the other option offered the viewing public, namely, that Juan Pablo marry his lover's mother in order to secure permanent resident status in Brazil.

17. Several homophobic campaigns linking AIDS to homosexuality and fomenting hysteria surfaced in the 1980s. A good example is the campaign by the former president and then-mayor of São Paulo, Jânio Quadros, to test all male dancers at the Municipal Theater ballet school to determine whether they were homosexual. I am grateful to James Green for this example of how the AIDS virus could be linked to other sources of anxiety about homosexuality. On this incident, also see Trevisan (1998: 98–99).

18. Care must be taken to avoid viewing the Brazilian gay and lesbian experience as paralleling or mirroring that of the United States. Lack of political awareness on the Brazilian side is the trait that most dramatically distinguishes the two experiences, for Brazilian gays and lesbians are members of a society that resists seeing sex as a political issue. However, students of the construction of homosexuality in Brazil, Peter Fry and Edward MacRae among them, have detected the emergence in the 1960s and 1970s of a new category of Brazilian male sexuality. Taking shape initially among middle-class urban male homosexuals, this new identity supplants the strict distinctions between *atividade* and *passividade* in same-sex practices—a binary opposition that mirrors the dominant heterosexually defined gender categories—in favor of a homosexual identity based on sexual object choice rather than gender roles. This more recent gender system coexists and sometimes competes with the older system built around *atividade* and *passividade*, which remains dominant in the rural areas of the North and Northeast and among the poor in the larger cities throughout the country. See Fry (1982); Fry and MacRae (1983); Green (1999); and Parker (1995).

19. An illuminating example of what can happen when transgression intersects with such social determinants of meaning and subjectivity as race and gender in Brazil is the so-called gay Zumbi incident, namely, the commotion caused when Professor Luiz Mott claimed for the gay ranks African Brazilian slave leader Zumbi dos Palmares (who died in 1695, not long before the Portuguese carried out the final massacre of Palmares, the maroon community he led). A group of black intellectuals reacted with accusations of racism against Mott, an indication of the sometimes uncomfortable clash of racial and sexual politics. The incident included an evident theatricality and it was also, unfortunately, the occasion for some serious threats to Mott's physical safety. See *Veja*, 24 May 1995: 57–58; and the debate published in *Folha de São Paulo* between Mott and the African Brazilian writer Fernando Conceição, 28 May 1995: sec.5; and 4 June 1995: sec. 5.

20. The Tupi were the indigenous peoples the Portuguese first encountered on the coast of present-day Brazil.

21. For a historical survey of the very old correlation between homosexuality and cannibalism, see Bergman (1991: 142–43).

22. On transvestism in Brazil, see Kulick (1998) and Hugo Denizart, *Engenharia*

erótica: Travestis no Rio de Janeiro/Erotic Engineering: Transvestites in Rio de Janeiro (Rio de Janeiro: Zahar, 1997); and Hélio R. Silva, *Travesti: A invenção do feminino* (Rio de Janeiro: Relume Dumará, 1993). On transvestism and carnival in Brazil, see Green (1999) and Parker (1991). For a negative review of Kulick's book see Luiz Mott's column in *Sui Generis* 43 (1999) 22. A more balanced reading is offered by Peter Beattie in *Luso-Brazilian Review* 36.2 (Winter 1999) 127-30.

23. Ambiguity and transgression also shape other key categories in Brazilian culture, be they sexual (*sacanagem*) or otherwise (*jeitinho* and *malandragem*). *Sacanagem*, "the thrill of doing what you are not supposed to and getting away with it" (Klein 1998: 28), is "a general term referring to a whole range of things sexual—above all else, to those aspects of sex that are considered especially marginal, prohibited or dangerous" (Parker 1991: 102). *Jeitinho* is a social currency that allows one to exchange favors (or the promise thereof), often bypassing formal or official procedure; *malandragem* is a strategy whereby one's wit and ability to outfox the system make the difference between survival and defeat.

24. Equally well known are the two more traditional notions of inversion, the Freudian and the marxist. As Freud (1958: 86), with deceptively disinterested language, puts it, "There are men for whom the sexual object is not woman but man, and there are women for whom it is not man but woman. Such persons are designated as contrary sexuals, or better, inverts, and the situation of such a relationship is called inversion. The number of such individuals is considerable, although it is difficult to estimate them accordingly." In the marxist view, "the conception of ideology as the 'inverted' consciousness [is] determined by what is itself an inverted social and historical reality. Thus, the capitalist market, a real set of relations, inverts the underlying reality of production relations by giving the appearance of a free and equal interaction to what is at base an unequal, coerced process of exploitation" (Larsen 1990: xxiii).

25. For most of its existence the theater in Brazil has had to cope with censorship. Types and degrees of censorship have varied with different regimes but the practice has more often than not been part of the concerns of theater practitioners in Brazil. In fact, at its inception Brazilian theater saw the creation of the Conservatório Dramático, which doubled as theater promoter and censorship office. See Khéde (1991) on theater censorship in the nineteenth century (including the role of the Conservatório Dramático); on twentieth-century censors see Khéde and, for the military period, Michalski (1985).

26. For more information on nineteenth-century Brazilian theater, see Severino J. Albuquerque, "The Theater in Brazil up to 1900," *Cambridge History of Latin American Literature*, vol. 3, 1996; João Roberto Faria, *Ideias teatrais: O século dezenove no Brasil* (São Paulo: Perspectiva, 2001); and Lothar Hessel and Georges Raeders, *O teatro no Brasil sob Pedro II*, 2 vols. (Porto Alegre: Editora da UFRS, 1979–86).

27. Reflecting demographic and urbanization trends in Rio de Janeiro (the traditional stronghold of the genre in Brazil), the *shows de travesti* have moved

from the downtown area of Praça Tiradentes to densely populated Copacabana. An example of the longevity of this form of transgressive theater is the clever musical comedy, *Quando elas chegam no céu* (When they reach heaven) by Lady Cristiny and Wander Filho and directed by Betti Pinho and Fernando Reski, staged at the Blair in 1997.

28. Roberta Close (Roberto Luiz Oliveira) is a cross-dresser and also a transsexual. The darling of the Brazilian media in the 1980s, she was at one point, and only half-jokingly, dubbed the most beautiful "woman" in Brazil; see her biography: Lúcia Rito, *Muito prazer, Roberta Close* (Rio de Janeiro: Rosa dos Ventos, 1998). Rogéria (Astolfo Barroso Pinto, b.1943) occupied the same space the previous decade; see Green (1999: 235–38) and Pinto's two interviews in a key counterculture journal: "Minhas memórias de alcova abalariam o Brasil," *O Pasquim* 107 (22 July 1971): 6; and "Rogéria," *O Pasquim* 223 (9 October 1973): 4–7.

29. Another stylist who preceded Clodovil as a television personality was Dener (Dener Pamplona de Abreu), a frequent guest on variety shows in the late 1960s and early 1970s. Dener, who died in 1978, seems to have consented to his being presented in such programs as an unlikable, effeminate snob. See Carlos Dória, *Bordado da fama: Uma biografia de Dener* (São Paulo: SENAC, 1998).

30. For more on the complex and fascinating figure of Madame Satã, see Durst (1985); Green (1999: 85–92); Sylvan Paezzo's *Memórias de Madame Satã: Conforme narração a Sylvan Paezzo* (Rio de Janeiro: Lidador, 1972); and the two excellent interviews in *O Pasquim* 95 (29 April 1971): 2–5, and *O Pasquim* 357 (30 April 1976): 6–11. See also the 2002 film *Madame Satã*, directed by Karim Aïnouz, with Lázaro Ramos in the title role.

31. For the most part the terms "modernist" and "neorealist" are used here as literary and cultural period markers. In Brazil, "modernist" refers to "*modernismo*," or the wide-ranging cultural and literary movement born, officially, with the Week of Modern Art of 1922 and stretching until 1945, the end of the Vargas dictatorship and World War II. *Modernismo* sought to liberate Brazilian thought and art from the tight grip of positivism, academicism, and other worn-out, late-nineteenth-century currents and traditions; in literature, *modernismo* was a rejection of Parnasianism while in the theater, as this chapter and the next explain, the movement wanted to do away with the so-called thesis play and the traditional comedy of manners and musical revues. In their place, *modernismo* attempted to introduce new, but likewise imported, ideas and trends from the European avant-garde, including futurism, cubism, dadaism, and surrealism. The imported, elitist, and bourgeois nature of the movement gave rise to a series of internal conflicts and dilemmas that were never resolved.

"Neorealist" refers to a trend among some fiction writers of the second period of Brazilian modernism (mostly regionalist novelists like Graciliano Ramos and Jorge Amado, as well as playwrights like Dias Gomes and Plínio Marcos) who used mostly realist techniques but threw in a good deal more social criticism.

32. Particularly enlightening are the writings of Herbert Daniel (1946–1992), especially his 1982 *Passagem para o próximo sonho* (A passage to the next dream), a kind of fictional autobiography that Daniel describes as "personal literature." Daniel was a guerilla fighter against the military regime of the 1960s and 1970s and lived in exile in France for most of the 1970s. Because he was never granted amnesty (in part because of his gay activism), he only returned to Brazil after the statute of limitations expired in 1981. In the early 1980s Daniel was deeply involved in the struggle for homosexual civil rights and later became a leader in the fight against AIDS in Brazil, writing books and participating in a number of organizations. For an excellent introduction to Daniel, see Borim (1994).

33. Homoeroticism (same-sex desire, attraction, or "tension") and homosociality (the practices and discourses of male friendship and alliances as forms of socialization), a general notion that refers to social relations in all-male or all-female organizations such as a soccer team and do not necessarily imply or constitute a prelude to or variety of, homosexuality.

34. Apropos here is a caveat Spivak (1987: 253–54) has formulated as she reasons against accepting elite methodology for apprehending subaltern material: "The position that only the subaltern can know the subaltern, only women can know women and so on, cannot be held as a theoretical presupposition either, for it predicates the possibility of knowledge on identity."

35. Apart from the few, minor lesbian characters in the theater of heterosexual males such as Nelson Rodrigues, Oswald de Andrade, and Plínio Marcos, there is a scarcity of lesbian roles in works by other playwrights, including women: the lesbian relationships between Marieta and Amália in Leilah Assunção's *Roda cor de roda* (1969, A wheel-colored wheel), Ana and Teresa in Isabel Câmara's *As moças* (1969, The young women), and Bárbara and Anna in Chico Buarque and Ruy Guerra's *Calabar: O elogio da traição* (1973, Calabar: In praise of treason). Perhaps the lesbian character with the most visibility ever on the Brazilian stage was, tellingly, in a foreign play, the title role of *As lágrimas amargas de Petra von Kant*, played by Fernanda Montenegro in 1982 in the Brazilian production of Rainer Werner Fassbinder's play, *The Bitter Tears of Petra von Kant* (from which he adapted and directed a film of the same title in 1972).

36. As has often been observed, one of the difficulties in writing about lesbians is the social invisibility accorded them by a society for which heterosexuality is the default category. In Brazil, as in much of the developing world, social, economic, and religious factors compound the heterosexist imperative. On lesbianism in Brazil, see Lígia Bellini's *A coisa obscura: Mulher, sodomia e Inquisição no Brasil colonial* (São Paulo: Brasiliense, 1989) and Luiz Mott, *O lesbianismo no Brasil* (Porto Alegre: Mercado Aberto, 1987).

37. On homosexuality in Qorpo-Santo, see Maggi (1999: 7–11). Other nineteenth-century Brazilian plays include several instances of role switching, gender bending, and the *double entendres* expected in farce; two of its exponents, Martins Pena

(Luis Carlos Martins Pena [1815–1848]) and Macedo (Joaquim Manuel de Macedo [1820–1882]), resorted to these techniques with some frequency in their comedies. A good example is Macedo's *Antonica da Silva* (prem. 1880), which drew the attention of the imperial censors who banned entire speeches and scenes they viewed as too racy. In addition, nineteenth-century *comédias* and *revistas* featured men in drag long after the revocation in 1800 of the ban on women on stage; see Galante de Sousa (1960: vol 1, 119–20, 145). Finally, overtones of homosexual behavior can be detected in early Brazilian theater, in the portrayal of devils in some of Anchieta's *autos*.

38. Teatro Ipanema also became the principal propagator of the theater of Spanish playwright José Arrabal in Brazil, staging outstanding productions of *Cemitério de automóveis* (Automobile graveyard) and *O arquiteto e o Imperador da Assíria* (The architect and the emperor of Assyria), both in 1970.

39. Unlike his predecessors (Cauby Peixoto, Ivon Curi, Agnaldo Rayol, Agnaldo Timóteo, and others) who would not comment in public on their sexuality, Ney Matogrosso spoke freely of his homosexuality and thus opened the way for gay or bisexual singers whose career started in the 1980s and 1990s, for example Renato Russo, Cazuza, Edison Cordeiro, and Emílio Santiago.

40. On Ney Matogrosso, see Green (1999: 258–60) and, especially, Denise Pires Vaz's *Ney Matogrosso: Um cara meio estranho* (Rio de Janeiro: Rio Fundo, 1992).

41. Some of these names were previously known in other capacities in Brazilian theater and culture: Arap, for example, was an established stage director. On Daniel see this chapter, note 32. Aguinaldo Silva was, with Gasparino Damata, João Silvério Trevisan, Glauco Mattoso, Darcy Penteado, and João Antônio Mascarenhas, one of the founding editors of the ground-breaking gay newspaper, *Lampião da esquina*, which circulated against enormous odds from 1978 till 1981. On the importance of *Lampião* and the career and work of its writers, see Green (1999: 273–77), MacRae (1990: 65–93), and individual entries in Foster (1994).

42. Other gay-themed foreign plays followed in the 1970s and 1980s. Among the most successful of these productions were adaptations of Jean Poiret's *La Cage aux folles* (*A gaiola das loucas*, 1974), Martin Sherman's *Bent* (*Bent*, 1981), Manuel Puig's *The Kiss of the Spider Woman* (*O beijo da mulher aranha*, 1981 [Puig, who was then living in Brazil, authored the stage version of his 1976 novel, *El beso de la mujer araña*]), Michael Bennett's *A Chorus Line* (*Chorus Line*, 1982), and Charles Ludlam's *Irma Vap* (*O mistério de Irma Vap*, 1989). Two of these stagings, *A gaiola das loucas* and *O mistério de Irma Vap* remain among the all-time top-grossing plays in Brazil.

43. Still, one must lament that Autran, in a position to influence society by speaking out on behalf of diversity and tolerance without fear of retribution, has chosen to remain silent on the issue of his homosexuality. In the series of interviews Alberto Guzik conducted with Autran in 1996 and 1997, the actor again refused to discuss the subject and Guzik, politely, perhaps too politely, did not

press the matter. See *Paulo Autran: Um homem no palco*, entrevista de Alberto Guzik (São Paulo: Boitempo Editorial, 1998) (personal interview with Alberto Guzik)

44. Among the numerous articles appearing in the dailies, see for example the long highly informative review Mauro Ferreira wrote for *O Globo* surveying some of the plays I examine in this book (Ferreira 1997).

45. It is of course safe to assume that a portion of such a public is made up of gay men and women. In addition, there is the issue of the often mentioned but vaguely defined "gay public." To the best of my knowledge the first-ever serious research project on a gay public in Brazil is being conducted by Carlos Alberto Messeder of the Communication Arts Department of the Federal University of Rio de Janeiro. On his work, see *Sui Generis* 38 (1998): 25.

46. I have chosen to use such terms as "gay-themed theater" and "homoerotic theater" instead of the more direct "gay theater" precisely because I want to avoid the false query, "What is gay theater?" This is a paralyzing question, and as Elizabeth Marchant (1998: 152) points out, when such questions as "Is there such a thing as women's writing?" are deconstructed, they reveal a desire to devalue and debase those endeavors.

47. This issue is, of course, related to a much ampler one, namely, the different representations of, and responses to, AIDS in various areas of Brazilian culture. Exposure to many of those areas has impressed on me the notion that the theater is but one of the many important responses the AIDS crisis has elicited from Brazil's diverse communities. I am comforted by the thought that the theater, although serving as a frequent tool to control representation, is also an eloquent vehicle for a host of attitudes and messages, including protest, intervention, resolution, and solace.

While several articles and books have appeared on the clinical, epidemiological, and anthropological aspects of AIDS in Brazil, there has been only one book-length critical examination of the representation of the syndrome in the arts (Bessa 1997). Chapter 4 is a contribution toward an understanding of those representations, at least where the theater is concerned. While I am indebted to the approach to AIDS representation prevalent in the United States (in particular Baker [1994], Murphy and Poirier [1993], Nelson [1992], and Pastore [1993]), I favor a much more inclusive strategy, one steeped in cultural studies, and ultimately colored by my Brazilian perspective.

48. In Brazil as elsewhere in the third world, persons with HIV face quasi-institutionalized discrimination and different forms of violence virtually sanctioned by the more traditional segments of the media, organized religion, and the political establishment. As our forced coexistence with the disease enters its third decade, considerable progress has been made, especially in the media and the scientific and medical establishments. However, pockets of organized religion continue their shrill denunciations of homosexuality and of people with AIDS;

these attacks are more prevalent in evangelical churches and among populist Catholic priests (for example, the invectives by Father Marcelo Rossi, the aforementioned young, media-savvy practitioner of the so-called charismatic school of the Catholic Church; see *Veja*, 6 January 1999: 79).

49. A more ample inquiry into the allegorization of AIDS in Brazil could include the reception of Brazilian versions of foreign plays that deal with AIDS allegorically. Other kinds of foreign texts that might be examined in an even broader study of the representation of AIDS in Brazil might include nonfiction (for example the translations of Randy Shilts's *And the Band Played On* [1987] and Susan Sontag's *AIDS and its Metaphors* [1989]).

50. I am grateful to Fernando Arenas for these insights on recent cultural changes in North America and Western Europe.

51. This issue is related to the fact that the history of gay-themed theater in Brazil is not easily broken into the tidy sequence of phases proposed by, say, Eric Lane in the preface to his *Actor's Book of Gay and Lesbian Plays* (1995: v-x). In her apt comments on Lane's evolutionary stages of the gay theater, Melissa Lockhart (1998: 67–68) detects the same problem Alberto Sandoval writes about in his reflections on periodizations of the history of AIDS theater and how they do not take into account the issues of race, class, and cultural diversity and thus strengthen the hegemonic nature of the representational process (see chapter 4, n. 1).

52. A positive sign are the growing crowds (over 200,000 people in 2001, a dramatic increase from the 2,000 in attendance in 1997) marching in São Paulo's Gay Pride Day Parade. The originality that has come to characterize so much of Brazilian queer performance has so far allowed the parade to avoid becoming a carbon copy of similar North American events.

53. These murders are outrageous examples of how visibility is punished when gay men and women take a more politically assertive stance in Brazil. Particularly revolting was the assassination of bisexual city councilman Renildo José dos Santos (with torture and castration preceding the execution) in the little town of Coqueiro Seco, in the state of Alagoas. The atrocities were carried out with the complicity of government officials, because of Santos's open discussion of his sexuality in a radio interview (Mott 1996: 64–66). Documentation of this and over two thousand other such murders (130 in 2000 alone) has been gathered by the most politically involved gay rights group in contemporary Brazil, Grupo Gay da Bahia, which is led by Luiz Mott (b.1946), a professor of history and anthropology at the Federal University of Bahia and Brazil's most visible activist for gay and lesbian rights. See also Mark Ungar, "Sharp Jump in Brazil Murders," *Amnesty International Members for Lesbian and Gay Concerns Newsletter*, Spring 1998: 1, 3; and "Violação dos direitos humanos e assassinato de homossexuais no Brasil, 1997," *Boletim do Grupo Gay da Bahia* 37 (January–February 1998): 1–48.

According to Jack Epstein, violence against homosexuals in Brazil has been used as grounds for the granting of asylum to at least ten (at the time of his writing)

Brazilian gay men by the United States, United Kingdom, Canada, and Australia ("Why Brazilian Homosexuals Find Asylum in the US," *The Christian Science Monitor*, 7 December 1998).

54. While in the United States a critic in 1998 could ask, "Is there anything left that is subversive about queer theater? Has it lost its transgressive edge?" (Lockhart 1998: 67), in Brazil the length of time until assimilation occurs has been longer and the debates louder and more colorful (suggesting perhaps a lesser degree of smugness in Brazil).

Chapter 2. Modernist and Neorealist Backtracking

1. An exception here is the work of Victor Hugo Adler Pereira (1998), who uses the figure of Nelson Rodrigues as the focus for his book on the relationship between the theater and the state in Brazil. Pereira's study, however, does not consider the years that preceded the Estado Novo period (1937–45) of Vargas's regime.

2. João do Rio's life coincides with the period when the term "homosexual" was imported into Brazil and he was instrumental in giving it currency in turn-of-the-century society. Because this chapter begins with the period immediately preceding the official inception of modernism in Brazil, terms such as "homosexual" and "homosexuality" need to be historicized to avoid applying identities in an anachronistic and culturally misguided fashion. While these words may have been used by a few intellectuals, the average man who was sexually interested in other men was unlikely to use them to refer to himself or his partners or friends. Formal language and scientific jargon preferred *pederasta* and *pederastia*, the old clichés of *sodomia* and *inversão* or euphemisms such as *actos libidinosos* and *o vício ignóbil*, while slang, then as now, used a wealth of terms, some of which were coined by members of the group in question. *Puto*, *fresco*, and *fanchono* were some of the more frequently used slang terms; the contemporary *veado* (or *viado*) and *bicha* were later coinages. James Green (1999: 25–34, 80–83) provides an excellent survey of such usages and their origins.

3. This included not only the occasional wearing of white or light-green suits to formal ceremonies but also encouraging speculation about heterosexual affairs he may have had with famous women such as the actress Aura Abranches and the dancer Isadora Duncan during her much publicized visit to Brazil in 1916. Even his funeral in 1921 had an air of glamour and celebrity to it, attracting an estimated 100,000 people.

4. I do not share the optimism expressed by João do Rio's biographer, João Carlos Rodrigues, when he states that "*João do Rio só não se tornou o patrono da Semana de 22 porque morreu antes*" (qtd. in Name 1996: 6) (had João do Rio been alive at the time of the Week of Modern Art, he would have been its patron saint).

5. Oswald's review is reprinted in *O Percevejo: Revista de Teatro, Crítica e Estética* 2 (1994): 34.

6. See, for example, the chapter on Mário in Rachel de Queiroz's memoirs, *Tantos anos* (1998: 115), where she writes of her good friend's "sufocado homossexualismo" (repressed homosexuality).

7. Another fascinating black homosexual figure of the period is the sailor João Cândido Felisberto (1880–c. 1970) who in 1910 led the mutiny known as Revolta da Chibata to demand an end to the use of whippings, or *chibatadas*, in the Brazilian Navy. In his *Pontos e bordados: Escritos de história e política* (Belo Horizonte: Editora da Universidade Federal de Minas Gerais, 1998), José Murilo de Carvalho has written an engrossing piece on race, class, and antihomosexual prejudice, using as focal point the embroideries João Cândido did while in prison. On João Cândido, also see Fernando Granato, *O negro da Chibata* (São Paulo: Objetiva, 2000).

One is immediately reminded of another (albeit fictional) black homosexual sailor of the period, Amaro, the Bom Crioulo of Adolfo Caminha's novel of the same title ([Rio de Janeiro: Domingues de Magalhães, 1895]; *Bom Crioulo: The Black Man and the Cabin Boy*, trans. E. A. Lacey [San Francisco: Gay Sunshine Press, 1982]), which is reputed to be Latin America's first novel to depict two male lovers as protagonists. For a good introduction to Caminha and *Bom crioulo*, see Eva Paulino Bueno's entry in Foster (1994: 94–100) and Robert Howes, "Race and Transgressive Sexuality in Adolfo Caminha's *Bom crioulo*," *Luso-Brazilian Review* 38.1 (Summer 2001): 41–62.

8. The changes affecting life in Rio de Janeiro at that period were also portrayed vividly by Benjamin Costallat (1897–1961) in works such as *Mademoiselle Cinema* (1923) that are less known but just as interesting as those of João do Rio. Rosalina, the Mademoiselle Cinema of the title, a *melindrosa*, or cocotte, born to an upper-class family rejects the strict morals of her family and class and adopts instead a hedonistic life guided by pleasure and the latest fashions from Paris, indulging eventually in drugs and lesbian affairs.

9. In her carefully researched book, Teresa A. Meade (1997) details not only the extent and depth of Rio de Janeiro's urban renewal but also how local movements resisted it, for these changes made life worse, not better, for the working poor, who constituted the majority of the city's residents.

10. There was an element of regional rivalry involved in this issue, as *paulista* modernists accused their *carioca* (as residents from Rio de Janeiro are known) counterparts of futility and irreverence, implying at the same time that such disregard for order and seriousness made Rio unfit to be the national capital. The *cariocas* turned the issue around, accusing their São Paulo colleagues of too much seriousness, saying that their inability to indulge in humor and good cheer invalidated their modernist aspirations. This was not as black and white a split as presented in some accounts, however (see, for example, the preface to Monica Pimenta Velloso, *Modernismo no Rio de Janeiro: Turunas e quixotes* [Rio de Janeiro: Fundação Getúlio Vargas, 1996]: 11–19); *paulistano* Oswald de

Andrade's iconoclasm and irreverence lent Brazilian modernism a great deal of its creative originality.

11. The emancipation of women was then at the center of national debate, due to the inception of a serious, organized feminist movement in Brazil and the creation, under the leadership of Bertha Lutz (1894–1970) and others, of the Liga para a Emancipação Intelectual da Mulher (League for the Intellectual Emancipation of Women) in 1922 and the Sociedade Brasileira para o Progresso Feminino (Brazilian Society for the Advancement of Women) in 1924.

12. Here, I am using the term "decadence" in the general sense defined by Elaine Showalter (1990: 169) as "the pejorative label applied by the bourgeoisie to everything that seemed unnatural, artificial, and perverse, from Art Nouveau to homosexuality, a sickness with symptoms associated with cultural degeneration and decay." Wilde and João do Rio, however, thought of decadence more as a post-Darwinian aesthetic movement, which, as explained by Showalter (1990: 169–70) (who, in turn, is using Jean Pierrot's *The Decadent Imagination*), held that "nature was 'an unfeeling and pitiless mechanism'; religion, a 'nostalgic memory'; and love, a biological instinct for perpetuating the species. Since these traditional consolations were meaningless, the only solution was to live in the experience of the moment, to seek the 'new, the rare, the strange, the refined.'"

13. It should be noted, however, that João do Rio was not Wilde's first translator in Brazil. He was preceded by Elísio de Carvalho, who translated *The Ballad of Reading Gaol* as *Balada do enforcado* (Rio de Janeiro: Editora Brasil Moderno, 1899) and *Poems in Prose* as *Poemas em prosa* (Rio de Janeiro: Tipografia Leuzinger, 1900) (Faria 1988: 134, 140).

14. But see the interesting intersections Raúl Antelo establishes between the two Barretos (Lima Barreto and Paulo Barreto, or João do Rio) in chapter eight of his *João do Rio: O dândi e a especulação* (Rio de Janeiro: Taurus-Timbre Editores, 1989).

15. I am alluding here to the subtitle of Ed Cohen's article "Writing Gone Wilde" in *Critical Essays on Oscar Wilde*, ed. Regenia Gagnier (New York: G. K. Hall, 1991): 68–87. By "closet of representation" Cohen means the symbolic displacement of homosexual desire onto the aesthetic or the linguistic codification of the erotic.

16. Some of these short stories and *crônicas* have been gathered in the volume *Histórias da gente alegre* (Stories of happy/gay people) in an edition by João do Rio's accomplished biographer and bibliographer, João Carlos Rodrigues, who also wrote a useful introduction ("A flor e o espinho") to the volume. See *Histórias da gente alegre: Contos, crônicas e reportagens da belle époque carioca*, ed. João Carlos Rodrigues (Rio de Janeiro: José Olympio, 1981).

17. Here I am borrowing terminology from Piontek (1992: 133–34), whose ideas on the literary and cultural ramifications of the closet of representation have been very useful to my application of that notion to the Brazilian scene.

18. For a thorough, year-by-year account of *revista* productions in Brazil, see

Salvyano Cavalcanti de Paiva, *Viva o rebolado! Vida e morte do teatro de revista no Brasil* (Rio de Janeiro: Editora Nova Fronteira, 1991); for a meticulous study of the creation and development of the theater district in downtown Rio de Janeiro, see Evelyn Furquin Werneck Lima, *Arquitetura do espetáculo: Teatros e cinemas na formação da Praça Tiradentes e Cinelândia* (Rio de Janeiro: Editora da Universidade Federal do Rio de Janeiro, 2000).

19. The three-act *O rei da vela*, which is dedicated to Alvaro and Eugênia Moreyra "for struggling to raise the abandoned child that is the Brazilian theater," constitutes a devastating denunciation of crass capitalism through the portrayal of a new class, the moneyed bourgeoisie, as it replaces the bankrupt landowners and coffee barons. By means of characterization and scathing satire, the play depicts both groups as equally corrupt and unscrupulous. The upper class characters' struggle to preserve their standard of living reveals their moral and financial corruption. The bourgeoisie is guilty on two counts, of prostituting itself in exchange for the aristocracy's name and tradition and of aligning itself with foreign interests. Nor does the intelligentsia fare much better, since its representative, Pinote, is a writer who peddles his dubious talents to the rich. That such a world holds no place for love is confirmed by Oswald's recasting of the famous medieval love story of Abelard and Heloïse. In *O rei da vela* the suitor is a predatory nouveau riche who comes in two equally insidious incarnations, Abelardo I, the usurer, and Abelardo II, the self-proclaimed socialist. When Abelardo I becomes Abelardo II nothing but his name seems to change, the point being that no substantive change will occur until the socioeconomic structure undergoes a radical transformation. Abelardo is intent on buying the tradition of distinction associated with Heloísa's family name, while the bride and her relatives see the courtship as an opportunity to regain their squandered fortune. At play's end, money's preeminence is reaffirmed as each side attains its goal and both classes lose, while foreign capital, represented by the American businessman Mr. Jones, asserts its control of the Brazilian economy.

20. As several commentators of the play have pointed out, prostitution, in a literal and a figurative sense, is an important issue in *O rei da vela.* Not only do we hear of Joana/João's act of prostitution, Heloísa's engagement to Abelardo can be read as an act of prostitution, as can, on a larger scale, Brazilian business practices in relation to foreign capital, as represented by Abelardo and Mr. Jones, respectively.

Prostitution was part of an intricate social agenda that controlled women's contribution to the economy and society in general. This setup included not only the cultivation of myths like the sanctity of marriage and motherhood and the repression of unrestrained sexuality but also more concrete issues like women's participation in the work force, especially as factory workers; see Margaret Rago, *Do cabaré ao lar: A utopia da cidade disciplinar; Brasil 1890–1930* (Rio de Janeiro: Paz e Terra, 1985).

Prostitution, real and allegorical, was prominent among Oswald's preoccupations in the early 1930s, as attested by his writings in the journal *O homem do povo*, which he published briefly in 1931. He may have been made aware of the issue by his then wife Patrícia Galvão (1910–1962), best known in Brazil as Pagu, a feminist thinker and novelist who was a frequent contributor to *O homem do povo*, where she too denounced prostitution. The journal was a mouthpiece for the exalted stalinist views of Oswald and Pagu, both of whom were members of the Communist Party at the time.

21. In the groundbreaking *tropicalista* staging of *O rei da vela* by Teatro Oficina in 1967, Joana/João's manly behavior contrasts sharply to that of a male actor dressed like Shirley Temple. In his analysis of this production of Oswald's play, Victor Hugo Pereira (1995: 177) alludes to this and other staging choices as a deliberate attempt on the part of the director, José Celso Martinez Correa, to stress the fragmented quality of the character. This lack of consistency in characterization signaled a rejection of realist portrayal and an attempt to expose the contradictions occasioned by the opportunism of the ruling class to which these characters belong.

22. On the early days of psychoanalysis in São Paulo, see Roberto Yukata Sagawa, "A psicanálise pioneira e os pioneiros da psicanálise em São Paulo," *A cultura da psicanálise*, ed. Sérvulo Figueira (São Paulo: Brasiliense, 1985).

23. The two young women's kiss on the mouth at the beginning of *Album de família* (Rodrigues 1981–90, 2: 57) was, to the best of my knowledge, a first in the history of Brazilian theater and took most of the blame for the play being banned from the stage for two decades (written in 1945, it was published in 1946 but only premiered in 1967).

24. Oswald's and Nelson's notions about homosexuality came from ill-digested outlines of psychoanalytical theory with which the former was first in contact in Europe and the latter in Brazil, and they were not exposed to the views of early twentieth-century thinkers who were not immediately translated into French and English. An example is Hans Blüher, whose views Andrew Hewitt (1996) explicates in *Political Inversions*. For Blüher, writes Hewitt, "homosexuality is not to be understood from the perspective of heterosexuality—as a failure of full development—but rather in terms of its own logic. It is not something that has to be explained, but rather something that, like Eros, makes explanation and meaning possible. Thus, Blüher refuses any explanation that reduces homosexuality to the level of symptom or even to the level of displaced desire or erotic substitution" (106).

25. One has almost come to expect this sort of posture from ideological positions that fall under the umbrella of nationalism—of the Left and Right alike—and other discourses that are fundamentally homophobic. More difficult to accept is Teatro Oficina's uncritical acceptance—thirty-four years after the play was written—of this shallow view of male and female homosexuals.

26. Although he was an escapee from a juvenile reform school, "Dorothy" moves

up the social ladder rather quickly when Dr. J. B. de Albuquerque Guimarães marries him to his daughter and makes him the head theater critic in one of the magnate's influential newspapers. When Nelson wrote *Viúva porém honesta* (which premiered in September 1957), he was still piqued by the negative reception accorded his previous play (*Perdoa-me por me traíres* [Forgive me for your betraying me], premiered June 1957) by some younger critics. As Nelson sought revenge, he could not think of anything more insulting than having Dr. J. B. state in the play that a young flaming queen would be just perfect to serve as his paper's new theater critic.

27. Oswald dedicated *O rei da vela* to Moreyra, who led (with his wife, Eugênia) the short-lived but important modernist group Teatro de Brinquedo; *Adão, Eva* was the group's best known effort. Another important playwright of the period, Joracy Camargo (1898–1973), author of the ground-breaking *Deus lhe pague* (1933; May the Lord reward you), was, like Oswald and Alvaro Moreyra, a member of the Communist Party in the early 1930s. *Deus lhe pague* reflects, albeit timidly, the inspiration of the Russian Revolution and its vibrant economic plans. Introducing Karl Marx's name (but not quite his ideas) to the Brazilian stage, Camargo played with the public's curiosity about communism and with the belief that the then-recent crash of the New York Stock Exchange had signaled the demise of capitalism.

Iná Camargo Costa points out the importance of the theater for the Russian Revolution and the subsequent interest in theater on the part of the Brazilian Communist Party in the late 1920s and early 1930s. In the specific case of Oswald de Andrade, she stresses *"a não-casualidade do empenho oswaldiano em se tornar dramaturgo imediatamente após a sua inscrição no PCB"* (146) (it is no coincidence that Oswald became determined to be a serious playwright immediately after he joined the Communist Party).

Like Marx's, Freud's name made a late debut on the Brazilian stage, and his ideas were equally simplified or distorted. The first mention appears in *Sexo* (Sex) (premiered 1934), so titled for shock value. Freud is no more than a conversation topic between two characters, one of whom, having never before heard of the psychoanalyst, is given a muddled explanation of the notion of inversion. The playwright, Renato Viana (1894–1953) made several attempts in the 1920s and 1930s to create an artistically valid theater in Brazil. Prominent among such attempts is the creation, in 1922, by Viana and two noted modernists, the composer Heitor Villa-Lobos (1887–1959) and the poet Ronald de Carvalho (1893–1935), of a group called Batalha da Quimera, based in Rio de Janeiro. The immediate aim of the group was to introduce expressionist theater onto the Brazilian stage. Their first production, however, Viana's *A última encarnação de Fausto* (Faust's last incarnation), staged in 1922, met with an intensely averse public and critical condemnation.

28. By 1996, however, Plínio Marcos still presents gay men as affected things

who are promiscuous and dangerous; see Lili the cook in *O assassinato do anão de caralho grande*, 132–34.

29. In *O homem e o cavalo* the antibourgeois revolution has triumphed worldwide. The play judges bourgeois civilization by the codes of a new Soviet society in the early 1930s, extolling the virtues of socialism. In a Brecht-like structure, the work's nine tableaux of cosmic proportions (the play was meant to be performed in a soccer stadium or to be filmed) and biting satire document the new regime's attempts to correct the inequities of the old order by destroying the myths perpetuated by capitalism and Christianity. With its revolutionary form and message, propagandistic monologues, large cast of characters (from Cleopatra and Jesus Christ to the ironically misnamed Mister Byron and Lord Capone, plus a dog named Swedenborg, Hitler crucified on a swastika, and tourists from Mars), and diversity of settings (the boat of Saint Peter, an interplanetary airport, the derby at Epsom, the largest socialist factory in the world, Heaven, and so on), Oswald's play is in many ways reminiscent of Mayakovsky's 1918 *Mystery-Bouffe* (for a comparative reading of the two plays see Fred Clark, "Oswald and Mayakovsky: *O homem e o cavalo* and *Mystery-Bouffe*," *Revista de Estudios Hispánicos* 16.2 [1982]: 241–56). Its main thrust is a denunciation of the past and present evils of capitalism, along with the celebration of a new era in which the peasant's horse, representative of the economic exploitation of the past, is replaced by the new symbol of proletarian liberation, the horse-power evocative of the collectively owned industries of the future.

Written in 1933 for the Teatro de Experiência, a short-lived avant-garde group led by the architect and artist Flávio de Carvalho (1899–1973), *O homem e o cavalo*, although published in 1934—apparently without major problems—was banned by the censors on opening night.

30. With the elaboration of the new fascist man, George Mosse (1996: 155) writes, "The history of modern masculinity . . . reaches a new climax. Never before or since the appearance of fascism was masculinity elevated to such heights: the hopes placed upon it, the importance of manliness as a national symbol and as a living example played a vital role in all fascist regimes."

31. See, for example, Pagu's article, "Saibam ser maricons" (How to be a faggot), published in *O homem do povo* 6 (1931), in which she attacks a "*corja de pederastas*" (gang of pederasts) whom she blames for trying to destroy the journal (Iná Costa 1996: 145).

The same term "*pederastas*" is used in Abelardo's dying speech, as he is about to be replaced by Abelardo II. Abelardo I berates Abelardo II as a "*produto do clima, da economia escrava e da moral desumana que faz milhões de onanistas desesperados e de pederastas*" (product of the climate, the slave economy, and the inhuman morality that creates millions of desperate masturbators and pederasts). He also calls him "*Febrônio dissimulado*" (a barely disguised Febrônio) in reference to Febrônio Indio do Brasil (b.1895) who was feared and hated by a society that did not understand or accept difference and thus imprisoned and tortured him for his homosexuality, sexual sadism, and shamanistic powers. See Peter Fry, "Febrônio Indio do Brasil: Onde cruzam a psiquiatria, a profecia, a homossexualidade e a lei," *Caminhos cruzados: Linguagem, antropologia e ciências naturais*, ed. Carlos Vogt (São Paulo: Editora Brasiliense, 1982, 65–80.)

In relation to the play's last scene, it is important to note here the directorial choice to stage Abelardo's death not as a suicide (as in Oswald's text) but as the result of being impaled with a candle. As described by Alberto Sérgio da Silva (who in turn is drawing from Etty Fraser's character sketches), in his book on Teatro Oficina, group director José Celso Martinez Correa staged Abelardo's dying moment thus: "*Abelardo I passava da posição vertical para a horizontal e ficava mesmo na posição clássica, de quatro. Abelardo II . . . postava-se ereto e com a vela na mão, a mesma que iria enfiar no ânus de Abelardo I. Este morria*" (149) (Abelardo I would go from a standing position to lying down and would even go on all fours. Abelardo II would then rise, erect and holding a candle, the same candle he was to insert in Abelardo I's anus. The latter then died). Unabashedly transgressive, Zé Celso indulges in some directorial liberty here but more than the visual allusion to anal penetration his decision was meant to emphasize the change in control, with the new "king," the one now in charge, portrayed as the penetrator, the male. The penetrated one, symbolically losing power at the moment the penetration occurred, and now a confirmed pederast, must die.

32. Attempts to deny homosexuality a presence can also be found among theater critics. In his (mixed) review of *O rei da vela*, Décio de Almeida Prado (1917–2000), often referred to as the doyen of twentieth-century theater criticism in Brazil, seems to be bothered by the number of homosexual characters in the play, and also possibly among the cast of the Teatro Oficina, of which Prado was not quite enamored. He was likewise never very keen on Oswald or the Left in general. Prado (1987: 224) spices his expression of surprise with remarks both outlandish (the claim that there were only two or three "obvious" homosexuals in São Paulo in 1930) and downright insulting (claiming to be quoting a statement by an unidentified "French writer," Prado writes, "*é extraordinário . . . como eles se multiplicam sem se reproduzir*") (how remarkable it is . . . that they can multiply without being able to reproduce).

33. Although a penitentiary is usually perceived as an environment totally apart from the outside world, the violence taking place within its walls has severe repercussions to society at large. For an account of the realities of the Brazilian penal system, see Armida Bergamini Miotto, *A violência nas prisões* (Goiânia: Editora da Universidade Federal de Goiás, 1983). A 1994 study conducted by the State of São Paulo Department of Corrections showed that inmates learn to rape while they are incarcerated and add sexual violence to the crimes they commit after being released from prison; the study linked forty percent of sexual assaults committed in São Paulo in one year to former prison inmates (*Veja* 39 November 1994:54).

34. The play, published in 1966, was premiered the year before in Rio de Janeiro's Teatro Serrador, under the direction of Zbigniew Ziembinski, whose collaborations with Nelson Rodrigues famously included the staging of Nelson's *Vestido de noiva* (premiered in December of 1943, in Rio de Janeiro's Teatro Municipal), a production that most critics agree both marks the beginning of modern theater in Brazil and is the best Brazilian play of the twentieth century (interestingly enough, Ziembinski (1982, 6: 188) thought *Toda nudez* was a better play than *Vestido de noiva* . *Toda nudez* has been staged several other times, most notably by Antunes Filho and Grupo Macunaíma, as part of their important Nelson Rodrigues cycle of the early 1980s, *Nelson Rodrigues: O eterno retorno* (1981; The eternal return) and *Nelson 2 Rodrigues* (1984); see David George, *Grupo Macunaíma: Carnavalização e mito* (São Paulo: Editora Perspectiva, 1990) 93–100, 112–21.

Toda nudez has been translated into English as *All Nudity Shall Be Punished* (Rodrigues 1998) by Nelson's son Joffre Rodrigues and Toby Coe, and adapted and translated into Spanish (*Tramoya* 40–41 [July–December 1994]: 35–55) by Antunes Filho. The film version of *Toda nudez será castigada*, directed by Arnaldo Jabor in 1973, received public and critical acclaim, winning, among other awards, the Silver Bear in the 1973 Berlin Film Festival; see Randal Johnson, "Nelson Rodrigues as Filmed by Arnaldo Jabor," *Latin American Theatre Review* 16.1 (Fall 1982) 15–28.

35. Psychoanalytical criticism sees a latent homosexuality in Herculano, who is obsessed with "obscene penetrations," dreams of his son's rapist, and is accused by his lover of having faggy mannerisms. Two such critics, Martuscello (1993: 226) and Venturelli (1982: 89–93) see father and son as one, with Serginho functioning as a fantasy in which Herculano projects his homosexual desire—his "*obsessão*" (obsession)—the term Nelson chose as the play's subtitle.

36. This notion of salvation through rape reverberates into metaphorical use. An example is found in an interview with Leon Goes—the actor who plays Serginho in the 1998 production of the play under the direction of his brother, Moacyr Goes, in which he refers to the theater's role in helping him find harmony in his life: "*o teatro foi o meu Ladrão Boliviano*" (theater was my Bolivian Thief); *Sui Generis* 35 (1998): 20.

37. Peter Schoenbach (1976: 252–53) points out that "the violence and ugliness [in *Barrela*] are on a par with that of such works as [Kenneth H. Brown's] *The Brig*, which was shocking American audiences at about the same time."

38. For a semiotic reading of *Barrela*, see Elzbieta Szoka, *A Semiotic Study of Three Plays by Plínio Marcos* (New York: Peter Lang, 1995): 53–88.

39. In his account of his transition from the circus (where he worked as a clown) to the theater and his first steps as a playwright, Marcos acknowledges the enthusiastic support of several people, including that of Pagu, now married to the novelist Geraldo Galvão Ferraz. Marcos writes that Pagu, one of the first people to read the *Barrela* manuscript, was fascinated with the play and worked hard to see it staged (it was she who gave a copy of the text to Paschoal Carlos Magno,

who was instrumental in releasing the play). Convinced that Marcos had at least as much talent as Nelson Rodrigues, Pagu and Ferraz gave him books to read, encouraging him to intensify and diversify his reading and to become serious about a playwriting career (Marcos 1976: 6–7). Marcos offers additional recollections of Pagu in an interview with Elzbieta Szoka, "The Spirit of Revolution in Contemporary Brazilian Theater: An Interview with Plínio Marcos," *The Drama Review* 34 (1990): 70–83; his thoughts on Pagu are on pages 78–79.

40. The standing ovation, the packed theater, and the emotional reaction of the elated cast following the spectacle left an indelible mark on the dramatist, who considered *Barrela* his favorite play and believed that his fate as a playwright was sealed on that "unforgettable, unsurpassable night" of 1 November 1959 (Marcos 1976: 7).

41. The text also faced the censorship barrier and was not published until 1976; a film version, bearing the same title, was made in 1988, three years after the end of the military regime, directed by Antônio Cury. For a history of the play's battle with the censors, see Marcos (1976: 7–10) and Michalski (1985: 37).

42. Because of the havoc wreaked by censorship, that year was "*talvez o ano mais trágico de toda a história do teatro brasileiro*" (Michalski 1985: 33) (perhaps the most tragic year in the entire history of the theater in Brazil).

43. For my analysis I am drawing from Melissa Lockhart's "*Beijo no asfalto* and Compulsory Heterosexuality" which is, as far as I know, the first (and as of this writing, the only) article to deal exclusively with homosexuality in *Beijo no asfalto*, or, for that matter, in any of Nelson Rodrigues's theater.

44. Years later, a privileged agent in that process, the actor, director and critic Fernando Peixoto (1990: 61), wrote of Oswald's plays, "Not often do political subjects find such an uninhibited, radical, and brave form as they did in Andrade's texts."

45. For an easy-to-locate compilation of praise heaped on Nelson from all quarters of the Brazilian intellectual elite, see Paulo Moreira Leite, "Unanimidade burra," *Veja*, 29 May 1996: 118–20.

46. TEN was created and directed by Abdias do Nascimento (b.1914), the most distinguished name among African Brazilian playwrights and a tireless promoter of black theater in Brazil and elsewhere. Under Abdias, TEN was instrumental in training African Brazilian actors and theater technicians, encouraging the writing of plays that reflect black culture, and raising the consciousness of both blacks and whites about the existence of racism in Brazil's much-touted "racial democracy." The best plays—including Lúcio's *O filho pródigo*—commissioned by the group were later published in an anthology edited by Nascimento, *Drama para negros e um prólogo para brancos* (Rio de Janeiro, 1961). The acting careers launched by TEN include those of Aguinaldo Camargo (1915–1952), Zeni Pereira (b. 1925), and Ruth de Souza (b. 1929). For an excellent compilation of materials on TEN, see *Dionysos* 28 (1988), a special issue dedicated to the group.

Chapter 3. Beyond Evasiveness

1. Broadly speaking, opposition to the military had by then split into two different camps with contrasting political philosophies, the "serious," dogmatic Centro Popular de Cultura, or CPC (a part of the União Nacional dos Estudantes, or UNE), which felt they alone should determine the ideological validity of any resistance attempts, and the so-called *esquerda festiva* or the fun-loving left, which, while still opposing the dictatorship, did not, as its name suggests, renounce the celebratory component of human nature. *Esquerda festiva* included, among many other cultural manifestations, the performative groups of the early 1970s and the Banda de Ipanema (created in 1965 by Albino Pinheiro, Ferdy Carneiro, Hugo Bidet, and Sérgio Jaguaribe, known as Jaguar, who would soon thereafter start the key counterculture newsweekly *O Pasquim*). Jaguar's periodical was combated by the regime but the events were for the most part tolerated. Still, the censors were always questioning tactics such as, for example, the provocative use on the part of the Banda of apparently meaningless slogans like Yullesban Crisbeles.

Not surprisingly, the orthodox marxist CPC did not favor gay-themed plays. They endorsed instead an engaged theater such as that practiced by Augusto Boal and Oduvaldo Vianna Filho; see the play collection *O melhor teatro do CPC da UNE*, ed. Fernando Peixoto (São Paulo: Global, 1989).

On the CPC see Manoel Tosta Berlinck, *O Centro de Cultura Popular da UNE* (Campinas, SP: Papirus, 1984) and Jalusa Barcellos, *CPC da UNE: Uma história de paixão e consciência* (Rio de Janeiro: Nova Fronteira, 1994); on *O Pasquim* see José Luiz Braga, *O Pasquim e os anos 70* (Brasília: Editora da Universidade de Brasília, 1991); and on the Banda de Ipanema see Paulo Cesar Saraceni's film, "Banda de Ipanema, a Folia do Albino" (2000).

2. There is some autobiographical relevance here, for Zé Vicente was a clerk at Banco do Brasil when he was writing the play; as he confesses in his memoirs, he worked on his play when his supervisor was not around (Vicente 1984: 153).

3. For a more detailed study of verbal and nonverbal violence in *O assalto* see my *Violent Acts: A Study of Contemporary Latin American Theatre* (Detroit: Wayne State University Press, 1991): 245–48 and *passim.*

4. These are in many cases male characters, as most notably in Brazilian theater, Tonho and Paco in Plínio Marcos's *Dois perdidos numa noite suja* and in Spanish American drama, Lorenzo and Ignacio in Griselda Gambaro's *Los siameses* (1967; The siamese twins), but often the two characters are a woman and a man, as for example, Mariazinha and the anonymous invader in Leilah Assunção's *Fala baixo senão eu grito* (1977; Hush or I'll scream) and in Spanish America, Eva and El Merluza in Egon Wolff's *Flores de papel* (1970; Paper flowers); less often the two characters are women, as in Isabel Câmara's *As moças* (1969; The young women).

5. Though weakened and largely ignored, these cries were still heard in reaction

to the 1998 staging of *O assalto*, starring André Gonçalves and Cassiano Carneiro, under the direction of José Wilker.

6. The town lends its name to Alcides Nogueira's paean to Zé Vicente, which I examine in chapter 4. Several of the friends and family members mentioned in Vicente's autobiography have made their way into Alcides's play.

7. In his descriptions of these visions Vicente mixes politics and family history with religious faith, claiming the Lord had come to avenge the humiliation his family had suffered in their financial decline and to overcome the enemies of Brazil, most notably, for Vicente, the United States; see for example, Vicente (1984: 286).

8. In addition to *Santidade*, *O assalto*, and *Hoje é dia de rock*, Vicente's "teatro de juventude" also includes *Os convalescentes* (1970; The convalescents), *A última peça* (1972; The last play), *Ensaio selvagem* (1974; Wild rehearsal), *História geral das Indias* (A general history of the Indies), also called *A chave das minas*, (1977; The key to the mines), and *Rock and roll* (1983). Like *O assalto* and *Hoje é dia de rock*, *Os convalescentes*, *Ensaio selvagem*, and *História geral das Indias* were staged by Teatro Ipanema. The "teatro de adulto" is the trilogy he claims brought to a close his association with the theater. The three plays are imbued with Catholic faith and bear the titles *O povo de Deus* (God's people), *Satã* (Satan), and *A idade do ouro* (The Golden Age) (Vicente 1984: 286). Vicente also makes a brief mention of an adaptation he did with Antônio Bivar of Pope John Paul II's play, *A loja do ourives* (The goldsmith shop), never staged because he and Bivar failed to obtain the necessary permission from the Vatican.

In the foreword to his autobiography Vicente (1984: 8) also states that, aside from the printed text of his plays, *Os reis da terra* is his "*único livro: primeiro e último*" (his only book: the first one and the last). Since its publication in 1984 Vicente has led a quiet, secluded existence in a small town away from any "*cidade do Mal*" (city of evil).

9. *Greta Garbo, quem diria, acabou no Irajá* premiered in the 1973–74 season, directed by Leo Jusi and with stellar casts in both Rio de Janeiro and São Paulo. It debuted in Teatro Santa Rosa in Rio de Janeiro on 3 July 1973, with Nestor de Montemar as Pedro/Greta, Mário Gomes as Renato, and Arlete Sales as Mary. In São Paulo, Melo's play opened at the Teatro Itália on 19 March 1974, starring Raul Cortez as Pedro/Greta, Nuno Leal Maia (later, Marcelo Picchi) as Renato, and Pepita Rodrigues (later, Miriam Mahler) as Mary. *Greta Garbo* has since had numerous stagings, most of them forgettable. One of the most recent productions, however, at São Paulo's Teatro de Cultura Artística during the 1993–94 season starred Raul Cortez in a solid revival celebrating the twentieth anniversary of the role he immortalized in the 1970s.

10. The original film version of *La cage aux folles* (1978), directed by Edouard Molinaro and starring Ugo Tognazzi and Michel Serrault, was also a big box-office hit in Brazil in the waning years of the military dictatorship.

Gaiola das loucas has had several restagings over the years (including the 1998–99 production starring Jece Valadão, who for many years voiced *macho* bravado in Brazil in much the same fashion soccer player Renato Gaúcho would years later), but it is the original production under the direction of João Bethencourt and starring Jorge Dória and Carvalhinho that remains a classic in commercial Brazilian theater. It, and the crossover megahit of the 1980s, the Brazilian translation and adaptation of Charles Ludlam's *O mistério de Irma Vap*, are among the all-time top grossing productions in Brazil. The hilarious, superbly acted *Irma Vap* (directed by Marília Pera and starring Marco Nanini and Ney Latorraca) played for twelve years (in Rio de Janeiro, São Paulo, and on national tour) in the 1980s and 1990s. *Irma Vap* has had a counterpart in the 1990s, *A bofetada* (Slap on the face), played in *besteirol* style (improv and stand-up comedy) by the group Companhia Baiana de Patifaria based on texts (with frequent ad-libbing) by Mauro Rasi, Miguel Magno, and Ricardo de Almeida and performed by Wilson dos Santos, Diogo Lopes Filho, Frank Menezes, and Lelo Filho. Both *Irma Vap* and *A bofetada*, however, depart significantly from *Greta Garbo*, *Os rapazes da banda*, and *Gaiola das loucas* in that they abandon a key element—the neurotic older queen—in the plays of the 1970s and instead play up the campy, often outrageous scenes.

11. One assumes Mary's appearance was initially meant to validate the heterosexuality Renato vaunted in the beginning in order to bolster his desirability as a hustler. However, her physical presence may not have been necessary on stage, as demonstrated in *O assalto* where Hugo's heterosexual credentials are affirmed exclusively through his references to a wife and children (for whose sake he says he is ready to accept Vitor's offer of money and sex, until Vítor's extreme intensity and aggressiveness scare Hugo away).

12. The same insensitivity is found in the title of the play, which refers to the working-class district of Irajá in Rio de Janeiro and in the context of the play is portrayed as devoid of charm and cultivation.

13. This is said to be Brazilian theater's first full-blown male homosexual kiss shown on stage. The first male-male kiss in a Brazilian play seems to be that in *Beijo no asfalto*, which opened twelve years before *Greta Garbo*, but the kiss in Nelson's play is neither a homosexual kiss nor is it seen on stage. Apparently the first homosexual lip kiss on the Brazilian stage happened in 1958 in the Teatro Brasileiro de Comédia (TBC) staging of *Panorama visto da ponte*, the Brazilian version of Arthur Miller's *The View from the Bridge* (1957); the São Paulo-based TBC presented a new staging as part of the 1960 season with a slightly different cast. In that scene, one of the TBC stars, Leonardo Villar (in the role of Eddie Carbone) gives one of the young longshoremen a passionate liplock. Years later Miguel Carrano, who was one of the actors playing the role of the youth, gave this account of the kiss in the gay newspaper *Lampião da esquina*:

> *Quando eu levava um beijo do Leonardo Villar, o teatro inteiro vinha embaixo [sic]. Vaias, protestos, pessoas saindo, gritos de "Que viadagem!", era uma*

> *barra. Eu esperava, a qualquer momento, que o público invadisse o palco e nos linchasse.* (Moreira 1981: 13)
>
> [When Leonardo Villar kissed me, all hell broke loose. There was booing, protests, people walking out, some shouting "How faggy!" It was tough. Each time I was sure the audience was going to jump on stage and lynch us.]

Curiously, despite the homoeroticism between Eddie and the youth, the kiss is not explicitly called for in Miller's text nor is it mentioned in Décio de Almeida Prado's review of the TBC staging (*Teatro em progresso: Crítica teatral, 1955–1964* [São Paulo: Martins, 1964]: 93–96) or in Alberto Guzik's definitive study of the TBC, *Crônica de um sonho: O Teatro Brasileiro de Comédia, 1948–1964* (São Paulo: Brasiliense, 1986): 165–68; 189.

The 1960 TBC season also included another foreign play, *Um gosto de mel* (Shelagh Delaney's *A Taste of Honey* [1959]), this one with a gay male protagonist (played by Odavlas Petti). The sensitive, unhappy young man Geoff is befriended by a straight young woman (Natália Timberg) who lets him move into her apartment. Delaney's play, which was soon made into a film by Tony Richardson and starring Rita Tushingham and Murray Melvin, presented a sympathetic portrait of the difficult life of an openly gay young man in late 1950s industrial Manchester.

14. *Vera Maria de Jesus* was banned by the censorship apparatus when it was ready to be staged in 1969. When the five-year statute of limitation was about to expire in 1974, then Justice Minister Armando Falcão renewed the ban and stated the play was "*definitivamente*" (forever) banned in Brazil. To which, as Antônio Carlos Moreira recounts in *Lampião da esquina*, Fernando Melo fired off a brief telegram to Minister Falcão: "*Definitivamente?! Quá quá quá . . .*" (Forever?! Ha ha ha . . .) (Moreira 1981: 14). Although the text appeared in book form in 1981 without objection from the censors, the play remained banned from the stage until the end of the military regime in 1985.

15. *As tias* premiered on 7 May 1981 in Rio de Janeiro's Teatro da Lagoa, under the direction of Luis de Lima, in a Roberto Baker production starring Italo Rossi as Floro, Edney Giovenazzi as Arlindo, Paulo César Peréio as Juarez, Nildo Parente as Marcelo, Suzana Vieira as Maria de Lourdes, and Roberto Lopes as the chauffeur.

16. On *Lampião da esquina* see chapter 1, note 41.

17. Aguinaldo Silva wrote about half of the episodes of *Roque Santeiro* (1985), an adaptation of *O berço do herói* (Hero's cradle), the 1965 play by the distinguished playwright, Dias Gomes, who wrote the first and last thirds of the *telenovela.* A satirical view of the interplay of mysticism and politics in small-town Brazil, *Roque Santeiro* was the biggest hit in the history of Brazilian television, with nightly audiences often reaching levels above the 90 percent mark as measured by the IBOPE opinion poll institute.

18. Zeno Wilde's first produced play was *Daniel, Daniel* in 1974, followed by *A diva do barato* (The good trip queen) in 1976 and his best-known work by far,

Blue jeans (with Wanderley Bragança) in 1980. Virtually specializing, like Plínio Marcos before him, in the theatrical portrayal of social outcasts, Zeno subsequently wrote, among other plays, *O meu guri* (My own boy) in 1984 (for which the Associação Paulista de Críticos de Arte gave him an award for Best Author for that year), *Uma lição longe demais* (A lesson too far) in 1986, and *Sabe quem dançou?* (Know who's gone?) in 1990, winner of the Concurso Nacional de Dramaturgia for that same year (Timochenco Wehbi Award). In addition to his playwriting, from 1975 until his untimely death in 1998 Zeno Wilde was involved in the production of some of the most important plays of the period, including Fauzi Arap's *Pano de boca*, Chico Buarque's *Gota d'água* and *Opera do malandro*, and Oduvaldo Vianna Filho's *Papa Highirte*.

19. Whether or not they are former inmates of FEBEM (Brazil's juvenile reformatory system, depicted in the Hector Babenco film *Pixote* [1980]), these uneducated and unskilled teenagers often resort to prostitution for deceptively easy financial gain and end up ensnared in drug consumption. A number of them report physical and/or sexual abuse at home or the reformatory. Lonely, frustrated, and emotionally deprived, they are frequent agents of violence, including murder, unaware of their legal responsibilities and frequent victims of extrajudicial punishment.

20. Those involved with the production were reminded of the apparently large number of these men when members of the cast often received (after and sometimes even during each show) quiet proposals and silently passed pieces of paper with phone numbers (Zeno Wilde, personal interview).

21. In his book on *travestis* or transgendered Brazilian prostitutes, Don Kulick (1998: 159) examines the consensus among *travestis* that "a very large number of [males who seek transgendered prostitutes] want to be anally penetrated by the *travestis*." Kulick takes into account the difficulty in deciding the extent to which such a claim is "the reflection of some empirical reality and to what extent it is an element of *travesti* folklore" (160). His treatment of the situation is more balanced and more sympathetic than that of Hélio Silva, who in his 1993 book on transgendered prostitutes in Brazil reads such pronouncements as "a kind of guerrilla warfare against macho men, married men, family men, 'squares,' all those who under the cover of good behavior can slip, under protection, into practices that are not compatible with their public images" (translated by, and quoted in Kulick 1998: 161).

22. For example, the playwrights drew their material from over sixty hours of taped interviews with young male street walkers in Rio de Janeiro and São Paulo (Zeno Wilde, personal interview).

23. Other examples of such AIDS-occasioned changes include after-show lectures and debates and the distribution of free condoms and posters promoting "safe" sex.

24. In his account of the debacle surrounding the Brazilian production of *Hair*

in 1969, Yan Michalski mentions the final compromise reached with the censors whereby the nudity scenes were permitted as the lights were dimmed considerably. Michalski (1985: 39) reported that the stage was so dark the night he attended that he did not even notice the scenes had taken place.

25. By 1996 *Blue jeans* had had thirty-five different stagings throughout Brazil (Zeno Wilde, personal interview).

26. Another early 1980s gay-oriented play depicting full frontal center stage male nudity was an import, Martin Sherman's *Bent*, staged in Brazil in 1981.

27. As Charles Perrone (1989: 89) remarks, "Brecht's critique of early twentieth-century bourgeois mentality was no novelty to the Brazilian public, since it was staged in 1964 in São Paulo and 1967 in Rio de Janeiro."

28. For a political interpretation and historical background of the period see Luiz Werneck Vianna, "O americanismo: Da pirataria à modernização autoritária (e o que se pode seguir)," published as an introduction to the play (Buarque de Hollanda 1978: 5–15).

29. Expressing his fear of a possible gathering of minority groups, the reactionary Duran lists blacks and gays along with a number of victims of disease. His contempt for difference does not however keep him from seeing the political danger in a coalition of these groups that together form a sizeable segment of the population:

> *tanta gente imunda e miserável . . . os aleijados . . . os leprosos, os bêbados, os toxicômanos . . . Mais os tuberculosos, os maleitosos, os sifilíticos, os epilépticos, os débeis mentais, os menores abandonados, os velhinhos desamparados, as bichas, os pretos . . . e se prepare pra ver noventa por cento da população do Rio de Janeiro! (149)*
>
> [so many filthy, poor people . . . cripples, lepers, drunks, drug addicts . . . Plus those with tuberculosis, malaria, syphilis, epilepsy, mental retardation, and the street kids, the uncared-for old men and women, the faggots, the blacks . . . be prepared to see who make up ninety per cent of Rio de Janeiro's population!]

30. The Brazilian version of Manuel Puig's novel *El beso de la mujer araña* (1976), opened in Spain and later that same year in Brazil, to critical and public acclaim at Teatro Ipanema, starring Rubens Correa as Molina, an effeminate man arrested for "corruption of minors." Although not a Brazilian playwright, Puig (who lived in Brazil for several years in the late 1970s and early 1980s) contributed an important twist to the issue of homosexual seduction, with the gay man's sexual seduction of his heterosexual cellmate Valentín mirrored by the heterosexual man's political seduction of the previously apolitical Molina; after his release from jail, Molina is killed by the military while conducting a dangerous mission on behalf of Valentín's political group.

31. Trevisan (1986: 101) remarks on the fact that in the São Paulo production of *Opera do malandro* Geni was played by a "real" *travesti* (Andrea de Maio) but because he is more interested in discussing Andrea de Maio's prominence and wealth, he misses the chance to explore this issue further. Trevisan falls in the "authenticity" trap when he implies that Andrea was more suited to the role because she, like Geni, was a *travesti.* This fallacy is tantamount to holding that only a gay man could write gay male roles, a view amply disproven by Chico Buarque's portrayal of Geni.

32. Terms like *bicha* and *veado* (and its alternative spelling, *viado*) are used in Brazil as perhaps the most offensive epithets one can direct at a man because, both terms, in addition to holding nonhuman association, reduce a man to the status of a woman (see chapter 1). Chapter 2 considers the use of homosexuality by the Left as well as the Right as a tool to denigrate the enemy. The same is true in plays of the period under consideration in this chapter. A myriad of works of every stripe include occurrences of such use. In the early 1970s, as the political climate became increasingly hostile to the theater and the censors stricter, playwrights resorted to what came to be known as a *teatro de metáforas* (theater of metaphors). Some authors, particularly of the Left, used homosexuality as a metaphor for repression. For example, three stinging denunciations of torture—Augusto Boal's *Torquemada* (1972), Jorge Andrade's *Milagre na cela* (1977; Miracle in a prison cell) and João Ribeiro Chaves Neto's *Patética* (1978; Pathétique)—all set mostly in a jail, include abusive terms like *bicha*, *veado*, and *fresco* to disparage heterosexuals who worked for the military regime. More often than not, these usages are by heterosexuals attempting to hurt other heterosexuals, and even a politically correct character like Manguari in Oduvaldo Vianna Filho's *Rasga coração* (Heartrending) resorts to this kind of verbal violence. Furthermore, characters like jailors and torturers are discredited or demonized through a direct or indirect association with homosexuality, as is the case in Andrade's, Boal's, and Chaves Neto's plays. In Roberto Athayde's allegorical portrayal of the dictatorship, *Apareceu a Margarida* (1973; *Miss Margarida's Way* [1979]), Miss Margarida rants at her captive students calling them "faggots," the implication being that those who remain silent in a tyranny are despicable.

33. The term *homoternurismo* (homotenderness) was coined by the playwright in an attempt to distinguish the situation portrayed in his play from a homosexual liaison (Prata 9–10). Unfortunately Prata did not elaborate or expand on the term, as it would be interesting to contrast it with other terms like *homoerotismo* (homoeroticism) and *homossociabilidade* (homosociality).

34. The same discourse informs the playwright's foreword, "A ternura do olhar" [The tenderness of the gaze] in the typescript I consulted (the play has never been published).

The title of both the play and its foreword allude to "A noite do meu bem," the 1950s classic by singer and composer Dolores Duran.

35. On Herbert Daniel's political activism and literary career, see chapter 1, n. 32.

36. The playwright has objected vehemently to directorial liberties with his texts, including a staging of *A aurora da minha vida* in which a character to whom Naum had not given a gay identity is portrayed as such (Milleret 1995: 151).

37. Among the prestigious awards Naum has received are the Molière, the Mambembe, and the São Paulo Theater Critics Prize.

38. Naum, who grew up in a strict Protestant family in tiny Pirajuí, in the state of São Paulo, was for many years a schoolteacher before hitting it big in 1972 as the designer for the hugely successful *Vila Sésamo*, the Brazilian television version of *Sesame Street*. He drew from his experiences in the classroom and design studio to start the Pod Minoga, an acting workshop and theater group he headed for most of the 1970s. No other Brazilian theater practitioner of his generation has displayed such a range of talent as Naum, who in addition to his playwriting and set designing has directed plays (not only his own but also such works as *Dona Doida* [Crazy miss] based on the poetry of Adélia Prado, in 1990), musical events (including the landmark shows, *Falso brilhante* [Fake diamond] with Elis Regina in 1976, and *Mulheres de Hollanda* [Women from Holland *or* The women of Chico Buarque de Hollanda], based on the music of Chico Buarque de Hollanda, in 1990), dance (*Salão de baile*, 1993 [Ballroom dancing]), and in 1992 in the opera (*Opera dos 500* [The Opera of the 500th Anniversary of the Discovery]). Naum has redefined the dynamics of creating performing arts in Brazil to prove that high art and low can coexist, as is made evident by his contributions to television where, in addition to *Vila Sésamo*, his work has included scriptwriting (for the groundbreaking show, *TV Pirata* [Pirate TV] among others) and directing sitcoms, such as *Até que a morte nos separe* (Till death do us part), the Brazilian version of *Married with Children*. In addition to the trilogy, Naum has written other plays such as *Nijinsky* (1987) and *Suburbano coração* (1989; Love stories of the working class), which starred Brazilian theater and cinema *diva* Fernanda Montenegro in the main role and in which Chico Buarque songs offset three friends' often comic search for true love. He has also experimented with the monologue form (*Agua com açúcar* [1994; Sweetened water]) and been involved with children's theater, working with well known groups such as Nau de Icaros and Pia Fraus.

39. The three plays appear in this sequence in the *Trilogy* volume; the chronology is not based on the date of composition but rather on the protagonist's age in the three works. The carefully produced volume includes an introduction by Bárbara Heliodora in which the well-known critic completely avoids issues like homoeroticism and homosexuality.

40. As an artistic youth learning to come to terms with his homosexuality, Juliano is to some extent reminiscent of Tom Wingfield in Tennessee Williams's *The Glass Menagerie* (1944).

Chapter 4. AIDS, Subalternity, and the Stage

1. Alberto Sandoval (1994: 51) points out that "The first decade of cultural representations of AIDS was led by gay white males who had access to Broadway and off-Broadway," with little attention paid to "other experiences such as those of drug addicts, Haitians [singled out initially as a risk group, a measure whose racism escaped very few observers], hemophiliacs, and even heterosexuals with AIDS." Sandoval goes on to identify three stages in the evolution of gay theater on AIDS in the United States: anger and accusation; safer sex campaigning; and creativity (52). In the early period, "instead of showing people living with AIDS, they are seen dying of AIDS. Their life is a death sentence and anger and rage do not allow for negotiation and alternative experience" (65n. 4). The first two stages saw plays that are "educational and want to voice the gay experience. These are agit-prop pieces full of terror, anger, and fury. They vociferate discrimination, compassion, frustration, pain, confusion, grief, death, loss, helplessness, and activism" (52). The third stage begins when "AIDS theater moves from propaganda to creative theatrical and poetic forms" (52).

2. AIDS has hit the Brazilian theater hard, depriving theatergoers of a more thorough experience of the theatrical event and, above all, causing numerous and tragically untimely deaths, cutting short several highly promising careers. A short list of the lives Brazilian theater has lost to AIDS includes directors Luis Roberto Galizia and Carlos Wilson, set designers Alziro Azevedo, Flávio Império, Edmar Pereira, and Fernando Zimpeck, playwrights Vicente Pereira and Timochenko Webbi, and actors Erick Barreto, Thales Pan Chacon, Lauro Corona, Rubens Correa, Hugo della Santa, Caíque Ferreira, Cláudia Magno, João Alberto Pinheiro, Carlos Augusto Strazzer, and Paulo Vilaça.

AIDS hysteria has fueled powerful gossip mills within Brazil's theater circles, so much so that a code language has developed in which "*estar doente*" (to be ill), for example, has come to mean that one has AIDS symptoms. The news, and subsequent denials, were particularly tenacious in one such incident, thanks to the prominence of its focus, director José Celso Martinez Correa of Teatro Oficina and Uzyna Uzona fame; see *Folha de São Paulo* 3, 4, 5, and 7 June 1994.

3. Andreato has vast experience in directing and performing monologues that he has adapted from other genres, such as *Van Gogh* (1995), a biographical sketch of the Dutch painter, and *Escritos do cárcere* (1997; The Prison writings), a selection of passages from Oscar Wilde's *De Profundis* and *The Ballad of Reading Gaol.*

4. Aranha's work was the subject of a 1993 documentary (*Presságios* [Pressages]) by film director Renato Falcão (b. 1963) and inspired a series of twenty-one AIDS-themed gouaches by noted Brazilian painter Iberê Camargo (1914–1994). The paintings were first exhibited in an art museum (Museu de Arte do Rio Grande do Sul, in Porto Alegre) and then sold to the public, with the proceeds

going to Um Ato de Amor à Vida (An Act of Love for Life), the AIDS services organization created by Aranha.

5. Another example of this group of plays is Regina Antonini and Marcelo Sabak's *Bravissimo*, which premiered at the Teatro Villa-Lobos in Rio de Janeiro in August of 1997. With music by Breno Marques and Cristina Bhering and starring Edwin Luisi, Luisa Thiré, and Fábio Villa Verde, the play uses flashbacks and voiceovers to portray the story of a distinguished maestro whose love for the girlfriend of his youth is rekindled just as he learns he is HIV-positive. Though hardly innovative in its staging or narrative and occasionally verging on melodrama, the production is noteworthy for its rare portrayal of AIDS in a heterosexual setting and also for the financial support of Glaxo Wellcome, the producers of AZT. In addition to the normal stage-related costs, the multinational pharmaceutical paid for the intense publicity campaign surrounding the opening of the play, including a number of highly visible and intriguing billboards in several areas of Rio de Janeiro.

6. Still, it is important to note, the playwright had to arrange for private publication of his play.

7. Segregated by the result of HIV-antibody tests or for having full-blown AIDS, these women are representative of the real-life inmates who are victims of prison administration measures that violate their basic legal and human rights. Useless for stopping the spread of AIDS, segregation is clearly punitive, with denial of access to recreation, visitation, the canteen, the library, education, and job training (ACT/UP New York 139–40).

8. The Portuguese noun "*mancha*" (stain, blemish; [from the Latin "*macula*"]) and verb, "*manchar*" (to stain, blemish, taint) are used literally as well as figuratively; compare with the expressions "*manchar a honra ou reputação de alguém*" (to taint someone's honor or reputation) and "*deixar manchas*" (to leave lasting stains); in short, what has *manchas* is impure. To the benignly distant "*mancha branca*" (large white area observed on Saturn's surface) and "*mancha vermelha*" (large reddish-pink area observed on Jupiter's Southern hemisphere) is now juxtaposed this menacing "*Mancha Roxa,*" which in the singular, and capitalized, alludes to the threat of AIDS, the stigma of AIDS, the disgrace of AIDS. In lower case, singular or plural, the term refers to the Kaposi's sarcoma lesions that afflict some AIDS patients, the signs that have become markers of AIDS in stereotypical depictions of the condition. In a repressive and uncaring society, these lesions have become a latter-day "*mancha de Caim*" (mark of Cain) (Baker 1994: 191). The same connotations are also present in Caio Fernando Abreu's play, *O homem e a mancha*, examined below. At one point in Marcos's work (1988: 27), however, the purple lesions are likened to Christ's wounds, perhaps to signal compassion and redemption, sentiments absent in Caio's play.

Marcos also uses the word "*roxa*" (purple) to denote AIDS, be it as a noun ("*Morrer de roxa é feio,*" says Isa at one point [28] [it is shameful to die from purpleness), or as an adjective, when toward the end Tita remarks, in resignation, "*Ninguém ouve a voz roxa*" (35) (No one hears the purple voice).

9. Another way of looking at this figure, is that 25 percent were per force women and that infection among women was increasing dramatically. While in the nation as a whole gay men have borne and continue to bear the brunt of the disease, other populations have begun to show marked statistical changes. The following data help illustrate the progress of the so-called "*feminização da epidemia*" (femininization of the epidemic) in Brazil throughout the 1980s and 1990s. For the country as a whole, the infection ratio in 1984 was 126 men to 1 woman; ten years later it was 5 men to 1 woman (Parker and Galvão 1996: 8). In the hardest hit state (São Paulo) the infection ratio in 1985 was 43 to 1; in January 1994 it was 4 to 1 (at that time, in Canada it was 20 to 1, in the USA 8 to 1, and in parts of Africa 1 to 1). Deaths from AIDS in the state of São Paulo for the year 1997 showed a ratio of 2.6 men to 1 woman (*Problemas Brasileiros* 327 [May–June 1998]: 6). In the city of São Paulo HIV infection among women rose 2,800 percent between 1984 and 1995; in mid 1995 the infection rate in the city was 1 man to 1 woman (*Folha de São Paulo* 9 October 1995, sec. 1, p. 1, sec. 3, p. 1). And in July 1996 it was announced that AIDS was the leading cause of death among women 25 to 34 years of age (*Folha de São Paulo* 21 July 1996: sec. 3).

Among the incarcerated population, the situation is even bleaker: the State of São Paulo Department of Corrections estimates that inmate HIV infection in mid 1995 was 20 percent among men and 30 percent among women (*Jornal da Tarde* 3 October 1995). By early 1996, the *New York Times* reported that infection among incarcerated women in Brazil had climbed to 35 percent (22 March 1996: sec. A), having almost doubled in only nine years (it was 18.3 percent in 1987 [Castilho 1994: 65]). U.S. data show that "incarcerated women diagnosed with AIDS live approximately half as long as their male counterparts" (ACT/UP New York 1996: 139); the same study concludes that "given the lack of proper medical treatment in prison, entering prison is a virtual death sentence for many women" with AIDS (139)—both statements being safely applicable to the situation in Brazil. Conditions in Brazilian prisons are generally atrocious and the disregard for the human rights of inmates, especially those who are HIV-positive, is notorious. These issues are pointed out in books such as Drauzio Varella's *Estação Carandiru* (São Paulo: Companhia das Letras, 1999) and reports such as Hélio Bicudo and Roberto Braz Ianini's "Encarcerados no Brasil" (Prison inmates in Brazil) in *Direitos humanos no Brasil, 1992–1993*, published by the Justice and Peace Committee of the Archdiocese of Brasília (São Paulo: Loyola, 1994); see also Herbert de Souza (Betinho)'s lecture "Direitos Humanos e AIDS" (Human Rights and AIDS), in *Direitos humanos e medo, AIDS, anistia, Estado, literatura*, published by São Paulo's Justice and Peace Committee (São Paulo: Brasiliense, 1989).

10. It is a measure of the degree of social rejection of people who are seropositive and incarcerated that a large segment of the general population stood behind

the São Paulo police responsible for the October 1992 massacre in the Carandiru Penitentiary. An egregious example of such support is that of Roberval Conte Lopes in his 1994 *Matar ou morrer* (Kill or die)—which he had to publish himself for lack of editorial interest—asserting that the high incidence of AIDS and seropositivity in prisons such as Carandiru justified the mass killing. For a reliable account of the Carandiru massacre, see the report issued by the University of São Paulo's Núcleo de Estudos da Violência (Center for the Study of Violence) and Comissão Teotônio Vilela (Teotônio Vilela Committee for Human Rights), *Os direitos humanos no Brasil*, ed. Túlio Kahn (São Paulo: USP/NEV/CTV, 1993), 64–73. *Carandiru*, the highly acclaimed film version of Varela's book, directed by Hector Babenco, opened in early 2003; in just a few months it became the top-grossing Brazilian film of all time. The penitentiary itself has since been imploded by the state.

See also Varela's *Estação Carandiru*, a fascinating account by a physician who volunteered his time and expertise in a ten-year effort to improve conditions at the infamous penitentiary.

11. In *O abajur lilás*, which predates AIDS by one decade, the accusations involve tuberculosis but aim to stigmatize the prostitutes in much the same way the prisoners in *A mancha roxa* resort to HIV infection. The atmosphere is equally oppressive and the lack of perspective equally despairing for both groups of women.

12. The term "crisis of representation" involving AIDS and minorities in the United States is used by Sandoval to refer to the fact that mainstream plays and films about HIV-positive people are authored by and only represent white men. Women, Latinos, and other minorities are thus not being dramatically represented; their crisis is not being revealed. Sandoval does acknowledge that this is part of a larger problem, that of a lack of Latino-authored theater in the United States. It is not, he explains, that such plays do not exist—they just do not find their way to the commercial stage (Sandoval 1994: 49–58).

13. Uses of the acronym also occur in the title of Cuban American dramatist Ofelia Fox's play *Siempre Intenté Decir Algo / Alguien Importante Decidió Salir* (I always tried to say something / Someone important came out), which premiered in Miami in 1989, and in the name of the San Francisco-based group that pioneered AIDS theater in 1984—Artists Involved with Death and Survival.

14. This study is based on a series of interviews and observations conducted in Rio de Janeiro in August 1996. I wish to thank Vagner de Almeida for his generosity in sharing his materials and time during several meetings, in particular during a long interview at his Copacabana home on 21 August 1996; for giving me access to his files, manuscripts, and videotaped performances; and for allowing me to sit in on his Wednesday night discussion groups with at-risk individuals (some of whom have gone on to write and to perform in works such as *Cabaret prevenção* [Prevention cabaret]). I am also indebted to ABIA and especially to Richard Parker for their constant support and sharing of information.

15. Bowing to the reality of widespread bisexuality in Brazil and in the interest of reaching a population that is notoriously difficult to contact, the group decided to substitute in its name the sentence *"homens que fazem sexo com homens"* (men who have sex with men) for "gays" or *"entendidos"* (gay men). See Parker on bisexuality (1991: 83, 92–95, 168) and the different terms used for homosexuals and homosexuality in Brazil (43–54).

16. On Projeto Homossexualidades, see the Special Issue (October 1994) of *Boletim ABIA* dedicated to the Projeto; also see Almeida et al. (1996: 1–2). The project was funded by a host of governmental and nongovernmental organizations, including Family Health International, the Brazilian Ministry of Health, and the John D. and Catherine T. MacArthur Foundation.

17. For a good summary of the work of these and other groups, see Klein (1998); and Station (1995).

18. Another example of this type of theater is the work of another Rio de Janeiro group, Teatro Vida, whose most successful production, Paulo Sérgio Mag's musical *Le Cabaret*, opened in October 1996. Unlike the Oficina de Teatro Expressionista, Teatro Vida's cast includes women, and AIDS is only one of numerous themes treated, with loneliness, prostitution, drug abuse, and madness being other issues of concern to the group and to the professionals (doctors, attorneys, analysts, social workers) who volunteer their time to participate in the debates that follow their performances (see "AIDS tratada com música," *Jornal do Brasil*, 4 October 1996: sec. B).

Also of note is the outreach work of Programa Pegação, a project started in 1989 for HIV/AIDS prevention among *michês* (male sex workers) in Rio de Janeiro; see the account by its cocoordinator, Paulo Henrique Longo, "The Meeting of the Michês," *New Internationalist* (February 1994): 20–21. See also Nestor Perlongher, *O negócio do michê: Prostituição viril em São Paulo* (São Paulo: Brasiliense, 1987).

19. The work of these Brazilian groups in many ways parallels that conducted in the United States by the New York City People with AIDS Theater Workshop; on the American counterparts, see Jones (1993: 121, 2n. 13).

20. Before making comparisons with the much higher numbers related to a commercial production such as *A mancha roxa*, one is advised to consider Jan Grover's caveat in "The Convergence of Art and Crisis" (1986: 31): "In looking at gay or any other subcultural art-making, it is important to look at the work's production, circulation and reception *in relation to its subcultural powerbase*. This is an important distinction, because comparing subcultural with mainstream productions on the basis of mainstream criteria . . . can only distort the achievements of subcultural work. An important reality of illegal or marginal subcultures is that they have fewer artists and institutions for producing, circulating and rewarding work, as well as smaller audiences to view and read it."

21. The text, edited by Vagner de Almeida, was published two years after the performance (Almeida 1997).

22. For the title, 283 possibilities were suggested; a marathon cast meeting cut the list first to 20 and later to 7 finalists; from among those, the eventual title was chosen by ABIA directors. Examples of finalists are, "Docinho" (Candy), one of the more common euphemisms current in Rio de Janeiro among those who cannot or will not name AIDS; and "*Sei que vou morrer com ela*," a double entendre which can be translated as "I know I'll die with her" or the more relevant "I know I'll die of it."

23. Some of these scenes and transitions between them are reminiscent of passages in Marlon Riggs's 1991 film, *Tongues Untied*, which occasioned a vicious reaction from the American right-wing when it was shown on PBS in July 1991. The film attempts "to counteract the anguish engendered by the hate gay blacks experience not only from whites but from a large proportion of the African-American community" (Pastore 1993: 30). Like *Tongues Untied*, in comparison with other U.S. AIDS films, *Cabaret Prevenção* is considerably more direct in its sexual content than other Brazilian AIDS plays, including simulated gay sex (onstage gay sex scenes still being unthinkable in Brazil outside the realm of pornography).

24. This was occasioned in part by the realities of working with persons with AIDS. A meeting held three hours before show time each night would determine how far each actor could go that night, emotionally and physically; those not feeling their best would be given less demanding roles or be replaced by understudies.

25. Rudnick's stroke of genius as a playwright was to discern the change in mood from the high-art doom and gloom that dominated most of the 1980s to a more inclusive, more popular, AIDS culture. Thus, while Edmund White's essay, "Esthetics and Loss," [1989: 151] encapsulated such an attitude ("If art is to confront AIDS more honestly than the media has done, it must begin in tact, avoid humor, and end in anger"). Rudnick in essays and interviews has consistently defended the writing of AIDS comedy; unfortunately, he has not gone beyond generalities ("only laughter can make the nightmare bearable" [1993: 21]) and witticisms ("Laughter and flair and an occasional cashmere sweater are to be treasured, accepted, and charged whenever possible" [1996: 35]). A more substantive treatment is Román (1992; 1998), which focuses on camp as a survival tactic in Terrence McNally's *The Lisbon Traviatta*, Lyspinka's *I Could Go On Lipsynching*, and the Sodomoy Players' *AIDS! The Musical!*

26. In this light, it should come as no surprise that the most brilliant comedic treatment of AIDS by a Latin American playwright was done outside Latin America. In *Une Visite inopportune* the Argentinian French Copi (the pseudonym of Raul Damonte, 1941–1987) subverts death and "transforms the bleakest visions of reality into high farce, . . . succeed[ing] in transforming outrage and horror into delight" (Wetsel 1994: 121); see also Wetsel 1992: 104–7.

27. The Job sign appears in other Brazilian AIDS texts, although without the same degree of sophistication found in Abreu's play; see for example, Mário Justino's *Nos bastidores do reino: A vida secreta na Igreja Universal do Reino de*

Deus (São Paulo: Geração Editorial, 1995): 134. Allegorizations of AIDS might also be anchored in another biblical book, *Apocalypse*, which, at the time of this writing, is the announced theme of Araújo's next collaboration with Teatro da Vertigem. In the United States, apocalyptic imagery has had particular resonance within AIDS theater (e.g., Kushner's *Angels in America*); for a provocative study of apocalyptic imaging, reasoning, and utterances in the representation of AIDS see Dickinson (1994).

28. As David Moss and Barbara Misztal (1990: 3) point out in their introduction to *Action on AIDS*, when it comes to other epidemics, "The past is indeed another country for AIDS; and knowledge of its terrain offers very limited guidance for us now." For, they write, "previous epidemics, of which those metaphors were once literal descriptions, do not provide a simple history lesson for direct application to management of HIV infection. . . . [And] contemporary understandings of privacy, freedom from discrimination, and civil liberty have drastically transformed the constraints on responses."

29. Here and in subsequent quotations I use the English translation provided anonymously in the tastefully produced, richly informative playbill. In addition to Araújo's text, the booklet includes an elucidating commentary by the playwright and a summary of the activities of the ensemble Teatro da Vertigem.

30. The production had a revival in the same location in mid 1996. In addition, Teatro da Vertigem performed *O livro de Jó* during the Porto Alegre em Cena festival in October 1996 and in a vacant wing of São Francisco de Assis Hospital in Rio de Janeiro in March 1997. The group also performed *O livro de Jó* in the San Juan de Dios Hospital in Bogotá, Colombia, as part of the Fifth Ibero-American Theatre Festival held in that city in March–April 1996 and in the FD dselsanstalten Hospital in Aarhus, Denmark, as part of that city's theater festival in September 1997.

At least one other contemporary Brazilian play has successfully used a hospital wing as stage. Ivana Moura's *O crepúsculo de Van Gogh*, an exploration of the limits of reason and of theatrical language, was presented at the Tamarineira Hospital for the Mentally Ill; the play premiered in November 1998 as part of the Second National Theater Festival in Recife.

31. This reluctance to name the condition is also found in plays by Spanish-speaking Latin American playwrights. Most notable among these plays is Isaac Chocrón's *Escrito y sellado* (1993) (Written and sealed); for Chocrón's reflections on the genesis and writing of his play, including his reasons for not mentioning the disease by name in his work, see Moreno-Uribe (1993: 73–74).

32. The association is made even stronger by the use of bed sheets with the stamp for Hospital Emílio Ribas, a large hospital for infectious diseases widely known in Brazil as a center for AIDS treatment.

33. For a truly provocative discussion of the implications of actual blood on stage in the age of AIDS, see John E. McGrath's 1995 account of and response to

Martyrs and Saints, Ron Athey's 1993 performance work in which the artist, who is HIV positive, has his assistants run needles through his scalp and push darts into his body, with blood running down his body and onto the stage. McGrath's reaction to the challenge of Athey's performance (in addition to fainting twice while in attendance) includes celebrating the construction of a space for the HIV-positive person, "asserting pleasure, perversity, and spirituality within the context of a privileged understanding" and lamenting that "the panic of his blood, the breaking of his skin's barrier, destroys the theatre of the moment, allows no metaphors of mysticism or S & M to insert meaning into the spectacle" (25–26). It is precisely this panic, however, this "inverse of the theatrical experience . . . [this] non-experience of control" (27), this sense of being unsafe and at risk, this destruction of the theatrical context, its conventions and assurances—that disturbs the spectator into a new experience of the condition.

34. Nachtergaele's career took off after the rave reviews he got for his performance in *O livro de Jó*. He appeared in two major films of the 1990s, Bruno Barreto's *O que é isso, companheiro?* (*Four Days in September*) and Walter Moreira Salles's *Central do Brasil* (*Central Station*); both works were Oscar nominees in the foreign film category, in 1998 and 1999, respectively; the latter won the Best Film award at the 1998 Berlin Film Festival. Nachtergaele has also had key roles in two hugely successful miniseries: *Hilda Furacão* (a June 1998 adaptation of Roberto Drummond's eponymous novel; Nachtergaele played the drag queen Cintura Fina) and *Auto da Compadecida* (a January 1999 adaptation of Ariano Suassuna's play of the same title; he played the protagonist João Grilo).

35. The selection of George Michael was not accidental. He is widely known in Brazil as the lover of a designer, Anselmo Feleppa, who died of AIDS in 1993; the Brazilian press has reported on the affair and Michael's visits to the late man's family; see for example, *Veja*, 13 October 1993: 81.

Michael eventually came out following his much-publicized arrest for "lewd behavior" in a Los Angeles restroom in 1998.

36. The show, *Pela passagem de uma grande dor* (For the passing of a great sorrow), was a one-time event held in Porto Alegre on 25 February 1997, the first anniversary of Caio's death. It was conceived and directed by Luciano Alabarse and included the participation of actors Zé Adão Barbosa, Alejandra Herzberg, Lauro Ramalho, Zeca Kiechaloski, Rosângela Batistella, and Ivan Mattos. All of the texts used for the readings had appeared in print but for one of the songs, "Alegre" (Happy or Gay), which was a new piece Adriana Calcanhoto composed for and dedicated to Caio.

37. In Luso-Brazilian literature, since the middle of the nineteenth century a "*crônica*" is "a 'sketch' of life, be it historical, personal, or imaginary . . . an open-ended genre [with] few fixed rules . . . its theme and content rang[ing] from the lightly poetic to the bitingly satiric or even to black humor . . . its language . . . highly colloquial; its length . . . most often less than 1,000 words; it offers no direct

moral" (Stern 1988: 100). Because there is no exact equivalent in English, I am keeping the Portuguese term, as do other critics and translators, among them the late Giovanni Pontiero in *Selected Crônicas*, his English translation of Clarice Lispector's *Descoberta do mundo* (New Directions, 1996).

38. By "the theatrical" here, I mean not the recourse to the establishment and development of an identifiable conflict but the use of a first-person narrative as a means to reveal the hidden spectacle-ness in often pedestrian situations. Foremost among these "*crônicas*" is the series of three pieces written in the guise of letters to a friend and published in *O Estado de São Paulo* in August and September of 1994. In them, Caio creates the vivid image of a man trying to smuggle a written message to those who are "*além dos muros*" (beyond the outer walls), presumably an AIDS-free area (Abreu 1996c: 96–104).

39. In spite of his obvious importance, Caio Fernando Abreu (along with other key authors) was not included in the otherwise comprehensive reference book edited by David William Foster (1994), *Latin American Writers on Gay and Lesbian Themes: A Bio-Critical Sourcebook.*

40. In an elucidating interview he gave to the newspaper *Estado de São Paulo*, Caio claims to have pioneered the depiction of AIDS in Brazilian fiction with the 1988 short story, "Linda, uma história horrível" (Linda, a terrible story) (Castello 1995); the piece was later translated by David Treece as "Beauty" in *Dragons* (1990), the English version of *Os dragões não conhecem o paraíso*. However, Herbert Daniel's AIDS-themed novel *Alegres e irresponsáveis abacaxis americanos* (Happy [or gay] and irresponsible American suckers) was published in 1987; Daniel died of AIDS-related complications in 1992.

AIDS appears in numerous other works by Caio, including his 1990 novel *Onde andará Dulce Veiga?* (published in a 2000 translation as *Whatever Happened to Dulce Veiga?*), and in his own translations, such as his Portuguese version of Susan Sontag's 1991 novella, *The Way We Live Now.* After the confirmation of his diagnosis in 1994, AIDS becomes central to Caio's writing, as evidenced by "Depois de Agosto" (After August), included in his 1995 *Ovelhas negras* (Black sheep); and "Bem Longe de Marienbad" (Quite far from Marienbad), published posthumously in *Estranhos estrangeiros* (Strange foreigners) (1996c).

41. Of the eight theater texts in *Teatro completo*, "A maldição do Vale Negro" is the only one to have previously appeared in print (Abreu and Nunes 1988).

42. The other two, *Pela noite* and *Dama da noite*, were not included in *Teatro completo* because they were written as short stories. The former appeared first in *Triângulo das águas* (1983; The water triangle) and later in *Estranhos estrangeiros*; the latter first appeared in book form in *Os dragões não conhecem o paraíso*. Both had had previous stagings.

43. Directed by Flávio Rangel and starring the two top actors of the time, Paulo Autran and Bibi Ferreira, the show opened in Rio in 1972 and was a major box office hit, running for over a year. Part of the reason for its appeal was the

Portuguese lyrics (by Chico Buarque) for the song "The Impossible Dream," a prime example of the language of allegory then predominant in Brazilian art as a result of the intolerant censorship apparatus of the military regime. "Nonsuspect" materials (such as a Broadway musical) served as vehicles for artists to encode messages avidly deciphered by large segments of the art-consuming public. Attending a play or a music festival was in itself an act of defiance; being in a theater in the company of a large group of people who shared the same values was a statement of resistance to the dictatorship, then at its most repressive.

44. While both *"O homem com a mancha"* and *"O homem da mancha"* translate as "the man with the lesion," the former suggests togetherness, whereas the latter stresses physical appearance (as when describing someone, *"a mulher de óculos,"* the woman in glasses, or, *"o homem de bigode,"* the man with the moustache). When the noun indicates a place (as in Mancha), *"de"* (or in this case the contraction with a feminine definite article "a") denotes origin.

45. In the playbill, Breda writes of his discovery of *O homem e a mancha* precisely at a time when he was looking for a thesis topic for an M.A. in performance arts.

Caio willed his longtime friend Breda all rights to his plays and stage adaptations of narratives (Gilberto Gawronski is executor for television and cinema, and Gil França Veloso the literary estate executor).

46. For Caio's description of the occasion when Clarice dubbed him "Quixote," see Castello (1995).

47. I am indebted to Gilberto Gawronski for the wealth of information on his work he provided in a long interview in Rio de Janeiro, 15 January 1997.

48. One is immediately reminded of two other contemporary Brazilian plays, Chico Buarque's *Roda viva* (1967) and Leilah Assunção's *Roda cor de roda* (1973).

49. For a cogent analysis of the *"pós-tudo"* controversy in Brazilian thought and literary production, especially, poetry, see Perrone (1996: 149–68).

50. For a comprehensive survey and perceptive analysis of the different movements see James Green (1994).

51. Caio began working on *Dama da noite* at the Ritz bar (in São Paulo) in the early evening, continued to write at home later that night, and only stopped when the piece was completed the following morning at six o'clock (Castello 1995).

52. Renato Farias is a *gaúcho* (from the state of Rio Grande do Sul) as are Marcos Breda, Luiz Arthur Nunes, Gilberto Gawronski, and, of course, Caio Fernando Abreu. A lifelong admirer of Caio's work, he mustered the courage to knock on the writer's door one day in early 1994, bringing along a videotaped dramatic reading of *Pela noite*. Caio gave his permission on the spot and was enthusiastically supportive of the project, personally calling a number of people who were instrumental in the production's success (*Jornal do Brasil*, Programa, 30 August 1996).

53. Caio was an early proponent in Brazil of the long-established technique of

using American jazz in creating mood and evoking love pains. In his 1996 narrative *Keith Jarrett no Blue Note* (Keith Jarrett at the Blue Note), Silviano Santiago has augmented the scope of the device, giving it a structural role (and subtitling the book, "Improviso de Jazz" [Jazz improvisation]); each section of the work is named after a piece from the Keith Jarrett compact disk ("Autumn Leaves," "Days of Wine and Roses," "When I Fall in Love," and so on), setting up a focal tension as the narrative's gay sensibility is played out against the feelings evoked by such standards of heterosexual love (S. Santiago, personal interview).

54. The AIDS crisis has illustrated more strongly perhaps than any other event in recent Brazilian history the large extent to which the personal is the political and how strongly Brazilian society reacts when it is reminded of that fact. The immediacy of the crisis led numerous gay men to an openness to their own homosexuality and in many cases to become involved in some aspect of the production of AIDS plays. That their participation in such theatrical events challenged hegemonic views and constituted a political act was evidenced in the anonymous phone calls and written messages threatening the different casts and production crews with physical aggression and even death.

Afterword

1. For a recent example of the reverence for Magaldi, see the laudatory sections in George 2000: 119–28, 157, 159.

2. For a glowing account of Brazil's successes in handling AIDS and a report on U.S. tactics to pressure Brazil to abandon its production of cheap, generic AIDS drugs in defiance of patents held by U.S. pharmaceuticals, see Tina Rosenberg, "How to Solve the World's AIDS Crisis," *New York Times Magazine* (28 January 2001).

Works Cited

Printed Sources

Abreu, Caio Fernando. 1988. *Os dragões não conhecem o paraíso*. São Paulo: Companhia das Letras.

———. 1990. *Dragons*. Translated by David Treece. London: Boulevard Books.

———. 1996a. *Estranhos estrangeiros*. São Paulo: Companhia das Letras.

———. 1996b. "Palavras que jogam luz sobre a alma humana." *O Globo*, 11 August, Segundo Caderno.

———. 1996c. *Pequenas epifanias: Crônicas (1986–1995)*. Edited by Gil França Veloso. Porto Alegre: Editora Sulina.

———. 1997. *Teatro completo*. Edited by Luiz Arthur Nunes. Porto Alegre: Editora Sulina / Instituto Estadual do Livro.

Abreu, Caio Fernando, and Luiz Arthur Nunes. 1988. *A maldição do Vale Negro*. Porto Alegre: Instituto Estadual do Livro.

ACT/UP New York, Women and AIDS Book Group. 1990. "Prison Issues and HIV." In *Women, AIDS, and Activism*. Boston: South End Press. 139–55.

Aguiar, Flávio. 1975. *Os homens precários: Inovação e convenção na dramaturgia de Qorpo-Santo*. Porto Alegre: A Nação / Instituto Estadual do Livro.

Aguinis, Marcos. 1997. "Entrevista." *Jornal do Brasil*, 1 March, Caderno Idéias.

"AIDS tratada com música." 1996. *Jornal do Brasil*, 4 October, sec. B.

Albuquerque, Severino J. 1991. *Violent Acts: A Study of Contemporary Latin American Theatre*. Detroit: Wayne State University Press.

Alcoff, Linda. 1991–92. "The Problem of Speaking for Others." *Cultural Critique* 20 (Winter): 5–32.

Almeida, Vagner de. 1994a. "*Cabaret Prevenção*: Expressionismo e sexualidade no palco." *Boletim ABIA* Especial (October): 14–15.

———. 1994b. "Oficina de teatro expressionista para homens que fazem sexo com homens." *Boletim ABIA* 25 (July–August): 9–11.

———, ed. 1997. *Cabaret Prevenção.* Rio de Janeiro: ABIA.

Almeida, Vagner de, Maria Eugênia Fernandes, Jane Galvão, Richard Parker, Veriano Terto Jr., and Elisabete Meloni Vieira. 1996. "*Cabaret Prevenção*: Expressionist Theatre and AIDS Prevention in Rio de Janeiro, Brazil." Paper presented at the Eleventh International Conference on AIDS.

Alves, Maria Elisa. 1993. "O craque que joga em dois times." *Veja,* 15 December: 102–3.

Andrade, Oswald de. "Manifesto Antropófago." *Revista de Antropofagia* 1: 3, 7.

———. 1928. 1974. *Um homem sem profissao: Memórias e confissões.* Vol. 9 of *Obras completas.* Rio de Janeiro: Civilização Brasileira.

———. 1976. *Teatro (A morta; O rei da vela; O homem e o cavalo).* Vol. 8 of *Obras completas.* Rio de Janeiro: Editora Civilização Brasileira.

Anon. 1997. "Villela é aplaudido pelo público e respeitado pela crítica." *O Estado de São Paulo* February 28, Suplemento Cultura.

Arenas, Fernando. 1999. "Writing after Paradise and before a Possible Dream: Brazil's Caio Fernando Abreu." *Luso-Brazilian Review* 36.2 (Winter): 13–21.

Athayde, Roberto. 1973. *Apareceu a Margarida: Monólogo tragicômico em dois atos.* Brasília and Rio de Janeiro: Editora Brasília.

Babcock, Barbara, ed. 1978. *The Reversible World: Symbolic Inversion in Art and Society.* Ithaca, N.Y.: Cornell University Press.

Baker, Rob. 1994. *The Art of AIDS.* New York: Continuum Publishing Company.

Bataille, Georges. 1988. *Inner Experience.* Translated by Leslie Anne Boldt-Irons. Albany: SUNY Press.

Bech, Henning. 1997. *When Men Meet: Homosexuality and Modernity.* Translated by Teresa Mesquit and Tim Davies. Chicago: University of Chicago Press.

Bergman, David. 1991. *Gaiety Transfigured: Gay Self-Representation in American Literature.* Madison: University of Wisconsin Press.

Bersani, Leo. 1995. *Homos.* Cambridge, Mass.: Harvard University Press.

Berthelot, Pierre. 1993. "AIDS Prevention on Stage." In *A Leap in the Dark: AIDS, Art, and Contemporary Cultures,* edited by Allen Klusacek and Ken Morrison. Montreal: Véhicule Press. 305–14.

Bessa, Marcelo Secron. 1997. *Histórias positivas: A literatura (des)construindo a AIDS.* Rio de Janeiro: Record.

Boal, Augusto, and Gianfrancesco Guarnieri and Edu Lobo. 1970. "Arena conta Zumbi." *Revista de Teatro* 378 (Novembro–Dezembro): 31–54.

Boone, Joseph Allen. 1998. *Libidinal Currents: Sexuality and the Shaping of Modernism.* Chicago: University of Chicago Press.

Borim, Dario, Jr. 1994. "Herbert Daniel." In *Latin American Writers on Gay and Lesbian Themes: A Bio-Critical Sourcebook,* edited by David Foster. Westport, Conn.: Greenwood Press. 129–34.

Buarque de Hollanda, Chico. 1978. *Opera do malandro.* São Paulo: Livraria Cultura Editora.

Butler, Judith. 1991. "Imitation and Gender Insubordination." *Inside/Out: Lesbian Theories, Gay Theories.* Edited by Diana Fuss. New York: Routledge. 13–31.

———. 1999. *Gender Trouble: Feminism and the Subversion of Identity.* Revised edition. New York: Routledge.

Canales, Luis. 1981. "O homossexualismo como tema no teatro brasileiro." *Luso-Brazilian Review* 18.1 (Summer): 173–81.

Case, Sue-Ellen. 1988. *Feminism and Theatre.* New York: Methuen.

Castello, José. 1995. "Inventário irremediável: Caio Fernando Abreu fala da vida antes da morte." *Estado de São Paulo:* 9 December, Caderno Dois.

Castilho, Euclides, Pedro Chequer, and Cláudio Struchiner. 1994. "A epidemiologia da AIDS no Brasil." In *A Aids no Brasil, 1982–1992,* edited by Richard Parker, Cristina Bastos, Jane Galvão, and José Stalin Pedrosa. Rio de Janeiro: Relume-Dumará / ABIA / IMS-UERJ. 59–67.

Cixous, Hélène. 1990. *Reading with Clarice Lispector.* Translated by Verena Andermatt Conley. Minneapolis: University of Minnesota Press.

Cláudio, Ivan. 1995. "Sem anestesia." *IstoÉ* 1330 (29 March): 84–85.

Comodo, Roberto. 1993. "Uma peça escrita com fúria e ódio." *Jornal do Brasil.* 11 January, Sec. B.

Coronil, Fernando. 1994. "Listening to the Subaltern: The Poetics of Neocolonial States." *Poetics Today* 15.4: 643–58.

Costa, Iná Camargo. 1996. *A hora do teatro épico no Brasil.* São Paulo: Editora Paz e Terra.

Costa, Jurandir Freire. 1979. *Ordem médica e norma familiar.* Rio de Janeiro: Graal.

———. *A inocência e o vício: Estudos sobre o homoerotismo.* Rio de Janeiro: Relume Dumará.

Coutinho, Valdi. 1992. "Prostituição masculina em ritmo de música." *Diário de Pernambuco* (Outubro): n.p.

Crimp, Douglas. 1988. "AIDS: Cultural Analysis/Cultural Criticism." In *AIDS: Cultural Analysis/Cultural Criticism.* Ed. Douglas Crimp. Cambridge, Mass.: MIT Press. 3–16.

da Matta, Roberto. 1991. *A casa a e rua: Espaço, cidadania, mulher e morte no Brasil.* Fourth edition. Rio de Janeiro: Guanabara Koogan.

de Lauretis, Teresa. 1987. *Technologies of Gender: Essays on Theory, Film and Fiction.* Bloomington: Indiana University Press.

Détienne, Marcel. 1979. *Dionysos Slain.* Translated by Mireille and Leonard Muellner. Baltimore: Johns Hopkins University Press.

Dickinson, Peter. 1994. "'Go-Go Dancing on the Brink of the Apocalypse': Representing AIDS. An Essay in Seven Epigraphs." *English Studies in Canada* 20: 227–47.

Dollimore, Jonathan. 1991. *Sexual Dissidence: Augustine to Wilde, Freud to Foucault.* New York: Oxford University Press.

Duncan, Cynthia. 1994–95. "Introduction." *The Configuration of Feminist Criticism and Theoretical Practices in Hispanic Literary Studies.* Special Issue of *INTI: Revista de Literatura Hispánica* 40–41: 3–19.

Durst, Rogério. 1985 *Madame Satã: Com o diabo no corpo.* São Paulo: Brasiliense.

Faria, Gentil Luiz de. 1988. *A presença de Oscar Wilde na 'belle époque' literária brasileira.* São Paulo: Editora Pannartz.

Ferreira, Aurélio Buarque de Hollanda. 1986. *Novo dicionário da língua portuguesa.* Second revised edition. Rio de Janeiro: Editora Nova Fronteira.

Ferreira, Mauro. 1996. "O dramaturgo das metáforas volta à cena." *O Globo.* Segundo Caderno. 11 August. Segundo Caderno.

———. 1997. "Teatro gay sai do gueto para a grande cena." *O Globo.* Segundo Caderno. 16 January.

Fonseca, Maria Augusta. 1990. *Oswald de Andrade, 1890–1954: Biografia.* São Paulo: Art Editora; Secretaria de Estado da Cultura.

Foster, David William. 1999. *Gender and Society in Contemporary Brazilian Cinema.* Austin: University of Texas Press.

———, ed. 1994. *Latin American Writers on Gay and Lesbian Themes: A Bio-Critical Sourcebook.* Westport, Conn.: Greenwood Press.

Freud, Sigmund. 1958. "Inversion. Invert." *Freud: Dictionary of Psychoanalysis.* Ed. Nandor Fodor and Frank Gaynor. Greenwich, Conn.: Fawcett. 86–87.

Fry, Peter. 1982. "Da hierarquia à igualdade: A construção histórica da homossexualidade no Brasil." *Para inglês ver: Identidade e política na cultura brasileira.* Rio de Janeiro: Zahar Editores. 87–115.

Fry, Peter, and Edward MacRae. 1983. *O que é homossexualidade.* São Paulo: Brasiliense.

Galante de Sousa, José. 1960. *O teatro no Brasil.* 2 vols. Rio de Janeiro: Ministério da Educação e Cultura / Instituto Nacional do Livro.

George, David. 1995a. "Review of *Cinco textos do teatro contemporâneo brasileiro.*" *Latin American Theatre Review* 29.1 (Fall): 188–90.

———. 1995b. "Theatre of the Oppressed and Teatro de Arena: In and Out of Context." *Latin American Theatre Review* 28.2 (Spring): 39–54.

———. 2000. *Flash and Crash Days: Brazilian Theatre in the Postdictatorship Period.* New York: Garland.

Gillespie, Michael Patrick. 1996. *Oscar Wilde and the Poetics of Ambiguity.* Gainesville: University of Florida Press.

Gonçalves, Augusto de Freitas Lopes. 1975. *Dicionário histórico e literário do teatro no Brasil.* Vol. 1. Rio de Janeiro: Editora Cátedra.

Green, James N. 1994. "The Emergence of the Brazilian Gay Liberation Movement, 1977–1981." *Latin American Perspectives* 21.1: 38–55.

———. 1996. *Beyond Carnival: Homosexuality in Twentieth-Century Brazil.* Ph.D. Diss. University of California–Los Angeles.

———. 1999. *Beyond Carnival: Male Homosexuality in Twentieth-Century Brazil.* Chicago: University of Chicago Press.

Gross, Larry. 1991. "Out of the Mainstream: Sexual Minorities and the Mass Media." *Journal of Homosexuality* 21.1–2: 19–46.

Grover, Jan. 1986. "The Convergence of Art and Crisis." *High Performance* 36: 28–31.

Guarnieri, Gianfrancesco. 1981. "Guarnieri." [Interview] *O Pasquim* 607 (1 December): 8–9.

Hewitt, Andrew. 1996. *Political Inversions: Homosexuality, Fascism, and the Modernist Imagination.* Stanford, Calif.: Stanford University Press.

Hocquenhem, Guy. 1993. *Homosexual Desire.* Translated by Daniella Dansoor. Durham: Duke University Press.

hooks, bell. 1988. *Talking Back: Thinking Feminist, Thinking Black.* Toronto: Between the Lines.

"Ilusões e sonhos de Caio Fernando." 1996. *Jornal do Brasil,* 22 December, sec. B.

Jones, James W. 1993a. "Refusing the Name: The Absence of AIDS in Recent American Gay Male Fiction." In *Writing AIDS: Gay Literature, Language, and Analysis,* edited by Timothy F. Murphy and Suzanne Poirier. New York: Columbia University Press. 225–43.

———. 1993b. "The Sick Homosexual: AIDS and Gays on the American Stage and Screen." In *Confronting AIDS through Literature: The Responsibilities of Representation,* edited by Judith Pastore. Urbana: University of Illinois Press. 103–23.

Juhasz, Alexandra. 1995. *AIDS TV: Identity, Community, and Alternative Video.* Durham, N.C.: Duke University Press.

Kaminsky, Amy K. 1993. *Reading the Body Politic: Feminist Criticism and Latin American Women Writers.* Minneapolis: University of Minnesota Press.

Khéde, Sonia Salomão. 1981. *Censores de pincenê e gravata: Dois momentos da censura teatral no Brasil.* Rio de Janeiro: Codecri.

Kistenberg, Cindy J. 1995. *AIDS, Social Change, and Theater: Performance as Protest.* New York: Garland Publishing.

Klein, Charles. 1998. "Gender, Sexuality and AIDS Prevention in Brazil." *NACLA Report on the Americas* 31.4 (January–February): 28–32.

Klusacek, Allan, and Ken Morrison, eds. 1993. *A Leap in the Dark: AIDS, Art and Contemporary Cultures.* Montreal: Véhicule Press.

Kulick, Don. 1998. *Travesti: Sex, Gender and Culture among Brazilian Transgendered Prostitutes.* Chicago: University of Chicago Press.

Lane, Eric, and Nina Shengold. 1995. "Preface." *The Actor's Book of Gay and Lesbian Plays.* New York: Penguin. v–x.

Larsen, Neil. 1990. *Modernism and Hegemony: A Materialist Critique of Aesthetic Agencies.* Minneapolis: University of Minnesota Press.

Libertson, Joseph. 1977. "Excess and Imminence: Transgression in Bataille." *MLN* 92.5: 1001–23.

Lima, Janaína. 2000. "A volta do estilo 'vivencial' de fazer teatro. Entrevista com Guilherme Coelho." *Jornal do Commercio* [Recife], 30 July.

Lima, Mariângela Alves de. 1992. "Tendências atuais do teatro." *Revista USP* 14 (June–August): 16–21.

———. 1998. "Escritos esclarecem projeto cênico de Zé Celso." *O Estado de São Paulo*. 18 April. Caderno 2. (Review of José Celso Martinez Correa, *Primeiro ato: Cadernos, depoimentos, entrevistas, 1958–1974*, ed. Ana Helena Camargo de Staal [São Paulo: Editora 34, 1998])

O Livro de Jó. 1995. Playbill. São Paulo: Teatro da Vertigem.

Lockhart, Melissa Fitch. 1994. "*Beijo no asfalto* and Compulsory Homosexuality." *Gestos* 17 (April): 147–58.

———. 1998. "Queer Representations in Latino Theatre." *Latin American Theatre Review* 31.2 (Spring): 67–78.

Luis, Macksen. "1995. Uma verdadeira Pérola." In Mauro Rasi, *Pérola*. Rio de Janeiro: Record. 11–12.

MacRae, Edward. 1990. *A construção da igualdade: Identidade sexual e política no Brasil da "Abertura."* Campinas: Editora da UNICAMP.

Magaldi, Sábato. 1989. "*A mancha roxa*: Plínio Marcos retoma a violência." *Jornal de Artes Cênicas* (July–August): 18–19.

———. 1990. "Introdução." Nelson Rodrigues, *Teatro completo*. Vol. 4. Rio de Janeiro: Editora Nova Fronteira. 7–49.

Maggi, Armando. 1999. "The 'Natural Relationship': Qorpo-Santo's Plays and the Liminal Performance of Morality." *Luso-Brazilian Review* 36.2 (Winter): 1–12.

Marchant, Elizabeth. 1998. Review of *Entre resistir e identificar-se: Para uma teoria da narrativa brasileira de autoria feminina*, ed. Peggy Sharpe (Florianópolis and Goiânia: Editora Mulheres e Universidade Federal de Goiás, 1997). *Luso-Brazilian Review* 35.2 (Winter): 151–52.

Marcos, Plínio. 1975. *O abajur lilás*. São Paulo: Global.

———. 1976. *Barrela*. São Paulo: Global.

———. 1979. *Dois perdidos numa noite suja*. São Paulo: Global.

———. 1984. *Navalha na carne* (1968). Third edition. São Paulo: Editora Parma.

———. 1988. *A mancha roxa*. São Paulo: Edição do Autor.

———. 1996. *O assassinato do anão do caralho grande*. São Paulo: Geração Editorial.

Martuscello, Carmine. 1993. *O teatro de Nelson Rodrigues: Uma leitura psicanalítica*. São Paulo: Editora Siciliano.

McGrath, John Edward. 1995. "Trusting in Rubber: Performing Boundaries during the AIDS Epidemic." *The Drama Review* 39.2: 21–38.

Meade, Teresa A. 1997. *"Civilizing" Rio: Reform and Resistance in a Brazilian City, 1889–1930*. University Park: Pennsylvania State University Press.

Melo, Fernando. 1974. "Greta Garbo, quem diria, acabou no Irajá." *Revista de Teatro* 400 (Julho–Agosto): 45–68.

Mendès-Leite, Rommel. 1993. "A Game of Appearances: The 'Ambigusexuality' in Brazilian Culture of Sexuality." *Journal of Homosexuality* 25.3: 271–82.

Michalski, Yan. 1985. *O teatro sob pressão: Uma frente de resistência*. Rio de Janeiro: Jorge Zahar Editor.

Milleret, Margo. 1995. "Entrevista/Interview: Naum Alves de Souza." *Brasil/Brazil* 14: 137–52.

Molloy, Sylvia. 1996. "Mock Heroics and Personal Markings." *Publications of the Modern Language Association* 111.5 (October): 1072–75.

Moreno-Uribe, Edgar Antonio. 1993. *El arte del Sida*. Caracas: Vardell Hermanos Editores.

Moreira, Antônio Carlos. 1981. "O teatro é uma arte guei?" *Lampião da esquina* 37 (Junho): 13–15.

Moreyra, Alvaro. 1990. *Adão, Eva, e outros membros da família* (1922). Porto Alegre: Instituto Estadual do Livro.

Morrison, James. 1992. "The Repression of the Returned: AIDS and Allegory." In *AIDS: The Literary Response*, edited by Emmanuel S. Nelson. New York: Twayne Publishers. 167–74.

Moser, Gerald. 1976. "Artur Azevedo's Last Dramatic Writings: The 'Teatro a Vapor' Vignettes (1906–1908)." *Latin American Theatre Review* 10.1: 23–35.

Moss, David, and Barbara Mitszal. 1990. "Introduction." *Action on AIDS: National Policies in Comparative Perspective*, edited by David Moss and Barbara Mitszal. Westport, Conn.: Greenwood Press. 1–24.

Mosse, George L. 1996. *The Image of Man: The Creation of Modern Masculinity*. New York: Oxford University Press.

Mott, Luiz. 1988. *O sexo proibido: Virgens, gays e escravos nas garras da Inquisição*. Campinas: Papirus.

———. 1995. "The Gay Movement and Human Rights in Brazil." In *Latin American Male Homosexualities*, edited by Stephen O. Murray. Albuquerque: University of New Mexico Press. 221–30.

———. 1996. *Epidemic of Hate: Violations of the Human Rights of Gay Men, Lesbians, and Transvestites in Brazil*. Salvador and San Francisco: Grupo Gay da Bahia and International Gay and Lesbian Human Rights Commission.

Muñoz, José Esteban. 1999. *Disidentifications: Queers of Color and the Performance of Politics*. Minneapolis: Minnesota University Press.

Murphy, Timothy F., and Suzanne Poirier, eds. 1993. *Writing AIDS: Gay Literature, Language, and Analysis*. New York: Columbia University Press.

Murray, Stephen O., ed. 1995. *Latin American Male Homosexualities*. Albuquerque: University of New Mexico Press.

Name, Daniela. 1996. "Revelações do dândi e da crônica." *O Globo*. April 13, 1996. 6.

Needell, Jeffrey D. 1987. *A Tropical 'Belle Époque': Elite Culture and Society in Turn-of-the-Century Rio de Janeiro*. Cambridge: Cambridge University Press, 1987.

Nelson, Emmanuel S., ed. 1992. *AIDS: The Literary Response*. New York: Twayne Publishers.

Nunes, Luiz Arthur. 1997. "Prefácio." In, *Teatro completo*, by Caio Fernando Abreu, edited by Luiz Arthur Nunes. Porto Alegre: Editora Sulina / Instituto Estadual do Livro. 7–9.

Oscar, Henrique. 1974. "Introdução a Fernando Melo e a *Greta Garbo*." *Revista de Teatro* 400 (Julho-Agosto): 43–44, 68.

Parker, Richard. 1989. Review of Vagner de Almeida, *Adeus, irmão, durma sossegado*. *Revista de Teatro* 469 (January–March): 47.

———. 1991. *Bodies, Pleasures, and Passions: Sexual Culture in Contemporary Brazil*. Boston: Beacon Press.

———. 1992. "Sexual Diversity, Cultural Analysis, and AIDS Education in Brazil." *The Times of AIDS: Social Analysis, Theory, and Method*, edited by Gilbert Herdt and Shirley Lindenbaum. Newbury Park, Calif.: Sage Publications. 225–42.

———. 1995. "Changing Brazilian Constructions of Homosexuality." In *Latin American Male Homosexualities*, edited by Stephen O. Murray. Albuquerque: University of New Mexico Press. 241–55.

Parker, Richard, Cristina Bastos, Jane Galvão, and José Stalin Pedrosa, eds. 1994. *A Aids no Brasil, 1982–1992*. Rio de Janeiro: Relume-Dumará / ABIA / IMS-UERJ.

Parker, Richard, and Jane Galvão. 1996, "Introdução." In *Quebrando o silêncio: Mulheres e AIDS no Brasil*, edited by Richard Parker and Jane Galvão. Rio de Janeiro: Relume-Dumará / ABIA / IMS-UERJ.

Pastore, Judith, ed. 1993. *Confronting AIDS through Literature: The Responsibilities of Representation*. Urbana: University of Illinois Press.

Peixoto, Fernando. 1990. "Brazilian Theatre and National Identity," *The Drama Review* 34: 60–69.

Pereira, Victor Hugo Adler. 1995. "O rei e as revoluções possíveis." In *Oswald plural*, edited by Gilberto Mendonça Teles. Rio de Janeiro: Editora da Universidade Estadual do Rio de Janeiro. 163–79.

———. 1998. *A musa carrancuda: Teatro e poder no Estado Novo*. Rio de Janeiro: Fundação Getúlio Vargas.

Peres, Phyllis. 1994. "Subaltern Spaces in Brazil." *Dispositio/n* 19.46: 113–26.

Perrone, Charles A. 1989 "Dissonance and Dissent: The Musical Dramatics of Chico Buarque." *Latin American Theatre Review* 22.2 (Spring): 81–92.

———. 1996. *Seven Faces: Brazilian Poetry Since Modernism*. Durham, N.C.: Duke University Press.

Phelan, Peggy. 1993. *UnMarked: The Politics of Performance*. New York: Routledge.

Piontek, Thomas. 1992. "Unsafe Representations: Cultural Criticism in the Age of AIDS." *Discourse* 15.1 (Fall): 128–53.

Prado, Décio de Almeida. , 1987. "Navalha na carne." *Exercício findo: Crítica teatral, 1964–1968*. São Paulo: Editora Perspectiva. 216–19.

Prata, Mário. 1987. *Besame mucho*. Porto Alegre: L&PM.

Queiroz, Rachel de, and Maria Luíza de Queiroz. 1998. *Tantos anos*. São Paulo: Editora Siciliano.

Rasi, Mauro. 1993. *Trilogia: A estrela do lar, A cerimônia do adeus, Viagem a Forli*. Rio de Janeiro: Relume Dumará.

———. 1995. *Pérola*. Rio de Janeiro: Record.

Rich, Adrienne. 1980. "Compulsory Heterosexuality and Lesbian Existence." *Signs* 5.4: 631–60.

Richardson, Alan. 1993. "Notes on the Challenges of AIDS Education." In *A Leap in the Dark: AIDS, Art, and Contemporary Cultures*, edited by Allen Klusacek and Ken Morrison. Montreal: Véhicule Press. 296–304.

Rodrigues, João Carlos. 1996. *João do Rio: Uma biografia*. Rio de Janeiro: Topbooks.

Rodrigues, Nelson. 1981–90. *Teatro completo*. Ed. Sábato Magaldi. 4 vols. Rio de Janeiro: Editora Nova Fronteira.

———. 1998. *The Wedding Dress, All Nudity Shall Be Punished, The Lady of the Drowned, Waltz #6, The Deceased Woman*. Translated by Joffre Rodrigues and Toby Coe. Rio de Janeiro: Funarte.

Román, David. 1992. "'It's My Party and I'll Die if I Want To!': Gay Men, AIDS, and the Circulation of Camp in U.S. Theatre." *Theatre Journal* 44.3 (October): 305–27.

———. 1998. *Acts of Intervention: Performance, Gay Culture, and AIDS*. Bloomington: Indiana University Press.

Román, David and Alberto Sandoval. 1995. "Caught in the Web: Latinidad, AIDS, and Allegory in *Kiss of the Spider Woman, the Musical*." *American Literature* 67.3 (September): 553–85.

Rossetti, Fernando. 1996. "Teatro leva sexo às escolas de Salvador." *Folha de São Paulo*, 1 September, Sec. 3,

Rudnick, Paul. 1993. "Laughing at AIDS," *New York Times*, 23 January.

———. 1996. "The Seminal Paul Rudnick, Part II." *Arts and Understanding* 20 (February–March): 32–36.

Ruiz, Roberto. 1988. *O teatro de revista no Brasil: Do início à Primeira Guerra Mundial*. Rio de Janeiro: Ministério da Cultura, Instituto Nacional de Artes Cênicas.

Sá, Nelson de, and Octavio Frias Filho. 1997. "A fúria do teatro: vingança dos 90" (Entrevista com José Celso Martinez Correa). *Folha de São Paulo* August 31. Caderno Mais!.

Said, Edward. 1983. *The World, the Text and the Critic*. Cambridge, Mass.: Harvard University Press.

Sandoval, Alberto. 1994 "Staging AIDS: What's Latinos Got To Do With It?". *Negotiating Performance: Gender, Sexuality and Theatricality in Latin/o America*, edited by Diana Taylor and Juan Villegas. Durham, N.C.: Duke University Press. 49–66.

Scarry, Elaine. 1985. *The Body in Pain: The Making and Unmaking of the World.* New York: Oxford University Press.

Schneider, Rebecca. 1997. *The Explicit Body in Performance.* New York: Routledge.

Schoenbach, Peter J. 1972. "Rio and São Paulo Theatres in 1970: National Dramaturgy." *Latin American Theatre Review* 5.2 (Spring): 67–80.

———. 1976. "Plínio Marcos: Reporter of Bad Times". In *Dramatists in Revolt: The New Latin American Theatre.* Ed. George Woodyard and Leon Lyday. Austin: University of Texas Press. 243–57.

Schulman, Sarah. 1998. *Stagestruck: Theater, AIDS, and the Marketing of Gay America.* Durham, N.C.: Duke University Press.

Scott, Joan W. 1986. "Gender: A Useful Category of Historical Analysis." *American Historical Review* 91.5: 1053–75.

Sedgwick, Eve Kosofsky. 1990. *Epistemology of the Closet.* Berkeley: University of California Press.

Shatzky, Joel. 1992. "AIDS Enters the American Theater: *The Normal Heart* and *As Is.*" In *AIDS: The Literary Response,* edited by Emmanuel S. Nelson. New York: Twayne Publishers. 131–39.

Showalter, Elaine. 1990. *Sexual Anarchy: Gender and Culture at the Fin de Siècle.* New York: Viking.

Silva, Aguinaldo, and Doc Comparato. 1981. *As tias: Tragicomédia em dois atos.* Rio de Janeiro: Achiamé.

Silva, Armando Sérgio da. 1981. *Oficina: Do teatro ao te-ato.* São Paulo: Editora Perspectiva.

Skidmore, Thomas. 1993. *Black into White: Race and Nationality and Brazilian Thought.* Revised edition. Durham, N.C.: Duke University Press.

Smith, Paul Julian. 1992. *Representing the Other: "Race," Text, and Gender in Spanish and Spanish American Narrative.* Oxford: Clarendon Press.

Souza, Naum Alves de. 1982. *A aurora da minha vida.* São Paulo: MG Editores Associados.

———. 1983. *No Natal a gente vem te buscar.* São Paulo: MG Editores Associados.

———. 1986. *Um beijo, um abraço, um aperto de mão.* São Paulo: MG Editores Associados.

Spivak, Gayatri Chakravorty. 1987. "A Literary Representation of the Subaltern: A Woman's Text from the Third World." *In Other Worlds: Essays in Cultural Politics.* New York: Methuen. 241–68.

———. 1988. "Can the Subaltern Speak?" In *Marxism and the Interpretation of Culture,* edited by Cary Nelson and Lawrence Grossberg. Urbana: University of Illinois Press. 271–313.

Stallybrass, Peter, and Allon White. 1986. *The Politics and Poetics of Transgression.* Ithaca, N.Y.: Cornell University Press.

Stam, Robert. 1982. "On the Carnivalesque." *Wedge* 1: 47–55.

Station, Elizabeth. 1995. "Activists Take on AIDS." In *Fighting for the Soul of Brazil*, edited by Kevin Danaher and Michael Shellenberger. New York: Monthly Review Press. 197–203.

Stern, Irwin, ed. 1988. *Dictionary of Brazilian Literature*. Westport, Conn.: Greenwood Press.

Stolberg, Sheryl Gay. 1997. "The Better Half Got the Worse End." *New York Times*. 20 July, Sec. 4.

Sullivan, Andrew. 1996. "When Plagues End: Notes on the Twilight of an Epidemic." *New York Times Magazine*, 10 November.

Terto Jr., Veriano, and Cecília Godinho. 1994. "O Projeto Homossexualidades faz um ano." *Boletim ABIA* 24 (Maio–Junho): 14–15.

Trevisan, João Silvério. 1986. *Perverts in Paradise*. Translated by Martin Foreman. London: GMP Publishers.

———. 1998. *Seis balas num buraco só: A crise do masculino*. Rio de Janeiro: Record.

Trexler, Richard. 1995. *Sex and Conquest: Gendered Violence, Political Order, and the European Conquest of the Americas*. Ithaca, N.Y.: Cornell University Press.

Velloso, Monica Pimenta. 1996. *Modernismo no Rio de Janeiro: Turunas e quixotes*. Rio de Janeiro: Fundação Getúlio Vargas.

Veneziano, Neyde. 1991. *O teatro de revista no Brasil: Dramaturgia e convenções*. Campinas: Editora da UNICAMP.

Venturelli, Paulo. 1982. "O discurso do não-manifesto: Nota de leitura da peça *Toda nudez será castigada*." *Estudos Brasileiros* 13 (Julho): 83–100.

Vicente, José. 1970. "O assalto." *Revista de Teatro* 375: 45–61.

———. 1984. *Os reis da terra*. Rio de Janeiro: Nova Fronteira.

———. 1981. "Teatro, representação litúrgica." *Arte em revista* 6: 76.

Wannamaker, Annette. 2001. "'Memory Also Makes a Chain': The Performance of Absence in Griselda Gambaro's *Antigona Furiosa*." *The Journal of the M/MLA* 33.3: 73–85.

Watney, Simon. 1987. *Policing Desire: Pornography, AIDS, and the Media*. Minneapolis: University of Minnesota Press.

Wetsel, David. 1992. "The Best of Times, the Worst of Times: The Emerging Literature of AIDS in France." In Nelson. 95–113.

———. 1994. "Copi." In *Latin American Writers on Gay and Lesbian Themes: A Bio-Critical Sourcebook*, edited by David Foster. Westport, Conn.: Greenwood Press.116–21.

White, Edmund. 1989. "Esthetics and Loss." [1987]. In John Preston, ed. *Personal Dispatches: Writers Confront AIDS*. New York: St. Martin's Press. 145–52.

Wilde, Zeno, and Bragança, Wanderley. 1985. "Blue Jeans." *Revista de Teatro* 454 (April/May/June): 52–64.

Wilson, Angelia R. 1997. "Somewhere Over the Rainbow: Queer Translating." In

Playing With Fire: Queer Politics, Queer Theories, edited by Shane Phelan. New York: Routledge. 99–111.

Wilson, Elizabeth. 1993. "Is Transgression Transgressive?" In *Activating Theory: Lesbian, Gay, and Bisexual Politics,* edited by Joseph Bristow and Angelia Wilson. London: Lawrence and Wishart. 107–17.

Wilson, Robert R. 1986. "Play, Transgression, and Carnival: Bakhtin and Derrida on *Scriptor Ludens.*" *Mosaic: A Journal for the Interdisciplinary Study of Literature* 19.1: 73–89.

Woodyard, George. 1969. "The Theatre of the Absurd in Latin America." *Comparative Drama* 3.3: 183–92.

Ziembinsky, Zbigniew. 1982. "Depoimento prestado ao Serviço Nacional de Teatro." *Depoimentos,* vol. 6. Rio de Janeiro: Ministério da Educação e Cultura / Serviço Nacional de Teatro. 169–90.

Interviews

Silviano Santiago	Rio de Janeiro	14 August 1996
Ana Maria Bulhões	Rio de Janeiro	14 August 1996
Italo Moriconi	Rio de Janeiro	20 August 1996
Vagner de Almeida	Rio de Janeiro	21 August 1996
Zeno Wilde	São Paulo	23 August 1996
Naum Alves de Souza	São Paulo	25 August 1996
Alberto Guzik	São Paulo	26 August 1996
Luis Alberto de Abreu	São Paulo	26 August 1996
Victor Hugo Pereira	Rio de Janeiro	20 December 1996
Luiz Arthur Nunes	Rio de Janeiro	14 January 1997
Marcos Breda	Rio de Janeiro	15 January 1997
Gilberto Gawronski	Rio de Janeiro	16 January 1997
Alberto Guzik	São Paulo	12 January 1999

Index